LISTENING TO *Poetry*

AN INTRODUCTION
FOR *Readers* AND *Writers*

JEREMY TRABUE

Listening to Poetry

ISBN: 978-1-943536-55-9

Edition 1.0 (Fall 2019)

Chemeketa Press

Chemeketa Press is a nonprofit publishing endeavor at Chemeketa Community College. Working together with faculty, staff, and students, we develop and publish affordable and effective alternatives to commercial textbooks. To learn more, visit www.chemeketapress.org.

Publisher: David Hallett
Director: Steve Richardson
Managing Editor: Brian Mosher
Instructional Editor: Stephanie Lenox
Design Editor: Ronald Cox IV
Manuscript Editor: Stephanie Lenox, Steve Richardson
Editorial Assistants: Nadia Isom, Taylor Wynia
Interior Design: Brice Spreadbury, Ronald Cox IV, Casandra Johns, Steve Richardson
Cover photo: © olly / Adobe Stock

Printed in the United States of America.

Contents

For Selby, Kelson, and Portia,
who kept believing it was worth it.

Chapter 1

Welcome Back to Poetry

Key terms: prose, form, understanding, appreciation, analyze, element, analyze/analysis, basic reading, paraphrase

Introduction to Poetry

I ask them to take a poem
and hold it up to the light
like a color slide

or press an ear against its hive.

5   I say drop a mouse into a poem
and watch him probe his way out,

or walk inside the poem's room
and feel the walls for a light switch.

I want them to waterski
10   across the surface of a poem
waving at the author's name on the shore.

But all they want to do
is tie the poem to a chair with rope
and torture a confession out of it.

15   They begin beating it with a hose
to find out what it really means.

Billy Collins, 1988

If you read a nursery rhyme to toddlers, they won't interrupt you to ask what it means. They certainly won't tie it to a chair and begin beating it with a hose. Instead, they'll laugh and clap and ask you to read it again—and again. They respond to the poem as people respond to songs, not as people respond to stories. The poem is delightful because of the rhyme, rhythm, and sound of the words, even if the words make no sense to toddlers—or to anyone.

Let's fast-forward fifteen or twenty years and check on those delighted toddlers as they sit down to take their first college literature class. If they now read a poem that makes no sense to them, they're not likely to be delighted by the rhyme, rhythm, and sound of the words. They want to know what it means. They don't respond to the poem as a song anymore, but as a story—or worse, as a problem to be solved, a code to be deciphered.

Something sad happened between preschool and college. The toddlers became students who unlearned their natural love of poetry, a love that is rooted in sound and surprise, pattern and play, discovery and delight.

This is sad because life can be dull and gray enough without cutting ourselves off from those amusements that are our natural birthright. And poetry is certainly one of those amusements. It's also sad because, to slightly misquote Robert Frost, if poetry begins in delight, it ends in wisdom. Poetry is not only one of our primal amusements, it's one of the best tools we have for rendering our lives comprehensible and meaningful.

Let's try to reverse this tragedy. Let's stop beating poems with hoses and relearn how to listen to them, have a conversation with them, enjoy them the way those toddlers did. This book will help you take the first few important steps in that direction. We'll start right away with a closer look at what poems are and how you can learn to really listen to them.

What Is a Poem?

Not knowing what to expect can be difficult. If you go to a football game without understanding the rules or that there are frequent and often long breaks between plays, you're going to be confused and bored.

It's the same with any art form. If you don't know what you're getting, or if you expect something different from what you're getting, then you're likely to be frustrated or disappointed. Your first job, then, is to make sure you know what you're getting into when you meet a poem.

A Poem Has Form

The first quality most people notice about a poem is the shape of the poem. When they see a poem on a screen or piece of paper, the look of the poem is what makes them think, "Oh. This is a poem."

Look again at the Billy Collins poem at the start of the chapter. It just looks different from the way most books or magazine articles or letters look. It's arranged in lines that don't run all the way to the right edge of the page. Normal **prose** writing—like the text you're reading right now—is shaped into paragraphs and made up of lines that run from one margin to the next. In the poem, however, some lines are longer and some are shorter, and they all stop and start according to some invisible, internal rule instead of reaching the end of the available space and wrapping around to the next line.

The shape of the poem is called its **form**. However, that term encompasses more than just the visual shape on the page that makes such an immediate impression. There are other elements of form that you might not notice as quickly. For instance, does every line start with the same word? Does every other line rhyme? Is each line only ten syllables long? The answers to those and many other questions are also part of the poem's form.

The rules that create the form of a poem often come before the poem is ever written. There are many traditional ways to arrange and limit the length and shape and sound of the poem. Sets of rules are passed down over time, imported from other cultures and languages, and reinvented from time to time. These sets of rules are called "forms," too, and they have names like "sonnet" or "haiku."

Even if a poem is composed free from prearranged rules and even if it isn't in a recognizable form, it still has form. It still has a shape of some sort on the page, in the mind's eye, and in the ear. The number and range of forms a poem can take is almost limitless, but all poems have form.

A Poem Is Like a Story, a Song, and a Picture

One of the first ways most students try to understand a poem is by reading it as a story.

The opening poem is not especially storylike, but it still tells a very short story. A teacher talks about the goals for the students and then explains how things really go. The students don't understand or appreciate the poems in the way that the teacher intends. The goals are never reached. It's sad. The poem tells this story by comparing the experience of reading and thinking about a poem to looking at a color slide, listening to a beehive, watching a mouse in a maze, walking into a dark room, waterskiing, and, finally, torturing a confession out of a prisoner.

Everything that defines a story is there. But is this a story? No. If for no other reason than the form, you instinctively recognize this is something other than a true story.

So, what is a poem?

You might have noticed how many poems are like songs. Like songs, poems may have verses, rhyme, a regular rhythmic pattern, repetition, and a variety of other sound patterns. Look at and listen for all the ways that this poem seems like a song:

The Yak

As a friend to the children commend me the Yak.
    You will find it exactly the thing:
It will carry and fetch, you can ride on its back,
    Or lead it about with a string.

5 The Tartar who dwells on the plains of Thibet
    (A desolate region of snow)
Has for centuries made it a nursery pet,
    And surely the Tartar should know!

Then tell your papa where the Yak can be got,
10   And if he is awfully rich
He will buy you the creature—or else he will not.
    (I cannot be positive which.)

Hilaire Belloc, 1896

It wouldn't take too much effort to set this poem to music. It's organized into sets of four-line "verses." All the lines are roughly the same length and rhythm without being monotonously identical. Repetitions of all sorts of sounds, including lots of rhymes, create a musical effect and remind you of the language of song lyrics.

But again, although the poem shares some qualities with song, it's still something other than a song. To begin with, you're reading it on a page. That means you can read, reread, pause, or skip ahead. These possibilities affect not only your experience in reading the poem but also the author's experience in writing it. Even if the poem is performed aloud, it's spoken, not sung. There's no instrumentation or accompanying music, no singer to create meaning or feeling with changes in tone or pitch, and even on the page, there's no score. It's only made of words.

This poem also makes use of elements that songs don't use. White space—those blank lines between lines of text—and the arrangement of the lines on the page are part of the poem. It tells a story, which some songs do but some do not. Once again, then, we recognize that while a poem can be songlike, it's something else, something other than a song.

So, what is a poem?

For hundreds of years, most poems have been written for the page and are read alone in silence. They are visual objects that often use the tools and techniques of design and even illustration.

Notice how the opening poem uses white space—those blank lines between lines of text—to emphasize transitions in the story? Each description of reading a poem is isolated by it. Sometimes the white space coincides with the end of a sentence, but sometimes it interrupts one. These visual elements are not overpowering or dramatic, but they are a part of the overall presentation and impact of the poem.

Some poems even use the printed words to create an actual picture on the page that in some way corresponds to the language content of the poem, as you can see in the following:

Sonnet in the Shape
of a Potted Christmas Tree

*

O
              fury-
         bedecked!
      O glitter-torn!
   Let the wild wind erect
bonbonbonanzas; junipers affect
frostyfreeze turbans; iciclestuff adorn
all cuckolded creation in a madcap crown of horn!
      It's a new day; no scapegrace of a sect
tidying up the ashtrays playing Daughter-in-Law Elect;
bells! bibelots! popsicle cigars! shatter the glassware! a son born
                  now
                  now
         while ox and ass and infant lie
      together as poor creatures will
      and tears of her exertion still
         cling in the spent girl's eye
      and a great firework in the sky
         drifts to the western hill.

George Starbuck, 1978

However, even this very picture-like poem of Starbuck's is not really
a picture. Its essence is language. What these words mean and how they
sound are both more important than how they are shaped to create an
image on the page. Poems share many qualities with pictures. Unlike a
picture, however, a poem can exist without the image of what it describes.
Unlike a poem, a picture can exist without language.

What then is a poem?

A Poem Is a Poem

We know now that a poem has form. We know that it can be like a story, like a song, and like a picture. In the end, though, we have to conclude that while a poem is like all of these, it remains different from all of them. It remains a poem and must be understood and appreciated as a poem.

As the opening poem wishes for us, we must be curious about what each poem is. We must talk to it and ask it what it is. We must sit with it and let it be itself. Most importantly, we must be quiet and listen carefully while its story and sounds and shape reveal themselves to us.

As a student of poetry, your greatest challenge will be to allow yourself to simply notice and enjoy all the ways a poem decides to act like a story, song, or picture—whether or not it makes sense in any of those ways. When you do that, without feeling the need to torture a confession out of it, then even if you don't understand it fully, you're off to a great start.

Common Mistakes

The first goal for this book is to give you the tools you need to understand poems no matter whether they choose to act like stories, songs, pictures—or all three. The second goal is to help you learn how to appreciate and enjoy the poems that you come to understand.

When most students first think about "understanding" a poem, they—like the students in Billy Collins's poem—assume that it's a riddle they must solve in order to get a decent grade. And to be fair to those students, that's not an unreasonable assumption. They've probably been trained to think that way by previous English classes. However, it's time for you to unlearn that lesson.

In fact, most poets write poems because they want to communicate with their audience. They want to share an idea, an experience, or a feeling. They want to tell a story or sing a song. They want to instruct or antagonize, to comfort or discomfort. They want to be heard, to feel less alone, and to give you a chance to feel less alone. They want to create an experience of beauty that others can share.

Whatever the specific goal, however, the point is to connect with the reader, to draw people together, to be heard and felt and understood—not to create barriers, distance, or confusion. A poem is an act of communication. It needs an audience. It's dying to confess.

That being said, some poems are hard to understand, at first, and your expectations are usually why:

You expect poems to *be* stories. If you try to put a glove on your foot, it's just not going to work out, no matter how well-made the glove is. If you insist on reading a poem as a story, it's not going work out, either. If you keep in mind that it might be doing almost anything other than telling a story, or the story it tells might only be part of what it's up to, it will suddenly become a lot less confusing.

You expect poems to be arguments about the world. It's certainly true that many poems express ideas about the world and human life, that they make arguments and assert moral lessons or offer instructions. But not all poems do that. Many poems barely have any ideas at all.

You expect poems to be direct. Poets tend to be of an indirect sort of mind. Sometimes they really try to put something into words that may not really fit into words. You can simply explore the poems and puzzle over the hints and enjoy that experience even if you never fully see a quietly concealed truth. And when you do see something, when you get that little flash of insight or understanding or empathy—it's pretty magical.

You expect poems to use normal sentences. Poets often use words to mean several things at once, or they use one word to suggest another through association with sound or shape. Likewise, poets often feel free to bend or break conventional rules of grammar and punctuation. If you expect the language of a poem to behave like normal language, you are asking for frustration.

You expect poems to speak just like you do. We keep reading poems long after their language has gone stale. Shakespeare, for example, wrote mostly for uneducated and even illiterate audiences. In the four hundred years since Shakespeare, however, English has changed. Many words common in his day are unused today. Grammar and punctuation changed. The more time that stands between you and the poet, the harder it becomes to understand the language.

These are all good reasons to find poetry difficult to understand. However, none of these are reasons to avoid poetry. You just need to take them into consideration as you explore each poem and come to understand and appreciate it for whatever it is.

Understanding refers to your intellectual and analytical response to something. **Appreciation** refers to your emotional and aesthetic response. Those toddlers from the start of the chapter can appreciate nursery rhymes even when they don't understand them.

It's valid to appreciate and enjoy a poem or something in a poem even if we don't fully understand what's going on or what ideas are being presented. Even something confusing can be beautiful and engaging. We have to just let ourselves be sensitive to the song in a poem as a source of beauty and delight that is separate from the sense of the poem.

Understanding often leads to appreciation, too. If someone points out the meaning of an obscure word, we might suddenly see and enjoy the cleverness of the plot or the development of a character. There's a thrill of appreciation for what the poem is doing. Even in that moment, however, notice how the realization and the thrill are different. The first is understanding. The second is appreciation.

As you learn to read poetry, pay attention to both. What do you understand? What do you appreciate? How do both of those responses evolve as you read and reread and work with a poem? Give yourself permission to like a poem you don't understand and to understand a poem you don't particularly like.

Analyzing a Poem

To **analyze** is to discover the structure that lies behind function or beneath surface appearance. When we analyze, we examine carefully with an eye to discovering not just what an object does but how it is put together and what makes it function. We learn to thoroughly understand a complicated system by isolating all the **elements**—the small pieces or processes within a system—and looking at how they work together to make the system work.

The first step in analyzing is to figure out the elements of the system. The elements of a martini, for example, are gin, vermouth, an olive, and ice. The elements of a car are the body, the engine, the drive train, the electrical system, and so on. Each of those elements is a complicated system in its own right, with its own elements, and so on right down to chemical elements—helium, uranium, lead, carbon—the basic building blocks of the physical universe.

A poem is also made up of elements that work together to create a whole. This process of **analysis**, of breaking a poem apart into elements and studying each element closely, is the key to an academic, intellectual approach to poetry. It allows us to better understand what a poem is doing, and it gives us more to notice and appreciate as we spend time with a poem.

You can also just read poems without analyzing them. But the object of studying poetry *in a college class* is to deepen your understanding of how poems behave as poems. This means learning to identify a poem's elements in isolation and explain how those elements work together to create a final total effect.

This is useful work in its own right, by the way. It develops your abilities to read, understand, analyze, and interpret in general, which are vital skills for college and life beyond. It can also be a lot of fun. Human beings naturally enjoy and are drawn toward complexity. Slowly unraveling and understanding a complex event or person or created thing is pleasurable for most people. It's an integral part of the fun to be found in life.

To succeed in learning to analyze poems, you'll need to learn a lot of new words that define and describe the elements of a poem. A large part of mastering any subject, from small-engine repair to organic chemistry, is learning that subject's special vocabulary.

The vocabulary of this subject presents some curious and difficult challenges. That's partly because it's so old. One of the very oldest textbooks is Aristotle's *Poetics*, from the third century BCE—and we still use some of its terms and concepts! The Greeks and Romans continued his work and developed sophisticated theories of poetry, and later English-language poets and teachers adapted those theories, including a lot of the vocabulary.

It's possible to streamline and modernize this vocabulary and adapt old theories and vocabulary to new materials and ways of thinking. Over the years, many people have done so. However, the older vocabulary has never gone entirely out of use. This means that there are sometimes multiple terms with the same meaning, and there are often multiple meanings for the same term.

This book will try to use the most common terms and to use them in the most widespread ways. As you journey forth into the wider world and learn more about poetry, you will find out just how slippery these terms can be within different contexts, but this is still a solid starting place.

There's a paradox here. On one hand, you should give yourself permission to appreciate a poem without understanding it, to let it be what it will be. On the other hand, working hard to figure out the complexity of a poem is inherently pleasurable. The resolution to this paradox is to stop thinking about the complexity of a poem as a kind of bomb that must be defused before it explodes—or a puzzle you must solve to pass the class, perhaps. Instead, think of a poem as being complex like a beautiful and mysterious stranger from a far-away place is complex. Exploring and coming to understand the mystery of that stranger shouldn't be a chore but a joy!

Let's try a different analogy: football, an extremely complex activity. It has rules, formal and informal; traditions, history; special symbols and vocabulary. It takes place in a historical context; it has economic and political ramifications; social concerns such as race, class, and gender relations impact the game and are in turn impacted by it, and so on. It has a rich cast of characters, both living and dead, who relate to each other in all sorts of complicated ways, on and off the field.

It is possible to watch a game without understanding any of this, and still enjoy it. It's exciting to watch these giant men crash into each other and run all over the field chasing a little ball.

But the more you understand, the greater your enjoyment. If you understand the formal rules and objectives of the game, you begin to appreciate the strategy unfolding before you. You can distinguish between the various formations and their purposes. If you recognize the players and coaches, the teams and their histories, the rivalries, the current standings in the playoff race, and so on, your enjoyment and appreciation are made even greater. And so on.

You can see where this is going. The more you understand the rules and history of any sport, the more you appreciate watching it played. Poetry is no different. Once you learn the rules of poetry—or even begin to learn them—you'll be amazed at how quickly you begin to understand and appreciate the poems you meet. It's possible that you might begin to love poetry, a little, even if it's been something you've always overlooked or avoided.

The Basic Reading of a Poem

This book regularly refers to a process for reading poems that is called the **basic reading**. You should practice this process so many times over the coming chapters that by the end of the book, it will be second nature to you. It may seem rather laborious at first, but stick with it. With practice, it will soon become comfortable and useful. Following these steps faithfully will make you much better at understanding and appreciating poems.

1. **Remember that it's a poem.** Don't expect it to be a story or to behave like other normal forms of writing. You have to be open to what you find. There might not be identifiable characters or events happening or other familiar parts you expect a story to have. There might be some of them but not others. It might not make sense in the normal linear way you expect from a story. Who knows?

2. **Be attentive and be receptive.** Remember that the poem wants to communicate with you. Listening to a poem means being actively and attentively receptive while at the same time holding back your own reactions and responses to the poem. When it reminds you of something from your own life, take that memory and set it aside.

3. **Actually listen to the poem with your physical ears.** This includes the following three sub-steps:

   a. **Read it out loud.** This can't be emphasized enough. Read poems out loud. Read poems out loud. Read poems out loud. You can read them to yourself in a whisper in the bathroom. You can perform them for your kids or parents or cats. You can take turns reading them to each other in class. A poem on the page is like a musical score. It exists to be performed.

b. **If possible, listen to the poem being read by someone else.** It's great to work with a classmate to read to each other, but family or friends can have fun with it, too. The internet is full of audio and video of poems being performed—sometimes by the poets themselves.

c. **Check in with yourself.** After you've read the poem out loud once or twice, take a minute to check in with yourself and note your reactions. Are you enjoying it? Are you bored, sad, curious, confused? Jotting down a few quick notes at this point is a good idea.

4. **Reread the poem and note questions.** Now reread the poem with a pencil in hand and make notes about whatever is confusing. There will be words you don't know and references you don't get. There may also be whole passages or lines that just seem out of place or confusing. Sometimes words mean something other than what you think they mean or what they normally mean. Look for places where a word or phrase might be used in a way that doesn't completely make sense or seems to take on an unusual significance.

5. **Answer your questions.** Once you've gone through the poem and noted all the questions, it's time to find the answers. Use a good, college-level, hardcover dictionary to look up definitions. The internet makes it reasonably easy to figure out references and allusions. Once you've found your answers, write them down next to the poem itself so that they're available when you go back and study the poem again.

6. **Get some context.** Poems are social artifacts. They always partake in at least a little of the environment in which they were created, and sometimes they're deeply embedded in it. The internet makes it easy to find basic information about the life and times of almost any poet. However, remember that poems are made

up. Don't try to use the poet's life and times as a decoder ring for the secret meaning of the poem. What you learn about a poet may not bear directly on the poem at all.

7. **Reread and paraphrase.** You now have a much better handle on the poem than when you started. You can test your understanding of a poem by rereading it and then writing a simple, informal paraphrase. A **paraphrase** is a restatement of a poem in your own words and in your own most natural writing style — but without omitting, altering, explaining, or interpreting anything.

8. **Talk about it.** Bring up questions or ideas in class, form a study group with your fellow students, or talk to the professor during office hours. When talking with peers, don't try to be right or solve the poem for them. Just bounce around ideas. Talk about what you appreciate as well as what you don't understand.

9. **Accept mystery.** The final step is to remember that there is no final step. There may be parts of a poem that never make any sense to you. It's also possible that if you reread a poem in another season of your life, you will get something altogether different from the poem. Some future conversation about the poem may crack the poem wide open for you.

The nineteenth-century British poet John Keats coined the term "negative capability" to describe this capacity for accepting mystery, and we'll take his wisdom on the matter as our closing thought for this section:

Negative Capability, that is when a man is capable of being in uncertainties, Mysteries, doubts, without any irritable reaching after fact & reason. . . . This pursued through volumes would perhaps take you no further than this, that with a great poet the sense of Beauty overcomes every other consideration, or rather obliterates all consideration.

Using this Book

Poetry is supposed to be fun. Kids instinctively enjoy poetry, even when they have no idea what it's about or what it means. Poems want to connect with their audiences. They are an act of sharing, of communication, of solidarity. Unfortunately, most people have this instinctive enjoyment smashed out of them in primary school. Instead of recognizing a poem as a joyful act of sharing, they've learned to imagine it as an enemy: incomprehensible, boring, and frightening.

You can reverse this unfortunate situation, and it starts with a couple of key facts about poems. First, a poem can be much like a story, and like a song, and in some ways it's even like a picture—but it is none of those things. Expecting it to behave just like any of them is the first mistake most student readers make.

Second, you must remember that understanding and appreciating are different things, though they may be related. You can understand something without appreciating it, and appreciate something without understanding it. Most of the time, however, one leads to the other in at least some measure.

Third, remember that a careful, intellectual, and analytical approach will paradoxically help you recover that natural joy in poetry and make it easy—and fun—to understand and appreciate poetry.

These final tips will give you a preview of the book—what it contains and how it's organized—and help you get the most out of it:

- It's best to read the book in order. Early chapters assume you're new to analyzing poetry and don't know many of the technical terms. Later chapters assume that you've been reading the book and thinking about the poems so that you understand the terms and ideas from before.

- At the end of each chapter, you'll find a few example poems with some suggested exercises that will help you practice analyzing the elements covered in that chapter. That's followed by four to six creative writing exercises. These writing exercises are not generally designed to produce poems but to help you practice and master the skills and knowledge from that chapter through your own writing.

- The book uses two poems over and over again throughout the first ten chapters to show you how sets of different but related elements overlap and work together in the same poem. "'Out, Out—'" by Robert Frost is the key example poem for chapters 3–8. "Counting-Out Rhyme" by Edna St. Vincent Millay is the key example poem for chapters 9–11.

- Chapters 2 and 12 each have their own key example poem, not shared with any other chapter.

- Chapters 13 and 14 pull together everything you've learned about analyzing a whole poem and explore what larger questions and arguments poems make—and what they might mean. It ends with some suggestions about how you can keep poetry in your life.

- After chapter 14, you'll find a glossary with definitions of the key terms from each chapter, a glossary of common and influential poetic forms, and a very brief introduction to writing about poetry.

Before we go forward, though, let's go backward to the Billy Collins poem that started this first part of the book. You don't need to interrogate poems. You don't need to torture them into submitting to your expectations of them. You need instead to put away the rubber hose and let them be what they will be.

Every poem is, in fact, dying to talk to you, to spill its secrets, to confess everything. All you have to do is listen to the poem. Be patient while you establish a bond with the poem. Once you learn to listen to it on its own terms and at its own pace, the poem will joyfully tell you all the secrets that it's holding back from those unhappy interrogators.

Chapter 2

The Form of a Poem

Key terms: content, form, line, end-stopped, enjambment/enjambed, caesura, stanza, couplet, tercet, quatrain/quartet, quintain/quintet, sestet/sextet, septet, octave/octet, triplet formal poems, received form/form, free verse/open form

Derecho Ghazal

And the high winds bore down, and the sky
built up that grey wall: *derecho*.

The taverns by the sea closed their shutters,
and the stands selling battered fries, *derecho*.

On the boardwalk, pieces of salt-water taffy, half-
eaten funnel cakes oozing grease and cream: *derecho*.

And the people on every highway, panicked, sought
a clear route for their exodus: *derecho*.

What's in your emergency backpack? Beef jerky, mineral
water, flashlight, solar cells? Snap in the sound of *derecho*.

Yesterday, white and blue sails pretty on the water;
sharp glint of skyscraper glass. Then this *derecho*.

Luisa A. Igloria, 2014

When we look at Igloria's "*Derecho* Ghazal," the shape of the lines and how they are arranged on the page tell us immediately that we're looking at a poem and not a story or newspaper article. What we're noticing is the form of the poem.

The word "form" has many meanings. Before we delve into our specialized poetry uses of the word, it's useful to consider it in a general sense. One easy way to do that is to contrast the words "form" and "content." **Content** is what you are saying—the information, ideas, emotions, and so on that we want your audience to understand. **Form** is how you say it—a phone call, a text, a birthday card. It's the method you use to get the content to the audience.

Let's say, for example, that you want to break up with your boyfriend. You've been putting this off for too long. It's time. The *content* that you want to transmit is: "I'm breaking up with you." You can use a variety of *forms* to transmit that content—a quiet conversation over dinner, a text, a phone call, an announcement on your Twitter feed that he is likely to see, a handwritten letter on scented paper that's dotted with fake tear stains. Those are all different forms, but they have the same content.

Now consider the way that the form you choose will modify or influence how your boyfriend receives the message. The content will be the same no matter how you break it to him, but the form greatly affects how he receives that content. *How* you say it becomes part of *what* you are saying.

In discussing poetry, we often use "form" in this general way to mean how a poem presents its content. We'll also use it in a more specific way to talk about the structure of any particular poem and how any poem uses a specific set of tools, or elements, to create structure. We'll also use "form" in a yet more specific way as a label for the patterns within and defining a poem, and even an established, prescriptive set of rules governing those patterns.

Form as Structure

To get a handle on the idea of form as structure, let's consider prose structure. Remember, **prose** is the "normal" writing you find in a newspaper, a crime novel, or a textbook. What you're reading right now is prose.

Prose structure is fairly simple. The basic tool, or element, of this structure is the sentence, which typically presents one idea. It begins with a capital letter and ends with a period, question mark, or exclamation mark. A sentence takes up as much space as it needs. It starts on the left of the page or after the last sentence and goes word by word to the right until it gets to the right edge of the page. If there is more to it, the sentence then keeps going onto the next line.

Sentences are organized into paragraphs that show readers how different sentences are working together to present a more general idea. Paragraphs are defined on the page by white space—indentations of the first line, as you see here, or lines of white space between paragraphs, as you often see in business letters. Sometimes long pieces of prose also have bigger structural elements like sections or chapters. Sometimes complex pieces of prose use elements like footnotes or sidebars to give structure to their ideas.

Poetry shares some elements with prose, but poetry has more elements that cover a wider spectrum of choices. As a general rule, form is more important in poetry than in prose. Prose is usually focused on presenting content clearly. Content is thus more important than form. Poets are often more interested in *how* they can say a thing than they are in *what* they have to say.

The two most important structural elements in poetry are the line and the stanza.

Lines

The basic unit of structure in a poem is the **line**. It is created first and foremost by white space. The words stop before they get to the right margin rather than running to the right margin and wrapping automatically into the next line like they do in prose. The poet ends one line and starts a new line as a matter of conscious choice.

Before the printing press, though, lines were defined by sound patterns. Manuscripts from the Dark Ages don't have visual line breaks. Lines were defined by rhythmic, rhyming, or other sound patterns. Lines are still defined by these patterns in many poems, and if you listen to these poems performed, you can still hear the line breaks.

Lines can also be structured by something other than arrangement on the page, white space, or sound. For example, lines might be defined and shaped by a pattern of repeated words or grammar structures, as in this example from Wordsworth's "Tintern Abbey:"

> Five years have passed;
> Five summers, with the length of
> Five long winters! and again I hear these waters . . .

Lines might fit into patterns like call and response, or they might be organized according to rhetorical patterns or repetitions of other elements, such as figures of speech.

Almost all poems are written using both sentences and lines, with these two patterns of organization working simultaneously. Line breaks sometimes coincide with the end of a grammar unit, like the sentence, clause, or phrase, as in this passage from Shakespeare's play *Julius Caesar:*

> Cowards die many times before their deaths;
> The valiant never taste of death but once.

Each line here could be a complete, sensible sentence all by itself. In that case, the end of the clause—a grammar term for a set of words that form a complete thought—coincides with the end of the line, a formal poetic unit. A line that ends at the end of a grammar unit like this is called **end-stopped.**

When a line break occurs in the middle of a grammar unit, on the other hand, it creates a different pattern and a different kind of energy. A line break in the middle of a grammar unit is called **enjambment.** We say that such a line is **enjambed.** Pay attention to how much of a contrast there is between the break in line and the grammar structure. For example, a line "is lightly enjambed" or "the poem is characterized by intense enjambment."

You can see several different kinds of enjambment in the first five lines of John Keats's *Endymion*. Pay attention to how you read across the line breaks. What happens to your eyes when they hit the end of the line? What happens to your brain? Is the experience different if you read out loud?

> A thing of beauty is a joy for ever:
> Its loveliness increases; it will never
> Pass into nothingness; but still will keep
> A bower quiet for us, and a sleep
> Full of sweet dreams, and health, and quiet breathing.

The first line is end-stopped. It sets up the lines that follow to be an explanation or list of the qualities that make a thing of beauty a joy forever. At the end of line 2, though, the main verb phrase of the sentence is broken in two. You know instinctively that "never" is modifying a verb — what never happens? — but to find out, you must move to the next line.

At the end of line 3, two distinct things happen. The first is that "still will keep" has three different meanings, any and all of which are plausible based on the first part of the clause. Does this mean "keep" in the sense of "continue," as in "still will keep / growing and growing in beauty"? If so, you want to know what it is going to keep doing. Or is it "keep" in the sense of retain possession of, as in, "still will keep / the fresh face she started with"? Or does "keep" mean "take care of, take responsibility for," as in "still will keep / house for us"? The many possibilities that arise from the enjambment between lines three and four are why we call the line "heavily enjambed."

Much of the language processing described above happens unconsciously. If you want to analyze the poem, though, you need to slow down and pay attention to these structural details and to your reactions to them. Bring the process into conscious thought and examine it.

Another aspect of lines is the **caesura**, a break or pause in the sound or rhythm of a line that comes from the content or the grammatical structure, which is usually marked with punctuation. In this example from "Mother and Poet" by Elizabeth Barrett Browning, the caesuras are marked with double vertical lines:

> What art can a woman be good at? || Oh, vain!
> What art is she good at, || but hurting her breast
> With the milk-teeth of babes, || and a smile at the pain?

Identifying caesuras can be tricky and subjective because punctuation does not always coincide with a pause. The length of a pause can sometimes be diminished or strengthened by the meaning of the line. The main technique is simply to be relentlessly attentive to what you notice and look for patterns in it. When heard aloud, does the poem show some sort of regular reoccurrence of perceived pauses in the middle of lines? If there's some sense of that, you can investigate more deeply.

Stanzas

Lines can be organized into a unit called a **stanza**, a recognizably distinct set of lines. Especially in modern poetry and in poetry that doesn't rhyme or have a regular rhythm, stanzas are often separated by white space. Sometimes this separation occurs between lines or with some form of indentation.

Like lines, though, stanzas weren't always separated by white space and don't have to be. A poem made up of lines uninterrupted by extra white space can still have stanzas divided by other principles, usually a sound pattern, such as rhyme.

Commonly, stanzas are named according to how many lines they have. These traditional names are taken from Latin or Greek:

A two-line stanza is a **couplet**.

A three-line stanza is a **tercet**.

A four-line stanza is a **quatrain** or **quartet**.

A five-line stanza is a **quintain** or **quintet**.

A six-line stanza is a **sestet** or **sextet**.

A seven-line stanza is a **septet**.

An eight-line stanza is an **octave** or **octet**.

There are also many types of stanzas, defined by other characteristics that have been given traditional names. Some of these are descriptive, some are nicknames, and some come from the types of poetry they're commonly used in. One example is the **triplet**, a tercet of any rhythmic pattern in which all three lines rhyme with each other.

Not all poems use stanza divisions. Some poems, especially long narrative or dramatic poems, let their lines run on indefinitely. Many short contemporary poems also don't bother with stanza divisions and are just a single short stanza, the size of which is of no particular significance.

Form as Pattern

All poems have lines and many have stanzas. These are the formal elements that give them structure. However, many poems also use those elements to create distinct patterns.

A pattern might be generated by the poem itself and be fairly slight, such as a repeating word at the beginning and end of every stanza. The pattern might be predetermined, in part or in whole, by a set of pre-existing rules that the poet inherits and follows. These rules might govern many aspects, such as length, syllable count, rhyme pattern, or almost any other characteristic of the poem. Poems that use the formal elements to create patterns are called **formal poems**.

Poetry has a broad spectrum of formality. On one end, you have very formal poems written according to tightly structured and prescriptive forms. As you move toward the other end, the poems become unstructured and not at all prescribed — not formal at all.

Writing poetry is thus a little like cooking. Sometimes you walk into the kitchen and throw together a meal based on whatever strikes your fancy and the ingredients you happen to have on hand. You don't follow any recipe in any conscious or specific way.

However, sometimes you cook straight from a cookbook. You shop for a particular recipe and follow it meticulously. The ingredients, preparation, techniques, and even the servings are all determined by a set of rules you follow.

And then, sometimes you start out with a recipe in mind but then modify it based on your own past experiences, creative instincts, whims — or even accidentally.

Formal Poems

So, at one end of the spectrum we have those poems that begin as a set of rules, like a recipe, that define some aspects of the poem ahead of time. We call these sets of rules—these recipes—**received forms** (or closed, fixed, or traditional forms), or often just **forms**. Some received forms determine almost every aspect of the poem—the length of lines and stanzas, the kinds of sound patterns, like rhythm or rhyme, the appearance on the page, and even the content. Some received forms only define certain aspects, and leave others more open. For example, a received form might dictate a certain kind of stanza, the lines of which are strictly predefined, while the number of stanzas differs from poem to poem and is not part of the "recipe."

Such a formal poem is automatically going to be read — by an educated audience—not just for itself, but also for how it relates to the rules of the form and how it relates to the body of other work in that form. Sometimes a form is part of a well-established tradition. Some of the entries in the Glossary of Forms are more than a thousand years old.

To stick with the idea of form as a recipe, let's think about actual recipes. If you choose to make your mother-in-law's frittata recipe—which, when *she* makes it, is considered famously delicious—dinner is not just dinner anymore. Your audience knows what a frittata should taste like. That's one pattern you must fulfill. However, because you're using your mother-in-law's recipe, your frittatas will also be judged by how well they match up against your mother-in-law's execution of that pattern. Your family has eaten this recipe when it was prepared by someone who does it quite well. How will your frittatas compare to those frittatas? You must contend, as well, with the way their love for her as a person is all wrapped up with their emotional response to this menu item. Good luck.

The complexity and richness of this "recipe book" of received forms separates poetry from other art forms. The more you know about these forms, the more you're going to understand and appreciate the poems that follow them. There are many, many traditional forms, and English-language poetry draws them in from other languages all the time. You have your own list, with explanations, in the Glossary of Forms.

Many closed form poems announce their form right in the title, as with our opening poem, "*Derecho* Ghazal." The title might seem confusing at first, but a quick trip to the dictionary tells you that "*derecho*" is a weather phenomenon and "ghazal" is an Arabic poetic form based on couplets all ending with the same word. So really this title is no more mysterious than titling your poem "Love Sonnet." It's a description of the poem that combines the subject and the form.

Now that you know that "*Derecho* Ghazal" is a poem in a closed form, you can find out the rules that define that form. Trying to find out the rules that govern ghazals, however, turns out to be sort of difficult. The form is very old, and it has migrated through the centuries, so now there are Arabic ghazal rules, Persian ghazal rules, Urdu ghazal rules, and English ghazal rules.

Even within each language tradition, there are varieties of ghazals, which shouldn't surprise you too much. It seems to be an inevitable law of human psychology that as soon as an idea is codified, the code must be revised and republished. At any rate, a bit of research will tell you that the basic rules of most English ghazals are:

- The poem is composed of five to fifteen couplets.
- The couplets are equal in length.
- Each couplet is grammatically complete, with no enjambment between stanzas.
- Both lines of the first couplet end with a repeated word or phrase preceded by a rhyming word.
- Each subsequent couplet ends with the same rhyme and repeated word or phrase.
- The final couplet refers to the author, usually including his or her name.
- Each couplet is independent in content.

Igloria's ghazal follows some but not all of these rules. There are five couplets of roughly equal length, and each is grammatically complete. Each couplet ends with the same word. However, the next-to-last rhyming word and the double refrain in the first stanza are entirely absent. The whole poem has unified content, too, and there is no apparent reference to the author in the last couplet.

So what's happening here with the form? The poet is simply taking what she wants from it and creating something new and original. She isn't following the strict English ghazal rules, which are themselves not following the strict Arabic ghazal rules, but she *is* entering into the ghazal tradition and adding her voice to that ongoing conversation.

Semiformal Poems

"*Derecho* Ghazal" has already moved down the spectrum from very formal to a little less formal. It's firmly based in a received form, but the poem varies or abandons many of the rules that define that form. Many poems use some patterns you might recognize from or associate with closed forms without really following any given form.

Semi-formal poems use the formal elements of line and stanza in structured, repeating patterns, but they do so in original, irregular, inconsistent, and surprising ways. They might borrow small pieces of a form, like just the length, or use some traditional tools of formal poetry, such as rhyme patterns. They might also invent their own pattern to follow and vary from.

"Three Days After" by Heidi Schulman Greenwald doesn't participate in any received or traditional form, and it isn't following any traditional rhythmic patterns. Notice, though, it does use rhyme and it follows a strict syllabic pattern. The stanza form repeats without fail, and the entire poem is strikingly shaped.

Three Days After

Heart
rides hills and vales
on the monitor, regular
as Monday's mail.
5   Shot

through
the slot today,
a cross-country package. My name
black-inked that he
10   drew

one
week before to
send media mail. Four-score scrawl.
Firm capitals
15   run

deep
in the mailer's
skin. There's a book inside. A note
I can't help but
20   keep.

Thought
you might like this.
Love, Dad. Words scraped like platinum
from a mountain
25   not

rich

in abundance,

simply arduous. Like the hills

outlining thin

30   stitched

beats.

His right hand and leg

rest oddly, short-circuited flesh

that blends into

35   sheets.

Sky

releases south-

bound kestrels one-by-one like his

voice, staccato,

40   wry.

Heidi Schulman Greenwald, 2019

What can we tell about the form of this semiformal poem? We notice quickly that all the stanzas are five lines long. They all start and end with one-word lines, and the second and fourth lines are longer but shorter than the central third line. There are eight stanzas, making forty lines total.

The first and last lines of each stanza rhyme. A lot of the rhymes look quite different, like "one" and "run," making them harder to notice at first. If we count the words in the remaining lines of each stanza, we won't find a consistent pattern. If we count the syllables in each line, however, a strict pattern emerges—one-four-eight-four-one. Even though this poem doesn't participate in any received form, it's not chaotic or unformed. In fact, it's highly structured, even if it isn't "in a form."

Is there any relationship between form and content here? Notice that the poem refers to a man who has suffered a cardiac trauma and is in a hospital hooked up to heart-monitoring devices. In stanza 1, we read: "Heart / rides hills and vales / on the monitor, regular. . . . " And in stanzas 6 and 7: "Like the hills / outlining thin / stitched / beats." In both references, the poem zeroes in on the shape of the lines on the monitor, comparing them to hills and valleys.

Notice too that the shape of the stanzas—entirely independent of what they say—looks just like a peaked hill, with a valley in between each. This also happens to be the shape of a regular heartbeat on a monitor screen. If you don't see that, turn the book on its side so the left margin is down and look again.

You might also consider the visual and sound pattern created by the extremely short first and last lines of each stanza. Do you hear a representation of the "thump-thump" of a heartbeat—expand, contract, pause? Remember you're not trying to guess if the poet "intended" that pattern to be there or not. You're just asking if it *is* there, and if it is, how it affects your understanding and appreciation of the poem. As you see, it is there, too. The form of the poem—line length, lines per stanza, syllable count—all give the poem a strong sound and visual structure, and they mirror and amplify the content.

Just like the creation of recipes, the construction of poetic forms is limited only by the human imagination and is happening all the time. Poet Gregory Pincus recently started publishing poems in which the number of syllables per line is derived from the Fibonacci sequence, a progression of numbers in which each number after the first two is the sum of the two preceding. This form has been named "The Fib," and it is undergoing a transformation from one poet's original notion into a shared recipe which other poets are trying out. When that happens, a semiformal sort of poem enters the realm of the received or traditional form.

Open Form Poems

Until about 150 years ago, there was a widespread consensus that poetry in English was defined by being formal—following, or modifying, the received forms, those poem-recipes of formal patterns and expectations.

However, starting around the middle of the nineteenth century and pervasively by the middle of the twentieth century, that consensus collapsed. Poetry that doesn't follow any received form, or indeed, any sort of apparent structural, rhythmic, or rhyme patterns, became increasingly common and eventually totally dominant. This sort of poetry is known as open form (or "**free verse**" or "**informal**").

Traditional formal poetry never goes away entirely, however, and it enjoys regular revivals. Much open form poetry also echoes, plays with, contains, and refers to elements that are traditionally formal. Many open form poems make use of rhythmic patterns, at least loosely or partially. Many rhyme, though perhaps just in a few places. Many use other devices of sound to create songlike effects.

In the end, all poems have form, even if not all poems are formal. In even the freest of free-verse poems, there are formal considerations and structures to analyze. Every poem has a shape of some sort, and it gets that shape from choices the poet made, formal choices. T. S. Eliot, a pioneer and master of free verse, once quipped "no verse is free for the man who wants to do a good job."

This next poem is representative of what people think of when they think of "free verse" or open form poetry. Nonetheless, it has form, and the form is important.

Love Poem # 7:
Something About Being an Indian

for Adrian C. Louis and Simon J. Ortiz,
"being poor and powerless. And refusing again."

1.

And we knew it as children: playing in tattered pants and
three day worn t-shirts, laughing at our slower cousin and
his hokey pokey hobble of a run, just starting to climb the
slope. We played king of the hill until night fall, scraped off
dried specks of blood from lips as we walked home bragging.

2.

And we proved it in high school basketball: the sweat still
drips from our foreheads, gym shoes squeak, and our shouts
echo through the court. Those are the remaining sounds of
our full court press. Our heads hung lower than our loose
hair after each playoff loss. We practiced back home on
black courts, scraped our knees and elbows on asphalt.

3.

And we finally acknowledge it in adulthood: our drunken
mouths whisper alcoholic nothings, accidentally though, in
each other's noses. We scrape together loose change and
take our beer cans back for the extra nickels. Hatred grew
more than our bones, replaced food and aspirations. It
slowly taught us how to love the ball of hand we call fists.

4.

There is something about being an Indian:
being poor and powerless. And refusing again.

5.

20 And do we ever feel Indian
as a Wasco would on his river
before meeting with Clark?
Are we still Nummu
after spending years
25 with only one sunrise
and the same sunset?
Can we ever peer from the Pueblo
and feel Acoma?
Did any of our ancestors
30 hear the words *Power* and *Less*
then think *Whites* and *Us?*
I don't know what to refuse
our past or our future.
What is derived from our poverty
35 that outsiders believe
we should keep as spirituality?

Jerry Brunoe, 2012

What can we observe about the way this poem uses formal elements? The first big structural element that jumps out is its division into stanzas. The stanzas are prominently numbered, with numerals on a centerline. The first three stanzas are roughly the same size and shape. The fourth stanza is smaller, just two shorter lines. The fifth stanza is a different shape. It's longer, but the individual lines are shorter.

If we look more closely, we don't find any rhyme or other obvious sound patterns. There are no regular rhythmic or syllabic structures, though as we already noticed, there is a pattern in the general line length. However, there are also stanza patterns. Each stanza except the fourth begins with "And." The fourth stanza repeats substantial elements from the title and epigraph. Each stanza is grammatically complete, too. There's no enjambment across stanza breaks. There is plenty of enjambment within stanzas, but not all lines are enjambed.

There's also a content element to Bruin's stanza structure. The first three stanzas move through time—first childhood, then adolescence, and then adulthood. The fourth stanza stops the narrative progression with an idea. The fifth stanza then asks a series of questions that refer back to previous four stanzas and point outwards toward life beyond the poem. Putting the description of each age range in its own discreet numbered stanza helps us understand that we're transitioning from one to the other, and that something new comes after the end.

The form thus gives structure to the content. Creating a somewhat predictable pattern, and then varying that pattern, helps us follow the ideas in the poem.

Final Thoughts

One of the most distinctive things about poems is their form—the way in which content is presented. In analyzing poetry, we use the word and concept of form in two distinct ways.

First, the form of a poem is what gives it shape and structure. The main structural elements of a poem are lines and stanzas. The line is the basic unit of the poem, which ends independently of the end of the page. It is part of the structure of the poem. Stanzas are recognizable sets of lines.

Second, form is a pattern of formal choices that can be recognized and described. A form may precede a poem—similar to a blueprint or recipe. The more important the form is for the poem, and the more the poem follows rather than generates its own pattern, the more "formal" we say it is. However, even very informal poems still have form in their structure and shape.

To finish off the chapter, here's a list of reminders, tips, and tricks to help you as you work with form in poetry:

- Form is seen in patterns, which may be patterns in sound, in appearance, in grammar—almost anything. Look for repetition, sequence, and variation.

- Patterns are often found within lines and between lines, and within stanzas and between stanzas. Ends and beginnings are often places to find a pattern and thus a form at work.

- Keep your mind open about what constitutes form. Make note of whatever creates structure, even strong patterns in content. Count whatever you can count.

- Pay attention to the title! Formal poems often label themselves.

- Use reference materials to match the patterns you see to received forms. The internet makes finding these forms easy, but this book has a Glossary of Forms that covers the most common received forms. There are also many other print references on the subject.

- If you can identify a received form, try searching online for a few other examples of the form and compare.

- The uniquely intense and complex relationship between form and content is one of the things that gives poetry so much energy and makes it distinct from other art forms. Understanding and appreciating this interplay can be a little odd, or feel alien, if it's not something you're used to paying attention to, but if it feels that way, stick with it. You will get used to it, and, hopefully, come to find it fascinating.

Exercises

This section gives you the chance to practice your understanding of these elements through a structured reading of three poems and through focused creative writing prompts. Your professor may or may not assign them. If not, they can still be completed independently if you wish.

For Readers

These three poems each present a clear and interesting situation in which to practice understanding and appreciating poetic form. If you're not given specific assignments by your professor, try doing this for each poem:

1. Complete the basic reading.

2. Jot down your own initial impressions: What did you understand to be happening on the literal level in this poem? Did you like it? Can you say how or why?

3. Identify and count the number of stanzas in each poem. Look for patterns in the stanza structure. Do they start or end with the same word or sort of word? Do the stanzas look visually similar?

4. Identify and count the lines in each stanza. Look for repetition. Are there rhymes? Does the stanza start or end with the same or similar words? Are lines regularly end-stopped or enjambed?

5. Identify and count the number of words and syllables in each line. If you know how to do it, identify and count the unstressed and stressed syllables. Mark them on the page.

6. Jot down descriptions of patterns you see, as well as length in lines and stanzas. Search online to see if the poem fits a traditional form.

7. Write as complete a description of the form of each poem as you can. There's no need to pass any judgments or solve any puzzles.

8. Supplement that description by a description of the relationship between form and content in the poem.

Poem 1

The formal elements at work in this first poem may be easy to spot for many student readers, but there is a danger in assuming too much ease and therefore giving up too quickly. Be patient with this one.

American Curse

May dark soldiers lead you through the mountains.
May you find the criminal weeping in his hands.
May the scent of whiskey rise from your horses.
May you build your mansion in the sands.

5　　May the beauty of your children be too great for kindness.
May the forest reappear when you close your eyes.
May your dogs grow wild as your heart goes tame.
May your bullet always meet with its aim.

Danielle Cadena Deulen, 2014

Poem 2

This next poem makes use of various near-rhyme devices, such as assonance and slant rhyme, which you will read about later in this book—or in a dictionary, if you're curious now. Especially in more contemporary poetry, it's not uncommon to take a form that calls for a pattern of exact rhyme and substitute these sorts of near-rhyme effects.

Three Arches

The droll postmaster says it's small but deep,
this village where the tourists come and go
like baby harbor seals who bask on the beach
awaiting their mother's safe bark back home.

5

This village has its share of idiots,
the local folk who simply will not leave
when driving torrents drive the others out,
they splash their boots in rainwashed, guttered streets.

10

Meanwhile, a mile from shore, huge dark haystacks
loom out of the dark sea. Misnamed the three arches,
a shuttered eye winking inside each rock
at low tide focuses in and watches

the humans with their lives so small and deep.
Forever the three arch eyes never sleep.

Nancy Slavin, 2015

Poem 3

The third poem is a passage from a book-length epic poem that was published in the seventeenth century. It is an imagined embellishment of the Biblical story of the creation of the universe up through Adam and Eve being cast out of the Garden of Eden. In this passage from near the beginning, Satan, "the lost arch-angel," has recently awakened to find himself and his companions in Hell. There they have been imprisoned after the failure of their rebellious war against God in Heaven.

This passage is a speech Satan makes to one of his lieutenants as he surveys what is around him and contemplates their current situation. When he says "he / Who now is Sovereign," he means God. He continues to refer to God in euphemistic ways: "he / Whom Thunder hath made greater" or by title: "th' Almighty." When he references "our faithful friends" toward the end of the passage, he is referring to the other outcast angels, lying stunned all around the lake of fire.

[Is this the Region] from Paradise Lost, Book 1

"Is this the Region, this the Soil, the Clime,"
Said then the lost Arch-Angel, "this the seat
That we must change for Heaven, this mournful gloom
For that celestial light? Be it so, since he
5   Who now is Sovereign can dispose and bid
What shall be right: farthest from him is best
Whom reason hath equaled, force hath made supreme
Above his equals. Farewell happy Fields
Where Joy for ever dwells: Hail horrors, hail
10   Infernal world, and thou profoundest Hell
Receive thy new Possessor: One who brings
A mind not to be changed by Place or Time.
The mind is its own place, and in it self
Can make a Heaven of Hell, a Hell of Heaven.
15   What matter where, if I be still the same,
And what I should be, all but less then he
Whom Thunder hath made greater? Here at least
We shall be free; th' Almighty hath not built
Here for his envy, will not drive us hence:
20   Here we may reign secure, and in my choice
To reign is worth ambition though in Hell:
Better to reign in Hell, than serve in Heaven.
But wherefore let we then our faithful friends,
Th' associates and copartners of our loss
25   Lie thus astonished on th' oblivious Pool,
And call them not to share with us their part
In this unhappy Mansion, or once more
With rallied Arms to try what may be yet
Regained in Heaven, or what more lost in Hell?"

John Milton, 1674

For Writers

The following exercises help you get to know and practice the concepts related to the form of a poem. They're not designed to produce whole, finished poems but to help you experiment with these important elements so that you can use them more effectively to create poems in your own time.

1. Identify any example you're familiar with of the same story being told in different forms. That might be a movie and a book, a myth and a painting, lyrics on the page and a performed song, and so on. Write an analysis or description of how these two forms present the same content differently.

2. Imagine you have an important announcement to make—you're graduating, getting married, getting divorced, moving to another country, joining the French Foreign Legion, starting a new job. . . Create three different announcements, each in a different form: a letter, a text message, a tweet, a Prezi or PowerPoint presentation, a handwritten letter. Now add a fourth announcement: a poem in one of the received forms described in the Glossary of Forms. Haikus are straightforward if the rules for the others seem overwhelming.

3. Concentrate on the idea of your next birthday. Let emotions and thoughts and associations come to the surface. Write them all down as they arise without editing or judging. Let this train of thought take you wherever it wants to go for ten minutes or so. Next, find and carefully and thoroughly read each of these very different poems:

   • "Sonnet II" ("When forty winters shall besiege thy brow"), by Shakespeare

   • "In a Station of the Metro," by Ezra Pound

   • "I Hear America Singing," by Walt Whitman

Write three poems about your next birthday. Imitate these three poems with your three poems.

4. Visit the website of the National Portrait Gallery of the US or England. Spend a while browsing the collection until you find one that really strikes you. Now imagine that the person in the portrait has some sort of problem—a goal he or she is not reaching, a question he or she can't get answered, and so on. The problem should be something that affects how he or she feels or sees the world, not just be an external difficulty. Write a paragraph describing the character and his or her problem.

Now, imagine the resolution of the problem—noting that "resolutions" aren't always happy. Write out a second paragraph describing that resolution.

Finally, relying on the rules from the Glossary of Forms, use these paragraphs as the basis of a sonnet. The main point is to focus on the idea of "the turn" and the compactness of the form, not the other requirements of the form. If those seem intimidating, just write a fourteen-line poem, each line having between eight and twelve syllables.

5. Write a letter to the editor of your local newspaper on a current topic—250 words or less. Then make the same argument eight different times using each of the received forms in the Glossary of Forms.

Chapter 3

The Voice of a Poem

Key terms: speaker, point of view, participant speaker, nonparticipant speaker, unreliable speaker, addressee, the lover, the beloved

'Out, Out—'

The buzz saw snarled and rattled in the yard
And made dust and dropped stove-length sticks of wood,
Sweet-scented stuff when the breeze drew across it.
And from there those that lifted eyes could count
5   Five mountain ranges one behind the other
Under the sunset far into Vermont.
And the saw snarled and rattled, snarled and rattled,
As it ran light, or had to bear a load.
And nothing happened: day was all but done.
10 Call it a day, I wish they might have said
To please the boy by giving him the half hour
That a boy counts so much when saved from work.
His sister stood beside him in her apron
To tell them 'Supper.' At the word, the saw,
15 As if to prove saws knew what supper meant,
Leaped out at the boy's hand, or seemed to leap—
He must have given the hand. However it was,
Neither refused the meeting. But the hand!
The boy's first outcry was a rueful laugh,

20   As he swung toward them holding up the hand
        Half in appeal, but half as if to keep
        The life from spilling. Then the boy saw all—
        Since he was old enough to know, big boy
        Doing a man's work, though a child at heart—

25   He saw all spoiled. 'Don't let him cut my hand off—
        The doctor, when he comes. Don't let him, sister!'
        So. But the hand was gone already.
        The doctor put him in the dark of ether.
        He lay and puffed his lips out with his breath.

30   And then—the watcher at his pulse took fright.
        No one believed. They listened at his heart.
        Little—less—nothing!—and that ended it.
        No more to build on there. And they, since they
        Were not the one dead, turned to their affairs.

Robert Frost, 1916

Stop. What did you just read? What did you just hear? It's time to listen carefully and start a conversation with a poem. In this and the following seven chapters, you'll frequently refer back to this poem, building an element-by-element analysis of its story. So be sure to first put the poem through a careful basic reading. Get the conversation off to a good start.

Every story is told by someone or something—there is always a voice we listen to. This chapter starts to explore the storylike elements of a poem, and it begins with that voice. It's common to pay more attention to the story being told than the voice telling it, but in this chapter, we're going to see that often the voice is far more important—and interesting—than the story it tells.

You'll learn what exactly a speaker is, the difference between the speaker and the author, and the many different kinds of speaker a poem can have. You'll also learn how a speaker's relationship to the story—its point of view—dramatically shapes your understanding and appreciation of the poem.

The Speaker

The voice of a poem is a persona, character, or active intelligence—the storyteller. When talking about prose fiction, it's called the narrator. When talking about poetry, it's referred to as the **speaker**.

The speaker may be a disinterested intelligence describing events that happened somewhere to someone, or it may be a fully fleshed-out character who takes an active part in the poem. There may be a lot of details about the speaker or none at all. The poem may describe the speaker directly, or it may only imply facts about the speaker. What we can know about the speaker may be crucial to understanding and appreciating the poem, or it may be almost totally irrelevant.

It's not very common, but possible, for a poem to have multiple speakers. A poem may go back and forth between the two, as if they're having a conversation. Others go through a whole sequence, perhaps letting a new voice speak every stanza. When the voice of the speaker seems to lack consistency, look carefully for evidence there are multiple voices speaking the poem. We should start our investigation of the speaker with all these possibilities in mind.

Speaker Versus Author

It's natural to assume that the speaker is the author, but they are not the same. In some poems, they are obviously not the same, such as poems in which the speaker is an inanimate object. For the purposes of analysis and definition, though, "speaker" and "author" are always different, no matter what. Even when the poem is told by a speaker who shares what seem to be biographical facts with the author, they are different.

Try this analogy: Every fast-food restaurant has a manager. There is also a district supervisor who supervises all the managers in the district. Those are two separate roles—two separate concepts. Imagine that you are a manager. The president calls you one day and says, "I'm going to promote you to district supervisor, but you need to continue to manage your restaurant."

Suddenly, you are both the district supervisor and a manager. You are one person who is filling both roles, but that doesn't mean there is no difference between the district supervisor role and the manager role. The district supervisor has one set of responsibilities and powers, and the manager has an entirely different set of responsibilities and powers—two roles, even if they are both carried out by the same person.

Author and speaker are similarly two different roles in a poem. It might be that the poem is 100 percent autobiographically accurate. That doesn't matter in the slightest. There are two different concepts—author and speaker. One is a real flesh-and-blood human being who wrote a poem one day. The other is an imaginary persona whose voice exists forever in the fiction of the poem.

This is also an important part of developing a disciplined approach to reading poems. You need to begin with the text on the page and not rely on any outside research, to start your reading confident that you don't need anything else in order to understand and appreciate it—except for a good dictionary, of course.

Wondering about the conditions of the author's life, his or her personal qualities and issues, or even his or her stated intentions in writing the poem can easily send you down a wrong path. You may start reading the poem as an historical episode instead of what it is, which is a piece of fictional art.

However, if you start with the idea that the author and speaker are two separate roles, it's not hard to later ask how much they have in common, if you become curious about that. In the meantime, pay attention to what the poem says. You're free to focus on what there is to learn about the speaker from the text, but your understanding isn't limited by what you can learn about the author's life.

Point of View

The **point of view** is the perspective from which the speaker tells the story. It is the relationship of the speaker to the story. The point of view of the speaker is either participant or nonparticipant. If the speaker takes part in the action, as if it were a story he or she is telling about his or her own life, that is a **participant speaker**. A participant speaker is also a character in the poem. When there is a disembodied voice telling a story about other people and places—a voice that does not belong to a character in the story—that's a **nonparticipant speaker**.

Participant Speakers

Much poetry focuses on the experiences, thoughts, and feelings of individuals, so participant speakers are common. Many poets are interested in the human mind—how it perceives reality, how it responds to stress, how it relates to others through language. The participant speaker is a great way to create that kind of poem.

When you find a participant speaker, try to get a clear picture of the speaker as a character. This next poem is a good one to start with.

After a Student Prefaces
Her Question About a Poem

I want to stop her, tell her I don't know much
about poetry either. I know about scrubbing toilets,
pumping gas and fixing cars, tearing apart
old fences and the rotting walls of sheds,
painting someone else's house. I've heard
the rhythms of engines breaking down,
wrenches dropped on concrete floors.

5

I taught myself to sing in filth, foot tapping in time
with ticking generators, dripping faucets, cooling
10   engines, pounding hammers. Trucks, garages,
basement workshops resounding with my voice:
ammonia, bleach, denatured alcohol, poly-
urethane, oil-based, latex paint, rubber gloves,
sawdust, rusty water running down cinder blocks.

15   I learned not to hold my breath for answers. Listen,
every poem poses a chance like this: we work our way
through its rooms — rubbing surfaces raw, stripping
walls to studs, putting them splinter by splinter back
till we're stuck with a pile of leftover parts —
20   and we raise a hand for help, asking to be
numbered among the great unwashed.

Brian Simoneau, 2008

What do you notice right away? The title sets the scene: A student is asking someone a question.

The first line directly continues the thought — and in fact, the sentence — that starts in the title. Rewrite that first sentence to get rid of the line breaks, and you have:

> After a student prefaces her question about a poem, I want to stop her, tell her I don't know much about poetry either.

That looks like a participant speaker. "I" is the subject of the first sentence. "I" is explaining how "I" reacted to what a student said before that student asked a question about a poem.

Can you learn anything about the speaker? Yes! To begin with, you see that the speaker is someone to whom students address questions — a teacher. What else? The first and second stanzas are mostly a description of the speaker's background, which is dominated by work that includes being a janitor, pumping gas, fixing cars, doing demolition and construction, and painting houses.

At the start of the second stanza, the speaker says, "I taught myself to sing in filth." "Sing" probably refers to writing poetry, not literally singing. This suggests that the speaker began to love and to write poems in this blue-collar life, before formally studying the subject.

So, you have learned that the speaker of this poem is an English teacher who came to teaching after a background in low-wage, blue-collar work, and who was self-taught in poetry before becoming a teacher.

Unreliable Participant Speakers

A participant speaker may not be reliable in how it tells the story. It may distort the story to make itself look good or to make other characters look bad or to control the audience's perception of events in some other way. It may tell a distorted story because it *cannot* tell that story accurately. It may labor under limitations of knowledge or perception or communication. Sensibly enough, we call such a speaker an **unreliable speaker**.

When you read a poem with a participant speaker, you need to watch for clues about how trustworthy it is. And when the reliability of the speaker is called into question, you must pay less attention to what is supposedly happening and more attention to the way it's being described.

Here's a poem with another participant speaker, but this one may not be very reliable.

Annabel Lee

It was many and many a year ago,
   In a kingdom by the sea,
That a maiden there lived whom you may know
   By the name of Annabel Lee;
And this maiden she lived with no other thought
   Than to love and be loved by me.
I was a child and she was a child,
   In this kingdom by the sea,
But we loved with a love that was more than love—

5

10   I and my Annabel Lee—
   With a love that the wingèd seraphs of Heaven
    Coveted her and me.

   And this was the reason that, long ago,
    In this kingdom by the sea,
15   A wind blew out of a cloud, chilling
    My beautiful Annabel Lee;
   So that her highborn kinsmen came
    And bore her away from me,
   To shut her up in a sepulchre
20   In this kingdom by the sea.

   The angels, not half so happy in Heaven,
    Went envying her and me—
   Yes!—that was the reason (as all men know,
    In this kingdom by the sea)
25   That the wind came out of the cloud by night,
    Chilling and killing my Annabel Lee.

   But our love it was stronger by far than the love
    Of those who were older than we—
    Of many far wiser than we—
30   And neither the angels in Heaven above
    Nor the demons down under the sea
   Can ever dissever my soul from the soul
    Of the beautiful Annabel Lee;

   For the moon never beams, without bringing me dreams
35   Of the beautiful Annabel Lee;
   And the stars never rise, but I feel the bright eyes
    Of the beautiful Annabel Lee;

And so, all the night-tide, I lie down by the side

Of my darling—my darling—my life and my bride,

40 In her sepulchre there by the sea—

In her tomb by the sounding sea.

Edgar Allan Poe, 1849

What can we learn about the speaker in this poem? In the first two stanzas, we learn that many years ago, he was in love with a "maiden" named Annabel Lee. In fact, this happened in his and her childhood. Their love, he says, was so great—"love that was more than love"—that it made the very angels of Heaven jealous. That love is why "a wind blew out of a cloud," killing Annabel Lee. Her family put her body in a crypt above ground, and he goes there to sleep beside her corpse every night.

Clearly, this is a participant speaker. The story is all about him. Therefore, he is *potentially* unreliable. How reliable does this speaker seem? How grounded in reality is his story? What about his state of mind is revealed by how he tells this story?

Blaming jealous angels for killing your childhood sweetheart and spending the rest of your life sneaking into a crypt to sleep beside her dead body is not sane behavior. Such a clear indication that the speaker is this detached from reality is your tip-off that he is an unreliable participant speaker. His whole story is suspect. Did Annabel Lee really love him back? Did they have any real relationship at all? How did she really die?

If you reread the poem with this unreliability in mind, you start to notice how jealous the speaker is of everyone. After her death, for example, her family doesn't just bury her. As he describes it, they take her away from him as if they were taking a thing that belonged to him. He also asserts their love was "stronger by far" than the love of those "older" and "far wiser." Someone older was in some way critical of their relationship. It's hard not to read the "far wiser" as sarcastic.

And how exactly did she die? He tries to convince you she was killed by angels. Is that normal angel behavior, to kill young girls because you're jealous of how perfect their love is? He gives us this story about the lethal jealousy of the angels, and then he spends the next stanza repeating it.

In lines 22–23, notice how he interrupts himself:

> Went envying her and me—
> Yes!—that was the reason (as all men know

He asserts the truth of his story—"Yes!"—and then adds the reassurance that "all men know" that it's the truth and that this is actually what happened. Because he argues so repetitively and nonsensically that this is true, you begin to wonder exactly who he's trying to convince.

This is a classic example of an unreliable speaker. We can reasonably question both his sanity and his motives. We have no idea what really happened to poor Annabel Lee or what their relationship was like—or if they had any relationship at all—but we are left with a striking and insightful portrait of an unhinged mind drawn from the inside out.

Nonparticipant Speakers

With nonparticipant speakers, the speaker is no longer a central element to consider. The focus shifts toward external events in the poem. However, there are still nuances of these speakers to be attentive to.

One complexity of nonparticipant speakers is how all-knowing they seem to be. Does the speaker describe the inner mental and emotional states of the characters? Does the speaker describe physical scenes or processes that are impossible to perceive with the human eye? Does the speaker race forward and backward in time? Does it know things that the characters do not or cannot know?

You should also note when the speaker is a nonparticipant but closely follows a single character. This restricts the audience's knowledge to the perspective of one character, but it doesn't necessarily make the reliability of the speaker an issue. The nonparticipant speaker who focuses on a single character is a common point of view, second only to the participant speaker. It's easily confused with the participant speaker, too.

Another thing to watch for is how much nonparticipant speakers comment on the situations they describe. Do they function as transparent presenters of their poems, or do they interject judgments and asides about the situations? In cases where they offer judgments, you need to distinguish between what the speakers describe and the comments they make. A speaker who interjects judgments about the situation often feels more like a character than most nonparticipant speakers. It's important to read carefully to see if such a speaker is participating in the story from a distance or just offering godlike commentary about it.

Be sure to read the whole poem all the way through before you start forming conclusions. Sometimes a nonparticipant speaker lets the characters speak directly, and in that dialogue they describe their own lives and action using first-person pronouns. They are addressing each other, not the audience, but it's easy to mistake a character's dialogue for the narration of speaker who is involved in the action.

Here is a poem featuring a nonparticipant speaker.

Quinceañera

The women of the house shook her from sleep,
and began to serenade, trying to mark
the air of another rite that seemed to come

too soon, the song her father should have sung
5   instead of barking, running her off, a song
with the momentum of a hand ready to skip

a stone across water, a hand which would
fall away soon as the song was done,
but not before a stone danced,

10   lifting and lifting off the face of water,
each time as if it'd never drop — past midnight,

the women sang, without ceremony,

without food, without a sense of how
to ready a girl to skip into the current
15   of her life, could only sing,

their voices cracked and strained, trying
not to wake her son who slept beside her,
a son who would grow up and dream of the night

these voices broke the air and raised a song
20   for the little girl his mother was,
for the woman she now had to become.

José Angel Araguz, 2014

No first-person pronoun appears. That's a good but not perfect indi-cator that we have a nonparticipant speaker. Does the speaker seem to be taking part in the events? No. Does the speaker mention interacting with any character, or mention being affected in any way by another character? No. The speaker describes what the characters do and know and intend, but the speaker is not a character in the poem. This, then, is a nonparticipant speaker.

The speaker is close to events of the poem, though. Notice how the speaker passes judgment on "the father" and on the timing of "the rite," that it's "too soon." The speaker has access to the thoughts and feelings of the women who sing, referring to their intentions and the gaps in their knowledge. The speaker knows the past and the future of the girl and her son. While not participating directly in the action of the poem, the speaker is intimately wrapped up in the lives of the characters.

Addressee

Before we leave the topic of speaker and point of view, we should consider another special character, the **addressee**—the person to whom a poem is addressed and the persona to whom the speaker is directly speaking.

In many poems, there is a direct addressee. The speaker uses the second-person pronoun, "you," and may make direct statements to or ask direct questions of some apparent listener. The listener is not the generic, impersonal audience but another character in the poem with the participant speaker. The whole poem becomes a speech made directly from one character to another, and the reader is put in the position of observer, overhearing an address that the speaker doesn't intend to be shared — but that the author is sharing.

One common set-up is for a participant speaker to be addressing someone he or she is in love with, and in such poems it's conventional to refer to the speaker as "**the lover**" and the addressee as "**the beloved.**"

The Speaker and Point of View in "'Out, Out —'"

Start your conversation with "'Out, Out —'" by listening carefully to the voice that you hear. What do you notice about the speaker? The point of view? One thing you're going to notice is that sometimes it's hard to determine the point of view with perfect clarity.

The voice presents someone else's story, the story of the buzz saw and the boy. Nowhere does this narrative voice indicate that it is a part of the story. It doesn't take any action or talk to any of the characters. It doesn't influence what happens. It describes something that happens to another group of people. You're inclined to describe this as a nonparticipant speaker.

However, there is a major complication. Notice line 10:

Call it a day, I wish they might have said.

There's the first-person pronoun, so the speaker does enter into the story, if only to express feelings about what's happening. The speaker seems close to the action. These are events that the speaker wishes had turned out differently. This makes the speaker feel less like a detached, impersonal narrator and more like someone relating a story about a relative or friend. That "I" and the sentiment it expresses thus push you to call this a participant speaker.

However, the speaker never expresses any other feelings about the event or makes any additional comments. Given the intensely sad story, the speaker seems remarkably detached. The speaker also suggests at points that it knows what the characters think or feel. In lines 22–25, it references the degree to which the boy understands what's happening to him. In lines 30–31, it knows what the people in the room think as the boy's pulse fades. In the final two lines, it knows the motivations and intentions of everyone present. It would be hard for any character to know any of those things, much less all of them. This suggests that the speaker is a nonparticipant.

The argument can also be made that all of those insights are reasonable inferences any observer might make—we see how people act, what they say, their facial expressions and body language, and we come to a conclusion about what they're thinking or feeling. If the speaker reports others' actions with more authority than is warranted, perhaps that's a sign that the speaker is unreliable. Perhaps it suggests something about the speaker's personality.

You can argue that the speaker is or is not a participant. Where you come down on the question may influence how you understand other parts of the poem. Ultimately, the point of view in this poem is ambiguous.

This ambiguity in the poem isn't a failure on your part or Frost's. It's a feature of the poem for you to notice and pay attention to, like any other.

Final Thoughts

Every story has a teller, every song has a singer, every painting has a painter—and every poem has a speaker. The speaker is not the author, no matter how similar they might seem. The speaker is a fictional persona an author creates to tell their poems for them. The speaker is a part of the poem that the author is writing, one of the tools the author uses in the crafting of a poem. Some poems have multiple speakers.

Speakers are of broadly two types. First, there are those who are characters themselves in the stories they tell. They are called participant speakers. Second, there are speakers who tell someone else's story from afar. These are referred to as nonparticipant speakers. Participant speakers cannot always be trusted to tell their stories accurately, so it's important to carefully assess how trustworthy, or reliable, a participant speaker is.

Don't stop wondering about the speaker until you're satisfied you've learned what you can about who's telling this story. To finish off the chapter, here's a list of reminders, tips, and tricks to help you as you work with the voices of poems:

- Always remember to ask the poem this: who is telling your story?

- Look for the main pronouns used by the speaker. When the speaker consistently uses first-person pronouns, such as "I," "me," and "mine," it's a good indication you have a participant speaker. However, remember that this is not a foolproof technique!

- Avoid jumping to conclusions. Watch out for participant speakers who start off describing other characters and what they're doing from a distance, without tipping you off to the fact that they're involved.

- Listen for clues about reliability if you think you have a participant speaker. Imagine you're overhearing a story or conversation in a dark room. There may be a lot of information there if you read between the lines.

- Ask yourself if there are inconsistencies in the speaker's story. Apply the same common sense you might when listening to a friend. Does it add up?

- Keep asking questions if you decide the poem has a nonparticipant speaker. What can you infer about the relationship of the speaker to the rest of the situation?

Remember that this is an open-ended conversation with a poem. You can't know ahead of time how much information there is or what it will be. Listen carefully to find what is there, and don't give up too easily. Ask questions about what seems unclear and listen for the answers. However, don't assume that every detail about the speaker is hidden in the poem somewhere. There may be little or no information to find. The information may be contradictory or inconclusive. And all that's okay, too. Keep listening!

Exercises

This final section of the chapter offers you the chance to practice your understanding of speaker and point-of-view through guided readings of three poems and through focused creative writing exercises. If a professor hasn't already assigned them, try them on your own. They're designed to be completed independently.

For Readers

These three poems present clear and interesting situations to practice your understanding and appreciation of speaker and point of view. Unless you've been given specific assignments, try doing this for each poem:

1. Complete the basic reading.

2. Jot down your own initial impressions: What did you understand to be happening at the literal level in this poem? Did you like it? Can you say how or why?

3. Identify the point of view and explain how you know.

4. Write a description of the participant speaker, if there is one. Note what you know for sure, what you have inferred, and how certain you feel about those inferences.

5. If you have a participant speaker, describe how reliable you think it is. Note the evidence in the text that supports your assessment.

6. If you have a nonparticipant speaker, explain the point of view.

Poem 1

As you read this first poem, know that much of what is vital is not said aloud. It is reminiscent of a famous line from an Emily Dickinson poem: "Tell all the truth but tell it slant." There are crucial passages in lines 6 and 10 that give you indirect information. Line 2 is more important than it seems on the first reading. What is being dreamed about in lines 13–15?

Burying Our Daughter's Teeth

I cleaned the house one hundred days after
the day of which we no longer speak

and set the baby's teeth inside your art
deco bowl. They looked so lost tinkering

5   around the matte aqua glaze, so I tucked them
in to sleep amidst their friends of ash and bone,

curled on downy potting soil pillows
as if I'd pulled my mother's old afghan around

their tiny saw-tooth chins. Inside this careful planting,
10   it will be as if she still sleeps in the clavicle space

between us. There on sheets with names like Dusk
and Smoke, we will dream together of curlicue

roots and the brittle red leaves placed
in her Buddha-doll hands, the writhing worm

15   plucked from her hungry latch-tongued mouth.
We will not notice the sour smell of our compost

heap gone wrong and the musty basement

out-gassing into the backyard, because it will be only

> your head on my lap,
20   our daughter on your cardigan chest

> in the late autumn sun — hemlock, whip stitch, peat moss.

Tiah Lindner Raphael, 2013

Poem 2

In this second poem, it's important to identify the addressee as quickly as you can. Notice the three-part structure. The first two stanzas work toward one purpose, and there's a shift in the third stanza and then another in the fourth. Also, the first stanza includes jargon. Look everything up. Information about the speaker and addressee is encoded in those references and in the proper nouns in the title.

"Willamette River, Marion Street Bridge: Pier Five, General Details"

The sun slams into us
like one of the pile drivers
down on the gravel bar. The crew I'm on
is erecting forms for concrete piers.

5   Machinery roars. Earth shudders.
Cottonwood leaves turn grey with dust.

Companions of duty,
is this our assignment? Simply to be here, packed
in these heavy bodies, dumbfounded,
10   while time drags
and the river slides quietly by?

I signal the sun to slack off a little,

But nothing happens.
I keep on signaling anyway.

Clemens Starck, 1995

Poem 3

This third poem relies entirely — at first — on the allusion in the title, so if you're not familiar with that allusion, be sure to look it up. Once you have a good picture of the speaker on the literal level, though, go back and reread it, paying particular attention to the possible double meanings of many words and phrases. There's a second, completely different way to understand and describe the speaker at work here, too.

Swan Maiden's Daughter

I was the eldest of her clutch. The one
who looked up when the wedge of swans
flew over, turned out my feet to match
their shadow on the grass. I who could feel
what might yet sprout from my shoulders
and break me open, what I had to fold in.

What kind of inveiglement plucks
a mother from her brood? I'll tell you:
it called to her stronger than kin. Her body
leaned away from us, the tremble of her
hands always upturning, rummaging,
seeking out the yearning of her skin.

Hiding it still failed to make her ours.
So many undone times my father found
her, passed out again in the reeds, face
half in the river, leeches latched
and glistening at her throat. The curve

of her thighs rising out of the mud.

My father told me how he took it:
20   gathering it up in his hands, turning
it over like a breathing thing. The shell
of it almost weightless, intricate feathering
of barbs and shafts needling his palms.
Vane after vane unzipping in his arms.

25   We presented her innumerable sweet
distractions: the wooden door with
bird-shaped knocker, down bedding trimmed
in eyelet lace, arrowgrass flowering
on the sill, fresh bread. The loop of our limbs
30   about her waist, kisses along her arched neck.

But of course she found it. Turned the world
upside down until it fell out of the sky. Slipped
into it arm by arm, lay back and let the plumage
wash over her, fingers fluttering like wings.
35   No man, no cygnet-girl could keep her.
Flying off behind her glassy eyes.

Brittney Corrigan, 2019

For Writers

The following exercises help you get to know and practice the concepts of speaker and point of view in your own writing. They are not designed to produce whole, finished poems but to help you experiment with these smaller elements so that you can use them more effectively to create poems in your own time. You might find that any of these exercises inspires you to start a poem, and that's great, too.

1. Start with an existing poem. It could be one of your own poems, but doesn't need to be. Rewrite the poem from two different points of view without major changes to length or form.

2. Meditate on some important events in your life that taught you some lesson. Jot down a line or two for each event. Narrow your options down to a single event. Tell the story in a short paragraph. Make sure the lesson comes through to the reader. Rewrite the paragraph using a nonparticipant speaker and fictionalizing at least three key components, such as the gender or age of the protagonist, the setting, and so on, but without altering the lesson learned.

3. List ten personality types or actual people whom you find irritating or contemptible. Pick one and write a poem from a first-person point of view, using that person as your speaker, which makes it clear to the audience just how awful this point of view or person is. Write a second poem, also told from that person's point of view, which gives the audience a chance to sympathize with and understand that person or point of view.

4. Write a 250- to 350-word description of a thing: a place, an event, or a person. Now imagine three people with very different backgrounds, education levels, cultures, and so on. Rewrite your description in the voice of each of those characters.

Chapter 4

The Feeling of a Poem

Key terms: tone, irony

In the last chapter, we started exploring the ways that poems can be like stories, starting with the fact that every story has a teller. There is always a voice that "speaks" the poem. That speaker is a fictional intelligence created by the author to tell the poem to us.

In this chapter, we'll look into another fact about stories—they're emotional. Stories are all about the exploration of emotional states and how they're created and changed. Not only are stories themselves inherently about feelings and full of feelings, but storytellers also have feelings about the stories they are telling. And because the speaker is always a part of the story, created by the author, then sometimes we can find in a poem *two* storytellers with *different* feelings about the same story. Both the fictional speaker and the real-life author may have distinct feelings about what happens in the poem.

You'll return to "'Out, Out —'" in this chapter, looking carefully at the feelings in the story and what the feelings of the speaker—or the author!—about the story seem to be. Go back and give it another reading now, reminding yourself of what you know, or think you know, about the speaker, and paying attention to the general feelings of the poem.

Tone

Tone describes a whole range of things in a poem. This term is used in a general sense to describe the overall emotional climate or mood of the poem—is it sad, angry, or happy? However, tone is also used in more specific ways to describe the apparent feelings or attitude of the speaker toward the content of the story being told, and, separately, the author's feelings about the content of the poem.

When the feelings of author and speaker overlap, analyzing tone is straightforward. When they diverge, as often happens, analyzing tone can be a more complicated process, requiring more careful rereading and thinking about those multiple overlapping attitudes and feelings.

Poems often have multiple tones because human emotions are complicated. People have the capacity to hold many, sometimes contradictory feelings about a subject at once. However, keep in mind that tone does *not* refer to how the poem makes you feel or how the characters in the poem seem to feel, even though those feelings may happen to be the same as the tone.

Below are two poems with different tones about the same subject—young English men going to war during World War I, and more specifically, their motivation for doing so.

The Call

Who's for the trench—
Are you, my laddie?
Who'll follow the French—
Will you, my laddie?
5   Who's fretting to begin,
Who's going out to win?
And who wants to save his skin—
Do you, my laddie?

Who's for the khaki suit—

10 Are you, my laddie?

Who longs to charge and shoot—

Do you, my laddie?

Who's keen on getting fit,

Who means to show his grit,

15 And who'd rather wait a bit—

Would you, my laddie?

Who'll earn the Empire's thanks—

Will you, my laddie?

Who'll swell the victor's ranks—

20 Will you, my laddie?

When that procession comes,

Banners and rolling drums-

Who'll stand and bite his thumbs—

Will you, my laddie?

Jessie Pope, 1915

The poem is addressed toward young men of fighting age—"my laddie." It asks the audience a series of questions, all of which are different iterations of the same question: Are you going to volunteer for the army and go to war in France? In this poem, going to war is a sign of character, bravery, and strength. It's guaranteed to end in victory, thanks, and parades. Not going to war is a sign of selfishness, cowardice, indecision, and it's guaranteed to end in a lifetime of regret. The war itself is barely described at all.

The tone of the poem is enthusiastic, excited, positive, patriotic, exhortative, admiring, mocking, a little stern, and maybe a little self-satisfied. We conclude that the poet is thus excited, enthusiastic, and positive about the war, seeing it as an occasion to build and prove strength. The speaker insists that young men sign up and go fight, is full of admiration for those who do, and mocks and humiliates those who don't sign up to fight. We may wonder, too, about the poet's attitude toward herself or those for whom she speaks. She seems satisfied with herself for doing her part to mobilize the troops.

Now, contrast the tone in that poem to the tone in this one. Watch how this poet chooses to describe the same topics — the choice to go to war, the meaning of being at war, the consequences of being at war, and the war itself.

Dulce et Decorum Est

Bent double, like old beggars under sacks,
Knock-kneed, coughing like hags, we cursed through sludge,
Till on the haunting flares we turned our backs,
And towards our distant rest began to trudge.
Men marched asleep. Many had lost their boots,
But limped on, blood-shod. All went lame; all blind;
Drunk with fatigue; deaf even to the hoots
Of gas-shells dropping softly behind.

Gas! GAS! Quick, boys! — An ecstasy of fumbling
Fitting the clumsy helmets just in time,
But someone still was yelling out and stumbling
And flound'ring like a man in fire or lime. —
Dim through the misty panes and thick green light,
As under a green sea, I saw him drowning.

In all my dreams before my helpless sight,
He plunges at me, guttering, choking, drowning.

If in some smothering dreams, you too could pace
Behind the wagon that we flung him in,
And watch the white eyes writhing in his face,
His hanging face, like a devil's sick of sin;
If you could hear, at every jolt, the blood

Come gargling from the froth-corrupted lungs,
Obscene as cancer, bitter as the cud
Of vile, incurable sores on innocent tongues, —
My friend, you would not tell with such high zest
To children ardent for some desperate glory,
The old Lie: *Dulce et decorum est*
Pro patria mori.

Wilfred Owen, 1920

The Latin phrase at the end is a quote from the Roman poet Horace: "It is sweet and fitting to die for one's country." Unlike in the previous poem, the war itself is described explicitly, in great detail, with first-person immediacy and full immersion.

This poem is also addressed to some specific group of people or person, though it's not revealed until the final stanza, when "you" enters the poem: "if . . . you could pace behind the wagon . . . and watch," "if you could hear," "My friend, you would not. . . ." The poem is addressed to people like the writer of the first poem, those exhorting young men to sign up and go to war by telling them lies about it. In fact, an early draft of this poem, which survives in manuscript, is actually dedicated to Jessie Pope, though Owen removed that dedication in later drafts.

The tone of the poem is seething with fury and rage and sadness. The poet is sick and angry about the war and the suffering of the men, but he's angrier about "the old lie" and the liars who tell it.

The two poems have the same subject but extremely different tones. The authors are talking about the same thing, but they have very different feelings about it. Notice too that this is not about ideas. You're not wondering what thoughts each author has or what ideas or arguments either poem might contain or imply. You're putting your fingers on the emotional pulse of each poem.

Tone in "'Out, Out —'"

What can we discover about the tone of the Robert Frost poem that we have been reading in recent chapters?

Let's map what outright expressions of feeling we can find:

- In line 10, we see regret as the speaker expresses a wish that things might have been different.

- In lines 11 and 12, the speaker talks about the pleasure a boy feels in a half an hour saved from work.

- In line 18, there's a peak of feeling with the speaker's interjection, "But the hand!" The incomplete thought and exclamation point mark some strong, incompletely spoken emotion.

- In the next line, the boy's "first outcry" is a "rueful laugh" — sad and full of regret. This is the second time we get the feeling of regret, of wishing things had been different.

- The boy's speech in lines 25–26 is full of fear and pleading.

- In line 30, the "watcher at the pulse" is afraid as it diminishes.

- In the next line, we see the shocked disbelief of everyone as the boy dies.

The feelings that are most clearly expressed are regret, sadness, shock, fear, and helplessness. The one positive feeling, the pleasure that "a boy" — though not this particular boy — feels at free time, is purely hypothetical. This boy doesn't get to feel that pleasure.

Given how tragic the subject matter is, that tone shouldn't surprise us. What might be surprising is how restrained the feelings actually are. In thirty-four lines about the violent accidental death of a child, feeling words are used in only seven places. We hardly see anyone's reactions to events. A great deal of space in the poem is given to describing the place. The saw is the most richly described character.

Notice how impersonal the language often is, too. The speaker describes the moment of the boy's actual death with "that ended it." And there's that final sentence after the boy has died. Everyone gets up and moves on with their business.

It's possible that the tone here is actually angry. Perhaps the poem condemns the indifference of the family and the world to the boy's suffering and death. In this way of thinking, the poem draws attention to the intensity of the sadness by not expressing it, like someone getting very quiet before they completely lose their temper. Maybe the poem expresses bitter cynicism about how quickly and selfishly the living forget the dead.

It's possible that there's a tone of profound despair running through this poem, which is emphasized at the end. Perhaps it's a statement of fact that everyone else, being still alive, goes on living. What else are they supposed to do? Lay down and die as well? There's nothing that says that his living relatives are not grieving for the boy, but no matter how deeply they grieve, an unbridgeable gap has opened between the living and the dead, and nothing can be done about it. The boy is dead, and the living must keep living. Anyone who has passed through grief should recognize this bizarre experience. The loved one is gone, yet somehow you must still be here, take out the garbage, feed the children, milk the cows.

Notice once again how much ambiguity there is in the tone of this poem. Don't be afraid of ambiguity. Poetry is often unclear and multifaceted. Sometimes all you need to do is be clear about the lack of clarity.

The Speaker's and Author's Attitudes

In the examples we've seen so far, the general mood of the poem and the apparent attitudes of the speaker and author are the same. But this isn't always the case.

The participant speaker is often a vehicle for the author to comment on social or existential conditions and how they affect us. By putting a speaker in a situation experiencing racism, for example, the author has a vehicle for exploring racism itself, how it manifests, how people do and could respond to it. This invites the reader into that experience and offers the chance to learn and reflect on it. The author may also try to teach a lesson or urge a certain course of action.

This gives rise to poems in which the values, attitudes, and experiences of the poem's speaker are far from the values, attitudes, and experiences of the poem's author. For instance, the author might explore the mental world of an animal, an inanimate object, or a psychotic murderer. A poem exploring racism might have a racist speaker. That doesn't mean the poem or its author are racist. The racist mind is the subject of the poem. It also gives rise to poems in which the speaker is someone in some mental extremity—facing great tragedy, confusion, or other difficulty.

As you try to piece together what you can about the speaker, keep these possibilities in mind. Stories conventionally invite you to sympathize with the central character, especially a participant speaker. But you should initially maintain some critical distance and appraise the state of mind of the speaker before extending that sympathy.

Here's a clear example of a speaker whose attitude is different from the author's:

[I Do Not Fret] from "Yoked"

Drop safety present, sir,
I am on duty, at the ready,
on alert, I am on guard, I
stand my ground.

5   My peers call me a chatterbox,
patched up, fixed up there and
here, but I don't fail my team,
my boys, the soldier

and his sons. He'll lift me from
my plastic lockup, show them
how to clean and hold me, cool
hands, steady, sure.

One by one, he'll bring them out,
teach them how to shoot,
kickass fun for both of us. And
once a year — I live for this —

his strong grip grabs me tight,
takes me on the hunt.
It is the rush of blood I love,
the pact with men, the power,

the way they talk about me,
our fresh meat on the table.
Home, I'm locked in dark
again, left alone to savor

our perfect partnership:
his aim, my execution.
Of late the taller boy,
close-mouthed like his dad,

waits till it's the two of us, strokes
me with his sweaty palms,
breathes in starts and fits.
When he's through he breaks

the rules of key and lock, of
unload and disarm, shoves me
underneath the bed, at ease
with 10-round magazines.

I do not fret. I do my job. So
when the boy with ragged breath,
stuffs me in a bag of ammo,
40   hauls me off to school on the yellow

bus, I stand my ground.
I am on guard. I am
on duty. At the ready. On alert.
Drop safety present. Sir.

Alida Rol, 2019

Before we can understand the differing attitudes of the speaker and the author, we have to identify this speaker. Our first read through should quickly discover that this is a participant speaker—the first-person pronoun is pervasive, and it's used to describe the speaker's interactions with the other characters and participation in events.

What else can we learn about the speaker? Through the first two stanzas, we might start to think that the speaker is a soldier, but the third stanza should radically alter our thinking about the speaker:

He'll lift me from
my plastic lockup, show them
how to clean and hold me, cool
hands, steady, sure.

What does this mean? If it's not clear yet, the following stanzas make it obvious that the speaker is a firearm—normally kept locked up, needing careful instruction on how to be cleaned and held, used to teach boys how to shoot, gripped strongly for hunting, and so on.

This firearm—probably a rifle or shotgun because it's used for hunting—describes its relationship to its owner and his sons, how it feels about hunting, what it sees as its duties and its pride. That's interesting enough, but in the seventh stanza, the action takes a dark turn as the older boy is described as hiding the gun, breaking the rules, obsessing over it, and keeping it loaded. Finally, in the last two stanzas, the speaker describes the boy bringing him and a "bag of ammo" onto the school bus. Clearly something terrible is about to happen.

And what is the speaker's attitude toward events? It is resolutely neutral. It passes no judgment on the boy's actions and expresses neither concern nor surprise. The speaker is clearly capable of strong emotions, of having preferences and passing judgments, but in this case, it is simply present and ready to do its duty.

Hopefully it's evident at this point that the author's attitude differs from that of the speaker. No one is neutral about a school shooting that is about to happen. No one could respond to such a situation as if it were simply another duty to be carried out. The tone of the poem, which reflects the attitudes of the author, is horror and dread and outrage. The attitudes of the speaker, however, are a resolute pride in duty, an eagerness to be ready, a love of power and execution of orders, and a studied indifference to the effects of that readiness.

The gap between tone and the speaker's attitude allows the author to create a character that the audience can judge—without judging the author. This tone and point of view also allow the author to set up a situation in which the audience might transfer its feelings or judgments about the speaker, which after all is a fantastical creation, to people who might hold similar opinions about guns and the role or place of guns in our society—without directly attacking those people.

Irony

The distinction between the feelings and attitudes of the author and the speaker or characters in a poem sets up the consideration of one particular type of tone, irony. **Irony** is created when what people say is purposefully different from what they actually mean or from what was expected. Irony works when the reader can understand both the stated meaning and, from the context, the actual meaning. Humans seem to get a delicious pleasure from this discrepancy.

Tone is often ironic because there can be a discrepancy between what the poem says, especially the words the author puts in the voices of speakers and characters, and what the author actually means. We see that in the Alida Rol poem. What the gun says and what the poem means are completely different.

Irony abounds in poetry, especially modern poetry. Here's an example:

Anti-Elegy

Your son shermed to death in makeshift car.
His loss was felt (but yours was felt the more).
Don't be a dad tonight, go to the bar.

His momma cries and prays to morning star.
5   She prays now that he reach celestial shore.
Your son, shermed to death in makeshift car.

Forgive us for not getting who you are,
but please forgive away from worship door.
Don't be a dad tonight, go to the bar.

10   A girlfriend mourns a body burned to char,
embalmed in a butane threshing floor.
Your son, shermed to death in makeshift car.

A whole church grieves in ways you feel afar
but you don't know the one they're grieving for.
15   Don't be a dad tonight, go to the bar.

Save the crying rap for the ripple jar,
the only brown thing you showed feeling for.
Your son, shermed to death in makeshift car.
Don't be a dad tonight, go to the bar.

Robert Lashley, 2014

This poem gives us a participant speaker who may be easy to mistake for nonparticipant, but notice in line 7 the speaker says, "Forgive us for not getting who you are." The speaker may be one of the congregation mourning the son, the one delivering the "anti-elegy" at the funeral, or possibly the collective voice of the whole community. Either way, it or they are involved in the action and speak directly to the father of the dead boy.

The speaker says to the father, who is apparently absent from the funeral, "Don't be a dad tonight, go to the bar." This command is repeated four times, including the final line of the poem. Do you suppose that the speaker genuinely wants the father to go to the bar instead of fulfilling his role as a father and joining the community in mourning? Do you suppose the author genuinely thinks that would be an appropriate response to the situation?

If you don't answer "no" to both of those questions, consider the evidence within the poem. In line 2, the speaker explains that the father's absence is felt more than that of the dead boy. In the second stanza, you see the contrast of the mother's behavior. In the third stanza, the collective speaker orders the father not to ask for their forgiveness to their faces. In the fourth stanza, the girlfriend's behavior is contrasted to the father's. In the fifth stanza, the speaker accuses the father of not knowing the son. In the final stanza, the speaker calls the father's tears false and makes it clear that whiskey — "the ripple jar" — is the only thing he ever cared for.

In this poem, the author and the speaker's attitude are closely aligned, but what they say does not consistently follow from that attitude. When the speaker commands the father not to be a dad, it is being bitterly ironic. It doesn't actually want the father to go to the bar, but it's outraged that this is what the father will do.

Some readers have a hard time recognizing irony. If this is you, start with the knowledge that sometimes what someone says is not what they mean. Whenever you find yourself shocked or flummoxed by the content of a poem because you understand what's being said on literal level but can't believe someone would say such a thing, look for irony.

Final Thoughts

People are feeling beings, and stories are all about feelings. Poetic story-telling is often especially emotional. Many poems are more about exploring and sharing emotions than facts or thoughts. There are often many feelings happening at once in a poem.

In particular, there can be differences between the general or overall mood of the poem, the attitude of the speaker toward the poem he or she is speaking, and even the attitude of the actual author toward the content of the poem—including the speaker! When the attitude, feelings, and opinions of the author are clearly different from those of the speaker—that is, the author is saying one thing in words but meaning something else—it creates a special kind of tone, irony.

Here are some tips and tricks to help you listen to the feelings and attitudes in a poem:

- Pay attention to how the poet sets up, treats, and describes the situation of the poem. What kind of details and descriptions are given? Do they seem to carry any judgments, positive or negative? Is important information omitted or glossed over?

- Look and listen for clues about attitude and feeling. Is there an overall emotional climate in the poem? Look for words that express opinions, judgments, or emotions, or that may imply the same.

- Be careful to not let your own emotional reaction to the content overwhelm the poem. Remember, you're listening, trying to understand and appreciate the poem's feelings, not getting in touch with your own feelings.

- Don't stop with a single tone. Make a note of the first tone and go back and look for more.

- Remember that tone is all about feeling. If you begin thinking too much about ideas, events, or anything else, you're getting off center.

- Tone is often conveyed through figurative language, especially allusions. Make sure you have explored those elements in a poem.

- Notice how the poem *feels* rather than what it *means* if a poem isn't making sense.

Understanding and appreciating tone in poems is not that different than listening closely as a friend tells a story and trying to understand how that person feels about what happens in the story. It's a little more challenging because you don't have clues like tone of voice and body language, but the basic idea is the same. If at first no attitude or feeling seems obvious, that's okay. Keep reading. Keep working on understanding and appreciating the rest of the poem. Keep being curious. As you deepen your reading, the tone may start to become clear.

Exercises

This section gives you the chance to practice your understanding of these elements through guided readings of three poems and through focused creative writing exercises. Your teacher may or may not assign them, but they are also designed to be completed independently if you wish.

For Readers

The following three poems each present interesting speakers who will help you to practice understanding and appreciation of tone. If you're not given specific assignments by your teacher, try doing this for each poem:

1. Complete the basic reading.

2. Jot down your own initial impressions—what did you understand to be happening at the literal level in this poem? Did you like it? Can you say how or why?

3. Identify and describe the speaker and point of view.

4. Underline all the feeling words in the poem or write out a list of them. How would you describe the general mood or emotional climate of the poem?

5. Answer this: How would you describe the tone? What clues can you find about the author's feelings and attitude?

6. Explain any differences between the general feeling of the poem and the attitudes of the speaker and the other characters.

Poem 1

The literal language in this poem is probably easy for most readers to understand, but accurately understanding and hopefully appreciating the tone may require a bit more care. At any rate, take this opportunity to not let your initial responses to the poem—or any feelings it may bring up in you—completely run away with you.

The Man and How We Plan to Stick It to Him

We'll prevail, because we're ruthless and we're honest and we're
Not afraid; we'd kill our mothers for a metaphor.
And oh, the fact that we're smarter and more talented than you,
Yeah it makes us better people.

5   They've got guns but we've got words,
No hail of bullets will hurt
More than the cut of our finely turned phrases.
And they've got jobs but we've got art,
Their wealth may set them apart,
10   But they'll never taste the richness of our inner lives.

We'll prevail, although it may look like defeat at first;
We're prepared to have to die before we're recognized.
But oh, in our paupers' graves,
We'll be mourned by future generations of liberal arts
15   educators.

They've got power and control,
They hold our student loans,
They've sewn up all the votes for the next ten elections.
We've got friends who drink too much,
Superiority complexes, broken homes,
And a horror of repeating ourselves.

The best way to stick it to the man is to write him a book that
　　he can't understand.

Justus Ballard, 2019

Poem 2

This second poem packs a lot of feeling into very few words. Listen for
the feelings that are not described.

Unemployment Diary, Day 92

I fumble with
The comfort

That perhaps you
Too, right

Now, are reminded
How difficult it is

To fold a bed sheet

By yourself.

W. Vandoren Wheeler, 2019

Poem 3

It may take you a little while to work through the third poem, but be patient. It's worth the effort. It is short but dense. As always, using your dictionary and reading out loud will really help. This is both a poem full of feeling and a poem about feelings, all at once.

[No worst, there is none.
Pitched past pitch of grief.]

No worst, there is none. Pitched past pitch of grief,
More pangs will, schooled at forepangs, wilder wring.
Comforter, where, where is your comforting?
Mary, mother of us, where is your relief?
My cries heave, herds-long; huddle in a main, a chief
Woe, wórld-sorrow; on an áge-old anvil wince and sing—
Then lull, then leave off. Fury had shrieked 'No ling-
ering! Let me be fell: force I must be brief.'"

O the mind, mind has mountains; cliffs of fall
Frightful, sheer, no-man-fathomed. Hold them cheap
May who ne'er hung there. Nor does long our small
Durance deal with that steep or deep. Here! creep,
Wretch, under a comfort serves in a whirlwind: all
Life death does end and each day dies with sleep.

Gerard Manly Hopkins, 1918

For Writers

The following exercises help you get to know and practice using the concepts of tone and irony in your own writing. They are not designed to produce whole, finished poems but to help you experiment with these smaller elements so that you can use them more effectively to create poems in your own time. You might find that any of these exercises inspires you to start a poem, and that's great, too.

1. Try expressing a feeling or attitude in writing without using any of the usual feeling or attitude words.

2. Pick any three emotions or attitudes. Imagine each as a person. Describe those people. Then write a dialog between them.

3. Make a list of poems or song lyrics that you associate with a particularly strong feeling. Go back and reread each carefully. Write a two-paragraph analysis of how each generates and sustains that feeling. As an additional exercise, try rewriting them to keep more or less the same content but alter the tone.

4. Experiment with irony. Write a short, sincere argument on a topic in a single prose paragraph. Rewrite the paragraph using as much sarcasm as you can to make your point. Then create a speaker who seems to be expressing very different or opposing feelings, but by doing so really makes your own point.

Chapter 5

The Situation of a Poem

Key terms: situation, setting, character, action

This chapter covers the questions closest to a reporter's heart: What happened? Who was involved? When did it take place? Where did it occur? These elements, familiar from prose stories, make up the **situation** of a poem. Some or all of them may not be present, or may only barely be visible, in a poem.

Readers often give up on finding the story in a poem a little too soon. Poems, especially shorter poems, tend to use condensed language, and the story of the poem is often only hinted at with a few quick details or references. We commonly need to infer facts about the situation from indirect clues. We can't demand that the poem act like a story, but we should be ready to hear the story if it has one to tell.

You'll return to "'Out, Out —'" several times in this chapter, examining it closely to see how it reveals its situation. It's a great example of how a poem can tell a story, even when it isn't one, often using only the slightest image to hint at the story elements. You should go back and give it another reading now, asking yourself when and where it's set, who its characters are, and what happens.

Setting

Setting refers to when and where a story takes place. That may be a single place and moment, or it may be multiple locations over long periods of time. It's often difficult to pinpoint, but if we can glean where and when the action occurs, that helps make the poem more sensible. Actions that seem incomprehensible in a suburban bungalow, for example, might make perfect sense on the moon.

The setting can also provide important clues about allusions, references, and the social context of a poem. The social context of the poem can make the actions and feelings of the characters much easier to understand. We may reasonably expect characters in a poem set in the Middle Ages to have different ideas about gender than most people do today. Although the setting may not provide us those answers by itself, it gives us a starting point to begin searching from.

Setting in "'Out, Out —'"

What information does this poem provide you about its setting? Lines 5 and 6 tell you that "five mountain ranges" are visible "under the sunset" — that is, to the west — "far into Vermont." That's pretty specific. Looking at a map tells you this must be in New Hampshire, probably in the White Mountains. Beyond that, a family working together out in the open air, cutting firewood, with mountains close by points to a rural setting, maybe a farm. It's somewhere a doctor can get to before the boy bleeds to death or dies from shock, though, which suggests a place not too far from town.

Can you find any clues about *when* the poem is set? There is a "buzz saw," and the doctor comes with "ether." A quick online search tells you that ether was first used by physicians in the 1840s but is rarely used now. Further searching reveals that the "buzz saw" was a tool used during the nineteenth and early twentieth centuries, powered by being attached to the drive train of a tractor. This background information reinforces the idea that this is a rural setting. It can also be useful to notice what's missing—no discussion of a telephone to call for help or a car to take the boy to help. This seems to push the setting earlier.

Now put the pieces together. You could say that the poem is set in New Hampshire, probably on a farm near a town and probably in the late nineteenth or early twentieth century. It's perfectly fine and even necessary, by the way, to use qualifiers like "probably" to indicate the degree of certainty you have about any given conclusion.

Types of Settings

Often a poem has no particular setting, or the setting is inconsequential. Sometimes a poem gives only vague clues to time and place. As you'll see in the following poem, it's possible that the only "location" that matters is inside the speaker's mind.

Bad Bad Baby Heads

Once I held a baby and I popped his head off like a dandelion.
Held his neck in the palm of my hand and POP with my
    thumb.
Don't worry, he was a bad, bad baby, and didn't go to waste.

5   I planted that bad baby head with my gardenias and out
came five more babies. Each with only a fifth
of that bad baby's evil.

I planted all five somewhat bad baby heads next to my azaleas:
Twenty-five babies grew. Each with only
10   one-twenty-fifth of that original bad baby's bad blood.

Now I have plenty of big beautiful babies.
Their soft spots flat and wide as the plains.
They make such lovely little door stops.

Allison Tobey, 2012

This poem mentions "dandelions," "azaleas," "plains," and "door stops," which tells you something. The speaker lives in a time and place where all those things are present, so it's probably not set in tenth-century Greenland. On the other hand, those items may not even be real, any more than the "bad baby heads" are real. The poem takes place in the speaker's mind. It's about ideas and feelings, expressed in imaginary images, not actual events.

Some poems make no sense without the setting. These poems usually don't make the setting too hard to decipher. But stay attentive to the importance of setting and the need to look for it.

Hunters

Dressed in their green spotted drabs to blend in
with trees, my brother and his new friends, then
nineteen, erected their dark tents and dug
a latrine, then gathered twigs from the edge
of their camp and the driest leaves, and at

5

twilight all of them assembled, then bent
their heads for a moment over their Tang
or their coffee or tea, and one boy sang
a little prayer in the unarmed quiet

10

(at night sometimes my brother still sings it),
and even the air began to settle
except for the occasional rattle
of insects and in the nearby distance
mortar fire from Da Nang, insistent.

Andrea Hollander, 1999

Let's look at how setting works in this poem. The title tells you the poem is about "hunters." The lines that follow describe a group of teenage boys pitching tents in the forest, making a fire, and getting ready for bed. This poem's setting remains unspecified until the final line, which completely changes your understanding. Everything gets quiet except for insects and, suddenly, "mortar fire from Da Nang." Mortar fire? Da Nang? If you don't know these terms, you should look them up. A mortar is "a short, smoothbore gun for firing shells at high angles." Da Nang is a port and city in central Vietnam that served as a US military base during the Vietnam War.

Now you know that the poem is set during the Vietnam War, the boys are American soldiers, and their camp is a wartime camp in the jungle, not far from the fighting in Da Nang. The setting completely alters how everything before is understood. Most readers first imagine the "hunters" are hunting for something like deer, camping out in the woods near their own homes, doing what they want to do. After first seeing them this way, you are forced to imagine them as something altogether different at the end of the poem. This abrupt shift makes a strong statement about what a strange and terrifying thing it is for them to be at war.

Characters

Characters are all the personlike beings in the poem. It's tempting to say "all the people," but poets frequently use animals, forces of nature, inanimate objects, or even abstract ideas as characters with humanlike qualities. If anything in the poem speaks, feels, thinks, or takes any kind of action of its own volition, it's a character.

Contemporary lyric poems are often about the thoughts and feelings of a single person. The central character is frequently the *only* character. Sometimes the central character interacts with a few other characters. When identifying the characters in a poem, look for whatever information you can about the biographical details or facts of the character. For example, the character might be a man, a doctor, a talking horse, a ghost, a small child, and so on. But you should also be on the lookout for information about the character's internal reality.

In addition to identifying the characters in the poem, pay attention to any evidence of change. Do the characters grow, or do they regress? Do they solve problems, become wiser, or gain experience? Are they defeated? Characters in poems, especially contemporary lyrics, are often just thinking, but you should still look for actions. Look for conflicts within the characters and between the characters. Look for motivations for their actions or feelings. Why do they do the things they do? There may not be answers to these questions, but sometimes just asking questions helps you see what you may have overlooked before.

Characters in "'Out, Out —'"

What can we discover about the characters in Frost's poem?

The central character seems to be the boy. Then there is his sister, some people working with the boy, a doctor, and a "watcher at his pulse." We don't know who this watcher is. It may be another medical professional or a member of the family. As discussed earlier, it's unclear if the speaker is a participant in the poem's action. And there is the somewhat mysterious "they" who turn "to their affairs" at the end. Does "they" refer to the doctor or the family or all of humanity? The reference is not clear.

Finally, there is the saw. It's described as a living thing that snarls and rattles. It makes dust and drops sticks of wood. The saw seems to be cutting wood all day on its own. In lines 14–17, the speaker makes it seem like the saw acted of its own free will when it "leaped out at the boy's hand, or seemed to leap." The speaker then revises the statement to say the boy "must have given the hand." The speaker undercuts this seemingly firm assertion by saying, "However it was." That is, maybe the saw leaped or maybe the boy gave the hand. Once again, the speaker attributes decision-making power to the saw with the statement that "Neither [hand nor saw] refused the meeting." But after that, the saw disappears.

We don't know much about the boy. He's a young teenager, perhaps. The speaker calls him a "big boy / Doing a man's work, though a child at heart." We know even less about the other characters. The sister is probably older, since he turns to her for help or comfort. Someone present has the authority to "call it a day" earlier but then doesn't. This might be the boy's parents, older relatives, or farm hands. The boy's parents are conspicuously absent. Why are they never mentioned? Why does the boy not call out to them?

Whoever "they" at the end are, they seem to move on quickly from the boy's death to whatever it is they have to do ("their affairs"). It seems exceedingly impersonal and uncaring, but can we really draw any conclusions about "them" as characters from this short passage?

Perhaps Frost is simply pointing out that the business of the living is to live. But who are "they," and what can we say about them from the evidence the speaker gives us? These questions are like a loose thread in a sweater. You pull on it, and more keeps coming. It's enough for now to note that looking into the characters leaves you with as many questions as it answers. You can set these questions aside until you explore the poem a little further.

Types of Characters

Here's another poem built around an entirely different sort of characters.

The Stapler

is weeping, the calendar is asleep
and the scissors yell *shut the fuck up.*
The stapler whispers *I'm lonelier than the moon*
and the checkbook cackles with laughter.
5   The flowered picture frame says
Hey, you want to talk about lonely
as the computer stares in disbelief,
and the purple desk lamp thinks it's raining.
The stapler glances over at the picture frame,
10   starts to say something but the stack
of blank journals curses and screams.
The empty camera case starts singing

You're once, twice, three times a lady . . .
and the phone book sneezes
15 and the unused day planner says
Look, at least you're married
and the stapler weeps and weeps.

Chrys Tobey, 2006

The characters in this poem are the stapler, the calendar, the scissors, the checkbook, the flowered picture frame, the purple desk lamp, the stack of blank journals, the empty camera case, the phone book, and the unused day planner. Nothing gives us any reason to think that these are goofy nicknames for actual human beings. In the fiction of the poem, the office supplies talk, scream, think, and feel. They have personalities and are acting as if they were people. That makes them characters.

It's important to read carefully, to make sure you're not missing any nonhuman or otherwise not obvious characters. But sometimes there's nothing to miss, as you'll see in this poem.

from "Towns in Color"

II Thompson's Lunch Room—Grand Central Station

Study in Whites

Wax-white—
Floor, ceiling, walls.
Ivory shadows
Over the pavement
5 Polished to cream surfaces
By constant sweeping.
The big room is coloured like the petals
Of a great magnolia,
And has a patina
10 Of flower bloom

Which makes it shine dimly
Under the electric lamps.
Chairs are ranged in rows
Like sepia seeds
15   Waiting fulfillment.
The chalk-white spot of a cook's cap
Moves unglossily against the vaguely bright wall—
Dull chalk-white striking the retina like a blow
Through the wavering uncertainty of steam.
20   Vitreous-white of glasses with green reflections,
Ice-green carboys, shifting—greener, bluer—with the jar of
    moving water.

Amy Lowell, 1916

This is only a short excerpt; in the whole poem, which is several hundred lines long, there are no characters to speak of, though some human beings make brief appearances mostly as bearers of color, or to interact with the inanimate objects and make them move. This poem is not interested in people, but places and the way colors fill and are found in them.

Action

Action means the sequence of logicallyrelated events that unfolds in the lives of the story's characters. These events are called "plot" when discussing prose fiction, but in discussing poetry, the term "action" is more common.

Action revolves around a central character with whom we usually sympathize and identify. The character wants something and is somehow frustrated in reaching that goal. It may be an epic, complex, and heroic goal, like throwing the One Ring into Mount Doom and saving the world. It may be a tiny, simple, and mundane goal, like getting a good night's sleep. Regardless, when forces prevent the character from reaching a goal, conflict results. This is what creates interest and excitement.

Action in "'Out, Out —'"

What can we discover about the action in Frost's poem?

This poem has a lot of straightforward action for a short lyric. The speaker gives a clear, mostly literal description and uses easy-to-understand figurative language. We see what happens and how events follow one another in a natural sequence of cause and effect.

A boy, perhaps a young teenager, cuts firewood with a power saw all day in his front yard. He's working with others. At quitting time, as he's called in to supper by his sister, there is an accident. He cuts his hand badly on the saw. It's so bad he's afraid it will be amputated, and he begs his sister not to let the doctor take his hand.

A doctor comes and puts the boy to sleep with ether. Under anesthesia, the boy's pulse gets weaker and weaker until his heart stops altogether, and he dies.

Notice how straightforward and perhaps even dull this is? The poem is built on this action, but it certainly can't be reduced to it.

Action in Imagination and Memory

Here's a short poem with surprisingly complex action. You have to work a little harder to put it together, but there's definitely a coherent story here.

Rimes of Salt

I imagine my father coming home to an empty house.
What did the spirits of the house convey
about our frantic escape?
The same phantoms my mother prayed to for protection
and made offerings to when we first moved in
failed to stop my father from bruising her face.

So when did my mother devise a plan to leave him,
saving enough to purchase five plane tickets, clothes,
and a couple of suitcases,
then hurrying her children aboard a plane,
from Columbus, Ohio to Long Beach, California?

The unmade mattress, the old grimy furnace and neighbors,
what tale will they tell when they share stories of a broken
        home?
I imagine the wind howling a song as mournful leaves rustle
        into twilight,
weeping because my father is too stubborn to cry for his wife
        and children.
I imagine the man finally breaking down,
when it all becomes too much to hold inside,
an ocean rushes from his eyes,
and he drowns.

kosal so, 2018

This poem starts with "I imagine." Is the speaker telling us an imaginary story? What really happens? Do events follow one another in a logical sequence?

In this poem, action divides into two parts, memory and imagination. Reading the first stanza closely, we see that the speaker imagines the father coming home to an empty house. The homecoming itself is not imaginary, but the speaker imagines what it was like because he was not there to witness it. The speaker wonders what the "spirits" told the father about "our frantic escape." Are the spirits literally real? We don't know.

This line moves from imagination to memory. "Our frantic escape" in this context refers to the mother and children. If their departure was "frantic," then things must have been pretty bad at home. The next few lines confirm this. When they moved into the house, the mother prayed to its "phantoms" for protection, but they did not stop the father from "bruising her face." Memory and imagination are intermingled.

The entire second stanza gives us more remembered action framed by a question. The speaker wonders how the mother was able to "devise" and fund a plan to leave the father and fly the family across the country. He doesn't know exactly how or what she did, but he knows how it turned out.

The third stanza slides back into imaginary action with a catalog of what the house still contains when the father arrives and how the father might have reacted. It even imagines him drowning in his own tears.

In memory, the family of father, mother, and four kids moves into a new house. The mother prays and makes an offering to the spirits she imagines inhabit the house, asking them to protect her from her abusive husband. They fail. Her husband continues to beat her. She makes a plan and saves up enough money to buy new clothes and luggage and fly the family far away.

In the imaginary action, the father comes home to learn that his family is gone. The wind howls a mournful song for the father, who is too stubborn to weep over his loss. At some point, he "finally" breaks down, and the speaker imagines him drowning in his own tears. This may be a figure of speech that suggests the father did actually die from the symptoms of his grief. Or it may just mean the speaker imagines the father is overwhelmed by sadness.

Not Much Action at All

Some poems have complex and fully developed action, and some do not. Many contemporary poems are reflections on experiences, descriptions of thoughts, or expressions of feelings. They may have slight or incomplete action, or no real action at all, even if they do have characters and setting. See if you can figure out what is going on in this poem.

Gentrification

—Hawthorne Boulevard, Portland

I'm worn out with these stud desserts. They leave me dysphasic
    as a father. The descant is snide.
(Where is that antsy dynast now, that golden eagle dreaming of
5   Elgin marble
Like the Golgotha loaded with grit?) The shops keep coming
    past 39th Street. Antiques and wine bars
Overtaking the auto bodies and head shops. The gentlewomen
    with their flag-draped prams

10 Morph into foggy homographs, foul-tempered, trumped with
    pills, cringing in fragmented Muzak
Of cunning, they're a horde of determination, a faction of
    mystique concrete.
They snort their ounces of Ouija as if sniffing sunlight when, or
15   if, it comes. And yet is this
The way we will meet, pleased to be the other's rag? Is this the
    way we trade our drought of kamikaze youth,

Out of earshot of the busking violinist, as his music, like the
    dervishes of order and odometers of ohm, goes mad?

David Biespiel, 2003

    The title and epigraph announce the general happening and setting, at least in place—gentrification on Hawthorne Boulevard in Portland. This may not mean anything to you right away. However, a quick internet search for "Hawthorne Boulevard, Portland" will tell you that Hawthorne Boulevard is a long street that anchors a neighborhood of the same name, filled with expensive houses, trendy restaurants, and lots of shopping.

    What about "gentrification"? *Merriam-Webster* reveals "the process of renewal and rebuilding accompanying the influx of middle-class or affluent people into deteriorating areas that often displaces poorer residents." That introduces the idea of conflict between existing, poorer residents and middle-class or affluent newcomers.

The speaker is a participant in the poem's action, described in the first line as "worn out with stud desserts." These "stud desserts" leave the speaker "dysphasic as a father." The speaker proceeds to complain about a variety of things, including the "antiques and wine bars / overtaking the auto bodies and head shops . . . the gentlewomen with . . . flag-draped prams . . . foul-tempered, trumped with pills."

There are many phrases in this poem that most readers won't understand. What's a "stud dessert"? What's a "drought of kamikaze youth," and how does one "trade" it? With whom? For what? This is the part where you have to remind yourself that this is not a story. It doesn't have to make sense. Maybe it just sings. If you read this poem out loud, you'll find it delightful in the mouth and in the ear.

That doesn't mean, though, that you have to totally give up on the possibility of a story. You've identified a speaker and point of view. You have a setting. You have characters. Is there any action you can find?

Lines 3 and 4 describe a never-ending tide of new businesses displacing old businesses. Lines four through seven describe apparent newcomers arriving with the new businesses: the gentlewomen with prams "morph into foggy homographs . . . cringing in . . . Muzak . . . snort . . . Ouija as if sniffing sunlight." "Homographs" are words that are spelled the same, so the speaker seems to suggest that the pram-pushing gentlewomen merge together into a foggy similarity. Again, you may not know exactly what that means, and it's hard to say exactly what's going on, but you can draw a few conclusions, and it's clearly not pleasant or positive.

To summarize the action in this poem, you might say that "the unhappy speaker describes the gentrification of Hawthorne Boulevard as new businesses and people flood into the neighborhood." Clearly, though, the story is not the heart of this poem, and some poems have even less of a story than this one.

Final Thoughts

From earliest childhood, we all know how to tell stories, and we tell stories all the time. Because we understand stories, then, it can be comforting to see a poem behave like a story. It makes things easier. However, the way poems tell stories is often much less direct and clear than we're used to, because the story really isn't central. Sometimes the stories poems tell are incomplete, and sometimes a poem tells no story at all. We have to be ready, on one hand, to work a little harder to find a story that is there but not so obvious, but on the other hand, we have to ready to accept that there may not be any story to be found.

As you look for and share what you learn about the story in a poem, remember that the story in a poem is called the situation. It's made up of a sensible sequence of events (action) about fictional personas (characters) that unfolds in particular places and times (setting). Don't stop wondering about the story until you're satisfied you've learned what you can about each of those elements.

To finish off the chapter, here is a list of reminders, tips, and tricks to help you as you work with the stories poems tell:

- Look for and pay attention to the title and the epigraph, if a poem has either. Many announce the precise setting or other specific information about the situation.

- Take a careful look for indirect clues or hints about setting, such as references to technology. If a poem includes a telephone, that tells you some things.

- Sometimes these subtle hints are in the form of allusions. A poem's setting may rely on a reference or two. Look things up! These references might be something as specific as the name of a particular business ("The Chelsea Hotel") or an event ("The Blitz").

- Be careful not to confuse the setting of the fictional events in the poem with the time and place a poem was written or published.

Look within the actual text for your information about when and where the action takes place.

- Learn about characters from what they say and do, especially how they interact with other characters. Can you find a struggle? Does someone in the poem want something they can't get? Don't wait for or rely on descriptions of them by the speaker.

- Locate action verbs, descriptions of time passing, indirect evidence of time passing, and changes in the condition of anything or anyone.

- Fill in the blanks. Poems are more likely than prose stories to leave out large chunks of the action, especially descriptions of progress from one important event to the next. Just don't add in anything that isn't supported by what is in the poem.

As you listen to the poem tell you its story, don't panic if you get confused. Just keep listening. Remember that this is a conversation, not an interrogation. Note what you can about the situation, then move on to identifying other elements, and be open to the idea that they will help you better understand the situation—or appreciate the lack of it! Give yourself permission to understand partially, or not at all, knowing that you'll come back for another look, and another.

Exercises

This section gives you the chance to practice your understanding of these elements through guided readings of three poems and through focused creative writing exercises. Your teacher may or may not assign them, but they are also designed to be completed independently if you wish.

For Readers

Here are three poems that present clear and interesting situations to practice your understanding and appreciation of setting, characters, and action—the situation of a poem. Unless your professor gives you other instructions, try doing this for each poem:

1. Complete the basic reading of the poem.

2. Jot down your own initial impressions. What did you understand to be happening at the literal level? Did you like it? Can you say how or why?

3. Review the elements of voice—speaker, addressee, point of view, and tone.

4. Summarize and paraphrase each poem as described in Appendix B.

5. Describe each of the poem's situational elements separately: "This poem is set in. . . ." "The characters in this poem include. . . ." "What happens in this poem is that. . . ." Include when you can't find evidence about something: "We don't know. . . ." or ". . . cannot be inferred from the evidence here."

6. Write a description of the situation in the poem that combines what you've discovered about the poem's elements. It's important to practice putting these separate elements back together.

7. Highlight each poem with three different colors: one for setting, one for character, and one for action. Practice being methodical about locating this information in the poems.

Poem 1

In this first practice poem, follow the clues to setting before you figure out the speaker and point of view. Take some time on the language. The slightly old-fashioned vocabulary may defeat less-complete dictionaries. Here are a few hints:

- "Ranks" in this context means "lines of soldiers in formation."

- "Hard-prest" is an archaic spelling of "hard-pressed," which means both "closely pursued" and "oppressed by serious problems or demands."

- "Foil'd" is a contraction for "foiled," which means "defeated."

- "'Tis" is a contraction for "It is."

- "Stanch" is not archaic, but it is uncommon outside of medical usage. It means to stop or limit the flow of blood from a wound.

A March in the Ranks Hard-Prest, and the Road Unknown

A march in the ranks hard-prest, and the road unknown,
A route through a heavy wood with muffled steps in the
    darkness,
Our army foil'd with loss severe, and the sullen remnant
5   retreating,
Till after midnight glimmer upon us the lights of a dim-lighted
    building,
We come to an open space in the woods, and halt by the dim-
    lighted building,
10 'Tis a large old church at the crossing roads, now an
    impromptu hospital
Entering but for a minute I see a sight beyond all the pictures
    and poems ever made,
Shadows of deepest, deepest black, just lit by moving candles
15   and lamps,
And by one great pitchy torch stationary with wild red flame
    and clouds of smoke,
By these, crowds, groups of forms vaguely I see on the floor,
    some in the pews laid down,
20 At my feet more distinctly a soldier, a mere lad, in danger of
    bleeding to death, (he is shot in the abdomen,)
I stanch the blood temporarily, (the youngster's face is white as

a lily,)
Then before I depart I sweep my eyes o'er the scene fain to
25 absorb it all,
Faces, varieties, postures beyond description, most in obscurity,
 some of them dead,
Surgeons operating, attendants holding lights, the smell of
 ether, the odor of blood,
30 The crowd, O the crowd of the bloody forms, the yard outside
 also fill'd,
Some on the bare ground, some on planks or stretchers, some
 in the death-spasm sweating,
An occasional scream or cry, the doctor's shouted orders or
35 calls,
The glisten of the little steel instruments catching the glint of
 the torches,
These I resume as I chant, I see again the forms, I smell the
 odor,
40 Then hear outside the orders given, Fall in, my men, fall in;
But first I bend to the dying lad, his eyes open, a half-smile
 gives he me,
Then the eyes close, calmly close, and I speed forth to the
 darkness,
45 Resuming, marching, ever in darkness marching, on in the
 ranks,
The unknown road still marching.

Walt Whitman, 1865

Poem 2

Tone is important in the second poem, which is not literally difficult or long. The language is clear and contemporary, but it's layered. As you read, pay close attention to references and implications. Things are mentioned and not explained or followed up. What can you reasonably deduce about what this poem implies?

January 22
—Summer Lake, 1928

Nineteen degrees. Wind from the east
like rolling pins over the dull xylophone
of our one-room schoolhouse. Mrs Reed
hates me. I can tell. And I miss Peter.

5   The Rexall. Soda fountain. Root Beer
float. Sweat on fluted glass. Hear that
wind? It wicks the woodstove's heat
down to the quick, then licks what's left

From the hearth. Hardly any warmth
10   touches our faces. Yet my pupils'
eyes are bright. They watch me pace.
They listen, intently, as I say:

Write a poem, of summer. Something
with lavender, or watermelons.

Scot Siegel, 2012

Poem 3

Next is a poem that has all the narrative elements of a short story and at least three interesting and developed characters. Pay attention to everything you can about the speaker's relationship to the rest of the characters. The title, by the way, is a play on words. "Surface Tension" means at least two very different things.

Surface Tension

The circle of smaller children
around Isaac's poised hand
draws itself in like a breath

as he splashes bubble solution
onto the top of the concrete block.
I scurry across the grass, ready

with a standard scolding
about waste, but stop short
when I see him crouch,

dip the hot pink wand
into the pooled solution,
and with his face hovering

just above the wet surface,
blow a lateral bubble whose edges
join themselves to the cement.

Filling it with slow, careful breath
it expands to the size of half
a cantaloupe. Then he pushes

20 back onto his knees and, together
with the group, watches colors
swirl and pulse and shift

from turquoise to fuchsia
to tangerine and electric yellow,
from purple to sapphire blue,

25 until Dymon, the girl named
for the hardest substance
in the world, smacks her hand

down hard and the bubble shreds,
its ragged edges rising and falling
30 like the gasp of a crowd.

I tense again, prepare
for Isaac's protest or tears,
maybe a fist flung in retaliation.

But instead, he laughs, as if to say,
35 Man, isn't that the truth?
then resumes, blowing

a series of new bubbles,
sometimes going for big,
sometimes for the shapes

40 of ladybugs or caterpillars
or burgeoning asters.
And Dymon, of course,

always going for broke.
I watch off to one side
45 until the bell breaks

the circle, scattering

the children over the blacktop.
They call, Bye, Isaac, bye!

and then they're at the walkway
again, where they all step back
into line. I bring up the rear,

humbled. Thinking beautiful,
breakable. Thinking, Yeah,
isn't that the truth?

Cindy Stewart-Rinier, 2011

For Writers

The following exercises help you get to know and practice the concepts related to the situation of the poem—setting, character, and action. They are not designed to produce whole, finished poems but to help you experiment with these smaller elements so that you can use them more effectively to create poems in your own time. You might find that any of these exercises inspires you to start a poem, and that's great, too. At any rate, keep the writing you generate here—there's no telling when it might come in handy.

1. "Pitch" is a term from the movie and TV industry that refers to a concise description of an idea for a movie or show, that gives the basic details about the movie's situation—the main characters, the setting, the conflict that drives the action—as well as important information about genre, production, and so on. Writers use pitches to sell their screenplays to producers. Imagine that you're pitching your poem ideas to your favorite poet. Here are a few things you might try with pitches:

   • Write pitches for six future poems. Your pitches should be under two hundred words and describe the whole situation.

- Find six poems that you know and like. Reduce them to pitches of no more than two hundred words that describe the whole situation.

- Try writing one haiku poem for each of your pitches for new poems or old favorites.

2. List three people you know at least sort of well. For each, list three prominent character traits. Then write a conversation between the three persons in which each reveals their character traits without ever explaining them directly. Your goal is to use dialogue to reveal character, but don't overdo it. They should only say things that they would actually say in conversation—and not because you want them to reveal their characters to your readers.

3. List six specific times and places that could be the setting for a poem. For each, write a list of three to six aspects, characteristics, or details that would make that setting clear to an attentive reader without naming the setting directly. Next, try grafting these details to an existing poem or poem draft of your own, one that don't really have a specific setting. Try two different approaches:

- Write a four-line opening stanza that sets a scene and leads into the rest of the poem.

- Try sprinkling the details throughout the poem to slowly reveal the setting.

4. For this final exercise, you need a partner or, better, a group, with whom you share things in common—events you've all experienced together, places you've all been, people you all know. Write indirect descriptions of these settings—give vivid details, but don't use names or other immediate identifying terms. Share your descriptions and see if people recognize what you're describing. If they don't, keep revising until they do.

Chapter 6

Structural Language

Key terms: diction, denotation, connotation, neologism, portmanteau word, syntax

Language has deep and inherent features that give it structure and meaning—rules and customs that define how words and phrases operate and that shape sentences to communicate ideas. Fundamentally, any language is a shared set of expectations that give structure to sounds and ideas.

Because poetry is art made out of language, the deeper your understanding and appreciation of language itself becomes, the better equipped you are to understand and appreciate poetry. It also really helps to keep in mind some hints about the particular—and, frankly, peculiar—ways that many poets think about, follow, manipulate, and sometimes outright defy the conventions of structural language.

As you proceed through this chapter, keep in mind that analyzing the structural language in a poem is never about finding the poem's structural language or deciding it if has any or not. Rather, the goal is to notice, carefully examine, and describe the structural language which every poem is made of.

"'Out, Out —'" reappears twice in this chapter, so you can take a careful look at the structure of its language. You should go back to Chapter 3 and give it another reading now, so it's fresh in your mind as you proceed.

Diction

Diction means word choice. It refers to the vocabulary in the poem.

Understanding the individual words in a poem is essential. Poets love words as things in and of themselves. Poets like to play with words the way that kids like to play with LEGO bricks. The words themselves are interesting in their inherent "wordness." It's difficult for people who aren't as excited about language to grasp or believe in this devotion that poets have. Every word in a poem is chosen and placed with great care, whether consciously or unconsciously.

Time and time again, students' confusion over or dislike of a poem is rooted in not knowing a word. Students most often make a quick but incorrect assumption about what a word means. When reading prose, it's not a bad idea to use the rest of the sentence to guess at the meaning of an unfamiliar word. When reading poetry, that's a terrible idea. You really have to stop and look up the meaning.

Poems might include words that fool you into *thinking* you know what they mean. Poets love to use obscure and archaic versions of words, to use words in unfamiliar ways, and to use words that can mean several things at once. Consider the word "junk." You already know it means "useless stuff" or "garbage." But it also has five other meanings! Poets love to tease you with the meanings you don't immediately think of.

As a careful reader, then, you have to develop a sensitive antenna for words. Your job is to notice when your understanding of a word might be contextually wrong. This is mostly a matter of guided practice. However, continuously reminding yourself that unfamiliar meanings, multiple meanings, and new meanings, even of words you thought you knew, are always possible in poetry is a solid start.

Diction in "'Out, Out —'"

What can we discover about the diction here? Frost's vocabulary is not difficult. We find very little specialized vocabulary and only a few uncommon words. Not only that, the words themselves are objectively easy. There are no words with more than two syllables in the entire poem. You might notice, if you're into that sort of thing, that most of the words have an Anglo-Saxon origin, meaning they tend to be shorter, simpler, and connected to physical things. There aren't a lot of Latinate words here, which are words that come from Latin and tend to be longer, more complex, and more conceptual.

There are a few exceptions. Most noticeably the crucial term "buzz saw" might legitimately refer to a variety of tools. To correctly understand and picture the exact tool the poem is describing requires a little research. In line 8, "ran light" and "bear a load" might not be clear to people unfamiliar with power tools. In line 19, "rueful" seems a little exotic compared to the poem's general diction. In line 28, "the dark of ether" may be hard to understand because the phrase is figurative, but also because "ether" is uncommon today.

If anything, though, the diction is so simple as to almost be simplistic. You might note the correlation between the content—a child's death—and a childlike vocabulary. You might also note the correlation between the setting and the diction. The diction evokes the reserved voice of the stereotypical New England farmer. You might notice how the straightforward, blunted vocabulary matches and supports the tone of the poem, too.

Denotation and Connotation

In your quest to understand and appreciate diction, it helps to be aware of the way words have two specific kinds of meaning. **Denotation** is what a word refers to literally—the verb is "to **denote**." **Connotation** is what it suggests through association—the verb is "to **connote**."

Denotative meanings tend to be referential. That is, they refer us to something else for an explanation. They are also descriptive, which means they try to appeal to our senses by showing us what a thing looks or feels like.

Connotative meanings, on the other hand, tend to be associative and emotional. They depend on situations associated with a word and point us toward feelings or states of mind. Consider the adjectives "obese," "plus-size," "overweight," and "fat." They share a single denotative meaning, but the connotations are quite different. Using any one of them in the wrong context would be offensive. Each transmits a slightly different feeling about the noun that it modifies.

Denotation is often explained as "the dictionary definition of a word," but a good dictionary usually includes at least some of the connotative meanings of a word. Cheap dictionaries or those accessed online may leave out important denotative meanings of a word. Even denotative meanings may be multiple and layered, so it's important to work with a good college dictionary to appreciate the full range of denotative meanings.

Connotative meanings are almost always multiple and subtle, but they are not always universal. Many connotations are bound to the associations of a word to a particular group of people at a particular place or time. The farther we are from the poet—whether culturally, in space or time, or whatever other sort of distance separates us—the harder it becomes to catch those intended connotative meanings.

Let's take a look at how connotation works in this next poem:

faded to blue, black

It's a bit meaningless
this breath
in this world overfull with boiled air
and my mother's theory
that the primary purpose of a family
is to make more babies.
What purpose then

5

but to grow up to make more
like the ten thousand black ants making a hill in my driveway
10   waiting for the natural disaster of my tire.
In a grocery store
the colors are on the bottom.
In my circle the most brightly lit flames
are always bottoms.

Leanna Crawford, 2019

One of the ways connotation influences our reading of a poem is by developing tone. The associations we have with a word often work in the background, laying down an emotional backbeat. Consider that the denotative meaning of "fade" is simply "to become less pronounced or intense." Sound can fade, pain can fade, and so on.

Nonetheless, "fade" most often describes a negative situation in American English. "My pain eased" or "my pain subsided," are more common, even though those phrases have the same denotative meaning as "my pain faded." We are much more likely to hear "the light faded" than "the darkness faded." There's already a slightly negative tone being developed in the first word of the title.

"Blue, black" comes next. These are just colors, but a pair like this has strong connotations. They suggest deep bruising and therefore injury, pain, and defeat. At the same time, "fade to black" is unambiguously negative, indicating coming to a close, the lights going out, death.

None of this means the poem has to be about something terrible, or even that its dominant tone is negative. What the author intended is irrelevant. For now, we're just noticing what's written on the page. Connotation here works like the soundtrack of a movie. It doesn't determine plot or direct conscious understanding, but it subtly influences our perception. By setting a certain mood, connotation predisposes us to see in a certain way. In this poem, connotation gives us the sad feelings before we even know what we're feeling sad about.

Connotation affects readers subtly and indirectly. On the other hand, a single word's denotative meaning can often determine the literal understanding of an entire poem. Here's such a one:

☺

In Wichita, we shot speedballs, and I thought
my heart would skitter onto the floor in Kenny's living room,
a wind-up monkey spattering smacks on a snare drum.
We watched *The Dukes of Hazzard*. Kenny was just out
5   of prison. Thrasher's dilated eyes showed the General Lee
floating through air. By four in the morning, we were
driving around trying to trade my Walkman and a 20
for another dime. I want to tell someone about the
flame beneath the spoon, how the bubbling drugs made music,
10   how we all went into the bedroom to shake Kenny's girl
awake, how Waylon Jennings singing made it okay.
"You got good veins," Kenny said, thumping my elbow pit.
I saw them rise to meet the needle, to greet, to say
Yee-haw and welcome, smile, have a nice day.

Tod Marshall, 2014

If you don't know what "to shoot speedballs" means, this poem is very confusing, at least until line 9, where it's spelled out more directly for us. "To shoot speedballs" means to inject a mixture of heroin and cocaine—or other drugs, but generally a stimulant and an opioid.

The poem doesn't intend to be mysterious. It announces exactly what's going on, trying to make the situation crystal clear right from the start. However, it does count on us getting that denotative meaning in order to follow along.

Uncommon Diction

In addition to thoughtfully considering the denotations and connotations of common words, poems often require us to work with uncommon words that require special efforts. Two types of uncommon diction are neologisms and archaisms.

Neologisms

One complication in understanding diction arises from the fact that, given how much they love words, some poets can't hold themselves back from inventing their own words. A made-up word is known as a **neologism** (Greek, meaning "new word"). Neologisms don't only arise in poetry, of course. Popular English constantly generates new words. The successful ones eventually enter mainstream usage and are no longer thought of as neologisms at all. Neologisms in poetry, though, are truly new words that are not found in other places, including the dictionary. While these can be challenging, the poem usually gives us the clues we need to understand their invention.

Many neologisms, like "spork," combine parts of other words ("spoon" + "fork"). This type of neologism has its own name, **portmanteau**, a word coined by Lewis Carroll, who was fond of creating them. "Portmanteau" originally referred to a large, hard-shelled suitcase that opens up into two equal halves.

Another common type of neologism is created by modifying a word with familiar but nonstandard suffixes or prefixes. For example, poet Kay Ryan created two new words when she took the adjective "bland" and made it into a noun, "blandeur" (synonym for blandness) and a verb, "blanden" (to make bland), as in "flatten / Eiger, blanden / the Grand Canyon."

Why make a new word? English already seems to have more words than we know what to do with. One reason might be pure fun. If you can make a new word, and it sounds amusing or strikingly original, why not? Poets like that kind of thing. But there's often more to it than that.

Neologisms might create desired musical effects, such as rhyming, where an existing word would not. Neologisms sometimes fill a hole in the language, too. There was no existing word for a spork, so someone had to invent one.

The new word may create a new connotation through association with other words. "Blandeur," for example, sounds and looks a lot like "grandeur," whereas "blandness" does not. In Ryan's poem, the speaker praises the blandness of the world and asks God to make everything duller. The neologism, then, creates a more positive connotation for "blandness" by making it sound and look like "grandeur," which you already think of as something wonderful.

If you encounter a word you don't know and that isn't in the dictionary, see if you can take it apart and find the meaning that way. Cautiously rely on context for clues. Pay attention to the music of it, as well. When Dr. Seuss writes, "How I like to box! / So, every day, I box a gox. / In yellow socks I box my gox," you don't expect "gox" to mean anything referential. A "gox" is a thing the speaker boxes, and "gox" is its name purely because it rhymes with "box" and "socks." Dr. Seuss creates musical and comic effects with a made-up word mixed in with real words.

Archaic Words

Diction becomes even more challenging if the poem is more than about one hundred years old. If you find yourself dealing with a poem like this, don't give up. With patience and a good dictionary, you may even find reading older poems rewarding. Anything people still want you to read after three or four hundred years—like Shakespeare, for example—is probably worth the effort.

When confronted with archaic or otherwise difficult diction, try this method:

1. Look up and write down the relevant definition of all the words that you don't know. Physically write them down in the margins of the poem or on a piece of notepaper.

2. Produce a "translation" of the poem by rewriting the whole thing, substituting words or phrases for all the words you had to look up.

3. Don't be afraid to tweak the sentence structure a little if you need to make the translation fit, but if the sentence structure is really confusing, skip ahead to the "Syntax" section.

4. Revise until you have something that makes sense to your modern ear.

5. Compare the original and your "translation" side by side. Make sure you haven't changed the meaning of the original.

A college dictionary will have definitions of all the older words, but you can also help yourself by memorizing some of the more common archaic words. You may have noticed, for example, that the pronouns "thee," "thou," "thy," "thine," "thyself," and "ye" are common in poems from before the twentieth century. Learning this short list of definitions will make your life a little easier:

- Thou = you (singular—used as the subject of a sentence: "*Thou* art lovely!")

- Thee = you (singular—used as an object: "And I love *thee.*")

- Thy = your (singular, possessive—used as part of a noun phrase in sentence: "*Thy* face is most fair. I really love *thy* face.")

- Thine = yours (singular, possessive—used as an object: "Press my lips to *thine.*")

- Thyself = yourself (reflexive—used as the object of a sentence in which *thou* is the subject: "Thou fool'st *thyself.*")

- Ye = you (plural: "*Ye* are good men and true.")

- Ye = your (plural possessive: "Take *ye* rewards and return home.")

Despite the fact that "ye" is commonly used as a substitute for *the* by modern writers attempting to mimic archaic language — as in "Ye Olde Pizza Shoppe" — it does not mean "the."

You may also have noticed that verbs sometimes take on odd forms, such as "dost," "doth," and "mayest." Here are some simple rules for verbs:

Verbs referring to the "thou" pronoun take an "-est" suffix. So instead of "you walk," it would be "thou walkest." "You may" becomes "thou mayest." Sometimes the ending is contracted, too — "thou walk'st" and "thou may'st."

"To be" and "to do" are exceptions to the first rule. You will see "thou art" and "thou dost" instead of "you are" and "you do."

The third person pronouns — he, she, it — have not changed over time, but the verb form for the third person has changed. Instead of an "-s" suffix, the "-eth" suffix was used. You will see "he walketh" and "she dieth" instead of "he walks" and "she dies."

This is obviously nothing more than the tiniest tip of a huge iceberg when it comes to archaic words, but if you can get these words and concepts firmly memorized, it will help tremendously.

You can practice on one of Shakespeare's most famous speeches:

[O Romeo] from *Romeo and Juliet*

O Romeo, Romeo, wherefore art thou Romeo?
Deny thy father and refuse thy name.
Or if thou wilt not, be but sworn my love
And I'll no longer be a Capulet.
5   'Tis but thy name that is my enemy:
Thou art thyself, though not a Montague.
What's Montague? It is nor hand nor foot
Nor arm nor face nor any other part
Belonging to a man. O be some other name.
10   What's in a name? That which we call a rose
By any other name would smell as sweet;

So Romeo would, were he not Romeo call'd,

Retain that dear perfection which he owes

Without that title. Romeo, doff thy name,

15 And for that name, which is no part of thee,

Take all myself.

William Shakespeare, 1597

Two medieval teenagers, Romeo and Juliet, meet at a party. Juliet has a massive crush on Romeo, but she doesn't know if he likes her or not. Her family, the Capulets, also have a long-running and bloody feud with Romeo's family, the Montagues. Juliet knows their parents would never allow them to have any future together, so of course, he is the perfect one for her. In this speech, Juliet is by herself in her room after the party, *imagining* that she is talking to Romeo about this problem and working things out in her own head.

How should you wrestle this difficult diction into submission? The first step is to look up the definitions of words you don't know:

Lines   **Definitions**

1   **wherefore**: "for what reason" — that is, "why"

art: archaic form of "are"

thou: an archaic pronoun corresponding to the contemporary "you"

2   **deny**: the modern definitions are "to refuse to admit the truth of" or "refuse to give," but the definition in Shakespeare's time was "to refuse access to someone," as in "to cut off" or "cut out of your life"

thy: an archaic pronoun corresponding to the contemporary "your"

3   **wilt**: archaic form of "will" (the helping verb that expresses future tense, as in "you will see her tomorrow")

Lines	Definitions

3   **be but sworn**: the sense of "sworn" here is as an *adjective*. The less common second definition, "determined to remain in the role or condition specified," makes sense. That "role" is as Juliet's love. So, "be sworn" means "be determined to be. . ." "But" is used as an adverb meaning "only" or "no more than." Modern usage would be "just."

5   **'tis**: a contraction of "it is"

       but: in the sense of "only"

6   **thyself**: an archaic pronoun corresponding to the contemporary "yourself"

7   **nor**: this word is typically used between two or more alternatives to indicate that they are all untrue. But in this line it's at the start of a list, not in between items. This uncommon usage means "not" or "neither."

12   **call'd**: a contraction of "called"

13   **owes**: the modern sense of "have an obligation to pay" doesn't make any sense. A special guide to Shakespeare's vocabulary, *Shakespeare's Words* by David and Ben Crystal, reveals that "most Shakespearean instances have a different sense: 'own, possess, have.'"

14   **doff**: the dictionary doesn't list this as archaic, but it's an uncommon word meaning "to remove (an item of clothing)."

15   **for**: it may not be clear that this is used in the sense of "in exchange for."

       thee: an archaic pronoun corresponding to the contemporary "you"

16 **myself**: contemporary dictionaries and grammar guides would call this use of a reflexive pronoun a mistake. Here Shakespeare uses it as "my (possessive) SELF (noun)"—"take all my self." "My self" means "me."

If you rewrite the poem inserting your more modern words, you get the following translation. It's not as pretty, but most will find it much more readable:

> O Romeo, Romeo, why are you "Romeo"?
> Cut yourself off from your father and reject your name.
> Or if you will not, just swear to be my love
> And I'll no longer be a Capulet.
> It is only your name that is my enemy:
> You are yourself, though not a Montague.
> What's "Montague"? It is not hand nor foot
> Nor arm nor face nor any other part
> Belonging to a man. O be some other name.
> What's in a name? That which we call a rose
> By any other name would smell as sweet;
> So Romeo would, were he not Romeo called,
> Retain that dear perfection which he owns
> Without that title. Romeo, remove your name,
> And in exchange for that name, which is no part of you,
> Take me.

This might still be rather confusing, or you might think you understand it and still be wrong. That's okay. You still need to explore the other set of norms that make up structural language—syntax.

Syntax

Syntax means word order—specifically, it means the grammatically significant arrangement of words into larger units of meaning such as phrases, clauses, and sentences. You may not have studied syntax formally, and you may not know the terms, but if you can understand English well enough to read this book, you have an inherent understanding of the "rules" of syntax.

Syntactical choices control meaning in sentences. They alter, create, preserve, and destroy it. In particular, syntax tells us who or what in the sentence is acting, what the action is, and if anything is being acted upon. You probably don't consciously think about it, but syntax is what determines your understanding of every sentence you read.

For example, we automatically understand that these two sentences — "The boy bit the dog." and "The dog bit the boy." — mean two different things. They contain the same words, but the order of the words creates the meaning. Any other arrangement — "Dog the boy the bit," for example — is just gibberish. That's syntax.

Because syntax is such a fundamental part of language, and because it's no longer carefully studied as part of a basic education, students rarely notice the syntax in a poem any more than they consciously notice the air they're breathing.

When the air is windy or filled with smoke or in some other way abnormal, however, we notice it. It affects us. Likewise, syntax that defies normal patterns can influence our understanding and appreciation of the poem. Peculiar syntax may affect our reading of the poem imperceptibly, without our understanding that's what's impacting us — just like rapidly changing air pressure can make your grandpa's elbows ache even though he doesn't know why.

Even when the syntax is "normal," however, it's important to pay attention to the patterns in the way the words are put together. Are the sentences long, short, or mixed? Are there lots of commas and parentheses and semicolons? You're not looking for the correct answer to these questions. You just need to slow down and be conscious of what is there, whatever it is.

One way to train yourself to see syntax is to copy the poem out by hand. Remove the line breaks and insert a space between each sentence. This way you can clearly see the text as sentences instead of lines.

Syntax in "'Out, Out —'"

Let's test out the method described earlier and rewrite "'Out, Out —'" without line breaks as a numbered series of sentences:

1. The buzz saw snarled and rattled in the yard and made dust and dropped stove-length sticks of wood, sweet-scented stuff when the breeze drew across it.

2. And from there those that lifted eyes could count five mountain ranges one behind the other under the sunset far into Vermont.

3. And the saw snarled and rattled, snarled and rattled, as it ran light, or had to bear a load.

4. And nothing happened: day was all but done.

5. Call it a day, I wish they might have said to please the boy by giving him the half hour that a boy counts so much when saved from work.

6. His sister stood beside him in her apron to tell them 'Supper.'

7. At the word, the saw, as if to prove saws knew what supper meant, leaped out at the boy's hand, or seemed to leap—he must have given the hand.

8. However it was, neither refused the meeting.

9. But the hand!

10. The boy's first outcry was a rueful laugh, as he swung toward them holding up the hand half in appeal, but half as if to keep the life from spilling.

11. Then the boy saw all—since he was old enough to know, big boy doing a man's work, though a child at heart—he saw all spoiled.

12. "Don't let him cut my hand off—the doctor, when he comes.

13. Don't let him, sister!"

14. So.

15. But the hand was gone already.

16. The doctor put him in the dark of ether.

17. He lay and puffed his lips out with his breath.

18. And then—the watcher at his pulse took fright.

19. No one believed.

20. They listened at his heart.

21. Little—less—nothing!—and that ended it.

22. No more to build on there.

23. And they, since they were not the one dead, turned to their affairs.

The syntax in the beginning is fairly conventional. None of these sentences is especially long. The second and fifth sentences are challenging to read, but rewriting them without the line breaks makes them clearer.

Notice how the sentence length and complexity changes. The first half of the sentences are a mix of long and short, though most are longer. After the eleventh sentence—when the boy "saw all spoiled"—the sentences become uniformly short and simple in structure. Multiple short sentences tend to read more slowly because all the starting and stopping slows us down. Most of the fast action of the injury itself is described in mostly long sentences. But the slow waiting quiet in which the boy dies is composed entirely of short sentences. Regardless of the author's intention, the pattern is there to notice.

Notice, too, how the word order reinforces the personification of the saw. In any sentence in which the saw is mentioned (sentences 1, 3, and 7), it is the actor, the character who does the action. The syntax reinforces the idea that the saw takes action rather than is acted upon. Nowhere does a person do things to the saw. The saw does things to the world.

Imagine if the first sentence began like this: "The boy and his father ran the snarling, rattling buzz saw. . . ." Adding the human subject and rearranging the order to make the saw the object changes the feeling and the impression of the poem. Once again, this is syntax at work.

Complex Syntax

At times, a poem's syntax may seem strange or even outright incorrect. This could be because the poem comes from a place and time distant from our own. As vocabulary changes over time and from place to place, so do conventions of sentence structure.

Complex syntax usually consists of longer sentences that involve lots of parts and ideas, all working together in complicated arrangements that are controlled by punctuation and rules of coordination and subordination of ideas. These sentences can be challenging to decipher even in prose, and your difficulty in understanding and appreciating poetry is often linked directly to complex syntax.

If you're having a hard time understanding a poem even on a literal level, try this key strategy: Break the poem down into individual sentences and then study those sentences one at a time. You can then break the sentences down into their parts and study those parts one at a time, too.

Let's take a careful look at the syntax of the passage from *Romeo and Juliet* from earlier in this chapter. We'll start by copying the poem out into sentences rather than lines, using the translated vocabulary:

1. O Romeo, Romeo, why are you Romeo?

2. Cut yourself off from your father and refuse your name.

3. Or if you will not, just swear to be my love and I'll no longer be a Capulet.

4. It is only your name that is my enemy: you are yourself, though not a Montague.

5. What's Montague?

6. It is not hand nor foot nor arm nor face nor any other part belonging to a man.

7. O be some other name.

8. What's in a name?

9. That which we call a rose by any other name would smell as sweet; so Romeo would, were he not Romeo called, retain that dear perfection which he owns without that title.

10. Romeo, remove your name, and in exchange for that name, which is no part of you, take me.

Joining the sentences together outside of the structure of lines may make the poem easier to understand. It certainly makes the question and answer structure more obvious. Sentences 1, 5, and 8 are questions, and each is followed by one or two sentences that answer or respond to the question. Then a final sentence transitions to the next question. It also makes clear that sentence 9 is far more complex than any of the other sentences. This may or may not impact our reading, but it's something to notice.

Beyond that, does any of this syntax seem nonstandard or confusing? Sentence 4 is a little weird. It seems to mean: "You are yourself, even if you're not a Montague." However, Romeo *is* a Montague. The problem here is punctuation, a specialized subset of syntax rules. Modern usage would add an extra comma after "though," as in, "You are yourself, though, not a Montague." This turns "though" into a transitional adverb like "however." The modern translation might thus be "You are yourself, however, not a Montague." That suggests that Romeo is his own person rather than just an extension of his family.

The rest of these sentences seem fairly straightforward until you get to that long, long sentence 9. It's made up of two independent clauses, which could stand alone as complete sentences, joined by a semicolon. If you broke them apart at the semicolon, you get this:

9 (A). That which we call a rose by any other name would smell as sweet.

9 (B). So Romeo would, were he not Romeo called, retain that dear perfection which he owns without that title.

That helps. The first half is still slightly confusing. Modern syntax would call for keeping the subject and main verb closer together, like this: "That which we call a rose would smell as sweet by any other name." That makes sense.

The second half, however, still has some strange structure. "So" refers back to the first half and can be changed to "in the same way." That's an easy fix. The passage "were he not Romeo called," is trickier. The verb is at the end, after the object. "Were he not called Romeo" restores the conventional sequence and makes more sense. "Were" also expresses a hypothetical possibility, and modern usage expects an "if he" in front of "were." That gives you "if he were not called Romeo." Let's reattach this revised phrase to the second half of the sentence:

> 9 (B). In the same way, Romeo would, if he were not called Romeo, retain that dear perfection which he owns without that title.

Good! Let's reassemble the whole thing:

> 9. That which we call a rose would smell as sweet by any other name; in the same way, Romeo would, if he were not called Romeo, retain that dear perfection which he owns without that title.

Our "translation" makes the diction and syntax more modern and conventional:

> O Romeo, Romeo, why are you Romeo?
> Cut yourself off from your father and refuse your name.
> Or if you will not, just swear to be my love
> And I'll no longer be a Capulet.
> It is only your name that is my enemy:
> However, you are yourself, not a Montague.
> What's Montague? It is not hand nor foot
> Nor arm nor face nor any other part

Belonging to a man. O be some other name.
What's in a name? That which we call a rose
would smell as sweet by any other name;
Romeo would, in the same way, if he were not called Romeo,
Retain that dear perfection which he owns
Without that title. Romeo, remove your name,
And in exchange for that name, which is no part of you,
Take all of me.

All this work obviously takes a lot of the beauty out of the original and makes it wordier. Hopefully, though, you can understand and appreciate the meaning of the passage better now.

Final Thoughts

Every poem has structural language—diction and syntax. These structural features are an inescapable part of language itself. When you're carefully reading and analyzing a poem, taking your time with syntax and diction can help you to solve problems with structural language. These kinds of problems are likely to arise when the diction or syntax are complex or difficult, as often happens when the poem is old or using a form of English you're not familiar with.

To finish off the chapter, here's a list of reminders, tips, and tricks to help you as you work with the language of poems:

- Use a dictionary—all the time—every poem. Don't get lazy. Don't guess or fill in from context. Look words up. The single greatest barrier between students and the understanding and appreciation of poems is vocabulary. It's also the easiest to overcome.

- Use a *good* dictionary, and carefully read through all the listed variants and definitions. Remember that those tricky poets like old and obscure meanings of words, the sort of definitions left out of small and free online dictionaries.

- Always be on the lookout for the multiple possible meanings of words. A word might very well mean several things at once within a poem. Depending on which meaning you hold in mind at a given moment, your sense of the line or the whole poem might change. Poets love that sort of thing.

- Rebuild the sentences in the poem by stripping away the line breaks. Focus your attention on the sentence as a unit rather than the line. Bring the background into the foreground.

- Just notice what you can notice about the sentences within poems if the complexity of syntax rules seems overwhelming. Where do the sentences start and end? Even noticing that simple pattern may help you find and understand some of the ways syntax is used in the poem.

Try to remember that you really do already understand the basics of English syntax — otherwise you wouldn't be able to read this book. It may be challenging to think consciously and critically about something you use without reflection, but it's mostly just a matter of realizing you need to care about it and then developing the habit. On the other hand, if you do want some extra help with understanding the concepts that underlie syntax, it's readily available from professors, in classes, and in excellent reference works like *The Chemeketa Handbook* — not to mention the internet.

Exercises

This section gives you the chance to practice your understanding of syntax and diction through guided readings of three poems and through focused creative writing exercises. Your teacher may or may not assign them, but they are also designed to be completed independently if you wish.

For Readers

The following three poems each provide a chance to practice understanding and appreciating diction and syntax. If you're not given specific assignments by your teacher, try doing this for each poem:

1. Complete the basic reading.

2. Jot down your own initial impressions. What did you understand to be happening on the literal level in this poem? Did you like it? Can you say how or why?

3. Summarize and paraphrase each poem as described in Appendix B.

4. Dig into the diction. Use a thick, college-level dictionary to look up *every* meaning of *every* noun, action verb, adjective, and adverb in *each* poem, regardless of whether or not you think you know what they mean.

5. Use the method you just learned for dealing with difficult syntax on all three poems, regardless of how simple or difficult a poem seems.

6. Explain how syntax affects your understanding, as in the examples discussed above. How would rearranging the syntax of any of the sentences alter the meaning? The feeling?

Poem 1

The first poem features modern but quite complicated syntax. There are only two sentences in the whole thing! Try rewriting these complex sentences into a series of simple sentences without changing the meaning.

Inheritance

As a man scoots behind them
    singing Hot Cross Buns
        in the middle of Pioneer Square,

as a train burrows in with a rumble
    and squeak to shake its passengers
        loose, as if a church bell had rung,

they turn at the same time, silver studs
    sparkling from their brows. Crows
        never prepared for flight with such

grace as they raise their arms
    around one another, and their
        hips and legs shift so the child

between them can throw what's
    left of her bread to the pigeons.

Darlene Pagán, 2019

Poem 2

Right from the title, wild diction takes center stage in this second poem. Don't take the meaning of anything for granted. What does the poem gain — or lose — from this kind of diction? If you think it could have been written with simpler or clearer words, ask yourself why it wasn't.

Cryophilia

What algid comfort curls the glacial ice worm
Supping the blush off watermelon snow
Wriggling meal of grey-crowned rosy finch
Itself ravened to sharpness by knifing winds

5   You may never be pierced by montane drafts
Prusik-sling out a transverse crevasse
But feel the frostbit, narrowly averted gaze
Hear the whistle cracked between moments
Space that fills your chest with steely scissors
10 Scoring, scarifying your chilblain heart
Sign of, signal to, further separation

And yet the ice worm somehow makes a home
Finds a crystal-cut purchase point
From which it feeds feathers, winged things

Jennifer Kemnitz, 2016

Poem 3

The author of this next poem is the same Jonathan Swift who wrote *Gulliver's Travels* and the satiric essay "A Modest Proposal." The diction and syntax may feel difficult because they're old, but take your time and work through it.

A Description of the Morning

Now hardly here and there a hackney-coach
Appearing, show'd the ruddy morn's approach.
Now Betty from her master's bed had flown,
And softly stole to discompose her own.
5   The slip-shod 'prentice from his master's door
Had par'd the dirt, and sprinkled round the floor.
Now Moll had whirl'd her mop with dext'rous airs,
Prepar'd to scrub the entry and the stairs.
The youth with broomy stumps began to trace
10   The kennel-edge, where wheels had worn the place.
The small-coal man was heard with cadence deep;
Till drown'd in shriller notes of "chimney-sweep."
Duns at his lordship's gate began to meet;
And brickdust Moll had scream'd through half a street.
15   The turnkey now his flock returning sees,
Duly let out a-nights to steal for fees.
The watchful bailiffs take their silent stands;
And schoolboys lag with satchels in their hands.

Jonathan Swift, 1709

For Writers

The following exercises help you get to know and practice using syntax and diction in your own writing. They are not designed to produce whole, finished poems but to help you experiment with the structure of language so that you can learn to use them more consciously to create poems in your own time. You might find that any of these exercises inspires you to start a poem, and that's great, too.

1. Take a contemporary poem and rewrite it using Elizabethan prepositions and verb conjugations.

2. Take a short contemporary poem and try replacing as many of the nouns, verbs, and modifiers as you can with archaic versions of the same words. However, do this without changing the basic situation in the poem. Do not use a thesaurus, but do use a dictionary.

3. Take an existing poem that's between fifteen and twenty-five lines long. Rewrite it as a prose paragraph, but alter the basic type of every sentence. Break compound or complex sentences up into simple sentences. Combine the simple sentences into compound or complex sentences. If you're not sure about the structure of compound or complex sentences, look those terms up in a writing handbook or online. Keep the line lengths and breaks as close to the same as possible. Then revise every sentence from the original poem into a sentence fragment or a run-on sentence. If you're not sure about the structure of those terms, you know where to look.

4. Try writing a "prose sonnet." Write a paragraph that is made up of four sentences. Each of the first three sentences must have exactly three clauses in it, and the final sentence must have two. In this way, the total number of clauses in the paragraph should be fourteen. If you're not sure about the structure of clauses, look those terms up in a writing handbook or online. If you're up to the challenge, try to make each of the fourteen clauses or phrases nine to eleven syllables long.

Chapter 7

Descriptive Language

Key terms: imagery/image figurative language/figure of speech, tenor, vehicle, implied figure of speech, personification, extended figure of speech, conceit

The last chapter showed you how language works under the hood with diction and syntax. This chapter looks at how language transmits information by describing the world around you and the world inside your own head. Describing those worlds—inner and outer—is central to most poetry.

The chapter divides the ways that poems use language to describe things into two main types that should be familiar to you from your own life, the conversations you have and the stories you tell every day. On one hand, you use language to describe things by explaining their actual physical attributes—how they look, feel, sound, and so on. On the other hand, you describe things by comparing them to other things.

Poetry uses both of those modes of description all the time, but many poets have a habit of using particularly rich, vivid, and sometimes complicated comparative descriptions, especially to describe unfamiliar things and inner experiences by comparing them to familiar and concrete things. Analyzing those descriptions carefully is a key to understanding and appreciating a lot of poems.

"'Out, Out —'" reappears twice in this chapter, so you can take a careful look at its descriptions. Before you get started, then, go back and give the poem another reading so that it's fresh in your mind.

Imagery

Imagery refers to anything in a poem that gives us a concrete description of the world and appeals directly to our senses. An **image** is a representation of some actual physical thing that is or could be in the world, using the details that we can perceive with our five physical senses. Most concrete nouns, such as "flower," "puppy," or "wind," are images, but abstract nouns, such as "patriotism," "love," or "weather," are not.

It's useful, when analyzing the images in a poem, to describe their quality in terms of specificity, richness, detail, or depth. For example, "apple" is an image, but it is not a very clear, specific, or vivid image. What kind of apple? "A tiny green crabapple" is very different from "a Pacific Rose apple four inches in diameter." Both of those images are more specific and rich than the first "apple." They are easier for us to *imagine*.

Looking at a pair of poems with very different use of images may help clarify the definition of imagery. Let's start with a contemporary poem:

Let the Light Stand

Let the light stand for nothing
but illumination. Let
the naked man and woman
out for air. Let the curtain hide
5   only another side of the
curtain. Let the food consumed
be consummated. Let the
consommé be a dish. Let the
dish into the bedroom
10   because she is there for the
cat. Let the cat be cool as Miles.
Let it all happen again
if you can. Let it happen again
if you can. Let the first word

15

spoken during intercourse be the
only definition you require. Let
need be need. Let love be need
also, if need be. And let
it all happen again because it can.

Corey Mesler, 2015

Very little imagery exists in this poem, and what images do occur are generic. A few concrete things are mentioned: "naked man and woman," "cat," "consommé," and "curtain," That gives us the slightest grounding in the world of the senses, but even these nouns are detached from any scene.

The poem seems to invoke the ideas of things rather than things themselves. Even the one proper noun, "Miles," which refers to a specific person, only makes sense if we know that "Miles" is Miles Davis and that this reference is used as a figurative way to describe the cat. Most of the poem is about thought rather than description of things.

Imagery in "'Out, Out —'"

Compare that that poem to "'Out, Out —'." It features detailed and vivid imagery appealing to more than sight. You hear the saw buzz, see the wood being cut, feel the breeze, and even smell the fresh-cut wood. The first three lines describe the saw at work, but notice the conspicuous absence of any people. The next three lines describe the mountain ranges and the sunset that fill the sky.

You hear the sound of the saw before you see the boy. Notice how abstract he is. There is no imagery of the boy at all. The sister has a single concrete attribute: the apron that she wears. After the accident, you hear the boy's "first outcry" and see how he turns holding his mangled hand. The damage to the hand, though, is not described with imagery. You understand the damage by how the boy responds to it.

The boy's final labored breaths engage your eyes and ears. How precise that description seems, the way the boy "puff[s] his lips out with his breath." The poem's imagery suggests the diminishing sound of his dying pulse, and, just barely, the sight of the people leaning in to hear the final heartbeats.

Ask yourself what effect the choice of images has on you. How would it be different if you could see and hear more of the boy and less of the saw? How would you react if the mangled hand were described in vivid, concrete imagery? What if you were not given the image of the mountain ranges at sunset?

Sometimes fully appreciating and understanding the imagery in a poem may require looking up details or terminology. Luckily, you looked up "buzz saw" when you were working out the setting for this poem in a previous chapter, remember? The specific noun "buzz saw" conjures up a clear and detailed image—not only of how a thing looks, but also of how it sounds and maybe even smells. Remember to take the time to understand the words and sentences, and the poem will happily make itself understood for you.

Imagery and Association

Images are by definition descriptive or representational, but they can also be suggestive and associative. They can bring to mind feelings, moods, or attitudes that they don't directly represent. This shouldn't seem unusual. It's a part of everyone's daily experience. When you reach into your pocket and feel the lanyard your child made for you at summer camp, you are flooded with all the complex love and memories you associate with that child. When you walk past a graveyard, all the awesome mystery of your own inevitable death floods your consciousness. Things are not just objects but gateways to thoughts and feelings.

The imagery in a poem is often there to evoke feelings and states of mind. However, this doesn't mean that the images are a puzzle for you to solve, or that you have to decipher or guess the author's intention in placing a particular image in a poem. Your job as a reader is merely to pay careful attention to what's in the poem, make sure you understand it, and notice your own reactions, feelings, and thoughts.

Evaluations and judgments do the thinking and feeling for you, but imagery lets you think for yourself. For example, "The man was overcome with sadness" is not imagery. "Sad" is an evaluation or judgment formed in response to the thoughts or feelings you have based on sensory data. On the other hand, "Tears ran down the man's red face, under his disheveled hair, and his breath came in wracking sobs" is imagery. The words in the first example tell you, while the imagery in the second example shows you.

Notice the way imagery contributes to a bleak, desolate feeling in this excerpt of a poem, even though no feeling words are used:

from "Preludes"

I
The winter evening settles down
With smell of steaks in passageways.
Six o'clock.
5   The burnt-out ends of smoky days.
And now a gusty shower wraps
The grimy scraps
Of withered leaves about your feet
And newspapers from vacant lots;
10   The showers beat
On broken blinds and chimney-pots,
And at the corner of the street
A lonely cab-horse steams and stamps.
And then the lighting of the lamps.

T. S. Eliot, 1917

The imagery in this poem creates an atmosphere of isolation and alienation. The second and fourth lines evoke the sense of smell with cooking steaks and smoke in the air. Lines 5 through 8 and lines 12 and

13 give us visual images—you see the wind blowing the leaves and news-papers around our ankles, the steam coming off the horse in the rain, and the gas lamps flickering to life. Lines 9 and 10, as well as line 12, call to your ears. You hear the rain beating against the blinds and chimneys and the horse stamping in the street. The horse is "lonely," but most people read that in the literal sense of it being alone on the corner, with no other horses there. It is not the horse that *feels* lonesome but the scene. The imagery creates this lonely tone.

Figurative Language

Figurative language is the definition, explanation, or presentation of one thing in terms of another thing. A **figure of speech** compares or replaces the original thing with some other thing that is surprisingly different. Often, figurative language explains or defines an abstract concept like "love" or "grief." It can define something presumed to be unfamiliar to the audience, like "my mother." Figurative language can also recast a familiar concept or thing by comparing it to something less familiar. We use figurative language all the time. When we try to explain something and compare it to something else—"Love is like chocolate"—we're using figurative language.

The many complex theories of figurative language go at least back to ancient Greek literary criticism. Learning to use figures of speech was an important part of Roman rhetoric. Broad definitions of figurative language include all nonliteral use of language, even irony, and arrangements of lan-guage, such as anaphora and chiasmus. Look them up if you're curious.

Some people spend a lot of energy classifying these terms and looking for the differences between them. While that can be interesting and fun, it's not anything you need to worry too much about for now. What all types of figurative language share in common is much more important than the distinctions between various figures of speech.

The Basic Structure of Figurative Language

Every figure of speech has two parts and shares this same basic structure:

- the thing being explained or defined (called the **tenor**)
- the thing that the tenor is being compared to (called the **vehicle**)

Once you find—or think you've found—any kind of figure of speech in a poem, begin by identifying the two parts shown above. Let's look at two simple examples.

Robert Burns wrote, "My love is like a red, red rose." He was trying to explain "my love," which is an abstraction that we can neither see nor touch.

- "My love" is the tenor, the thing being described.
- A "red, red rose" is the vehicle, the thing that "my love" is being compared to.

What does that comparison tell you about "my love"? How is it like "a red, red rose"? The connection is not obviously literal. How does thinking about, visualizing, and knowing a "red, red rose" help you better understand "my love"? When you answer those questions, you're well on your way to understanding this first figure of speech.

In a second example, Alfred, Lord Tennyson wrote of an eagle on a cliff: "He watches from his mountain walls, / And like a thunderbolt he falls." He was trying to explain the way "he falls," where "he" is the eagle diving.

- The way "he falls" is the tenor.
- "A thunderbolt" is the vehicle.

In this case, both parts of the figure are concrete. The vehicle, lightning, is presumably more familiar while the way an eagle dives, the tenor, may not be. What does that tell you about the way he falls? How is it like a flash of lightning? How does thinking about, visualizing, and knowing a flash of lightning help you better understand the way he falls? When you answer those questions, you're on your way to understanding this second figure of speech.

Implied Figures of Speech

All figures of speech have these two parts, the tenor and the vehicle. However, in an **implied figure of speech** one of these parts may not actually be written on the page. Instead, it's implied, which means it's logically demanded by the context.

If you say, "My love has soft petals but sharp thorns," the tenor is "my love." That's what you're describing. However, what are you comparing your love to? What's the vehicle? It's not "thorns and petals." Your love is not like those things. It *has* those things. What literally has those things? A rose. That means the figure of speech here is "my love is like a rose," even though "rose" never appears in the words on the page. It didn't have to appear—it was implied.

One particular kind of implied figure of speech is called **personification**. That is when a nonhuman thing is the tenor, and the vehicle is a human being. Personification also describes an implied figure of speech using a nonliving object as the tenor and defining it using a vehicle that implies animal or human characteristics. In personification, we rarely see an obvious comparison or definition like "the buzz saw is a wild and angry beast." Instead, we see "the buzz saw snarled and rattled." The vehicle is implied.

"My love is like a rose" was a nice, straightforward example. Implied figures of speech can sometimes be very subtle, though, and you have to be a careful reader to catch them.

Figurative Language in "'Out, Out —'"

The most prominent figure of speech in "Out, Out —" is the description of the buzz saw in terms of a living creature that possesses intelligence and volition. The buzz saw is the tenor. There is no single clear vehicle, however. The comparison is implied. What we get instead is a description that gives living qualities to the buzz saw.

First, remember from looking at the syntax of this poem that buzz saw is always the subject of any sentence in which it appears (line 1, lines 7–8, line 14, line 18). That gives us the impression that the buzz saw is the actor, that it does things.

Second, the saw "snarls" and "rattles" in lines 1 and 7. Those might be purely descriptive, but they are both noises that animals make — zgerous, angry animals.

Third, the saw "runs" and "bears a load" (line 8). These are terms anyone working with power tools might use, but in this context, they become part of the figurative description of the saw. Running and carrying a load are things that an animal, or a human being, might do.

Finally, the speaker imbues the buzz saw with perception, intelligence, and pride (lines 14–15). The saw hears "supper" and wants to prove it knows what that means, so it leaps at the boy's hand. The saw's motive in attacking the boy isn't the result of animal fear or hunger but a very human, violent pride.

The rest of this poem is almost completely literal. One exception is the figure of speech describing blood spilling from the boy's hand as "life" (line 22). Notice that again this is an implied figure of speech — the tenor, "blood," is not stated directly. All you get is what "the blood" is described as, "life." At the end of the poem, another implied figure of speech describes the act of caring for the wounded boy to "building." The pulse and breath, as minimum conditions of life, are described as things to "build on," the vehicle.

Extended Figures of Speech

Multiple figures of speech can share the same vehicle or the same tenor.
That is, one thing can be explained by comparing it to many other things,
or many things can be explained by comparing them all to one single
thing. Likewise, the same term or image can be the tenor of one figure of
speech and the vehicle of another at the exact same time.

Any of these descriptions is generally referred to as an **extended figure
of speech**. Here's an example of a fairly straightforward extended figure of
speech in which one figure carries through and controls an entire poem.

Shall I compare thee to a summer's day?

I better not. You'd boil at the thought.
Might I entice you toward an early spring?
You could explode through thaw like daffodils
or strut with stellar jays around our yard.
Or, how about the star magnolia tree
that beats out cherry, plum, forsythia
each year and risks a frost to be the first?
Something in you, my dear, desires to lead,
can't bear the thought of standing second best.

But let me clarify: there's just no way
you are the mower needing sharpening
nor peat that rests behind our garden shed
nor surly rains that shut a gardener in.
You've gleaned—withstanding twenty years
of partnering—I am the mower dulled
from summer's wear. I am the peat that waits
its spread as soon as coastal storms abate.
And, if you wish, I'd even be the shed.
Something in me feels worthy to protect.

20 But if these images still needle you
and you'd prefer the echo of a smile,
organic food consuming kitchen shelves,
the copper tint you splashed across our walls,
please humor me. Jot down on sticky notes
25 the things that speak to you of you. Arrange
them like perennials in tidy rows
near my writing pad and coffee cup.
I am an unlined page and cooling brew.

Carolyn Martin, 2014

The controlling figure of speech is launched in the title. Someone ("thee") is compared to "a summer's day." In addition to being a figure of speech, this is an allusion to Shakespeare's "Sonnet 18," which begins with the exact same question. That older poem develops one of the most famous extended figures of speech in English poetry, as the lover compares the beloved to a summer's day in various ways.

This contemporary poem immediately goes a different way. The lover admits that the beloved is not at all like a summer's day and then goes on to list four potential alternate vehicles: an early spring day, daffodils, stellar jays, or the star magnolia tree. Starting in the second stanza, the speaker lists three more vehicles that the beloved is definitely not—a mower needing sharpening, peat resting behind a shed, or "surly" rain that keeps the gardener indoors.

The poem then shifts to a new but related figure, which includes a number of vehicles that describe the lover rather than the beloved. This list begins with the first two vehicles the lover said the beloved definitely was not—the dull mower and the rain-soaked peat—or a shed. The lover could be a shed.

In the final stanza, the conversation turns back to the beloved, suggesting vehicles that might be preferable: the echo of a smile, organic food, copper paint on kitchen walls. The poem ends with the lover asking to be described by the beloved "on sticky notes" beside a "writing pad and coffee cup." Then, in the final line, these threads come together with the description of the lover as "an unlined page and cooling brew." The lover figuratively asserts her willingness to listen to and understand the beloved, as well as their unity as a couple.

This next poem offers an example of a complex extended figure of speech. The poet extends the figure by elaborating on the vehicle, adding details about the vehicle to more fully explain the tenor. This poem uses the original figure to extend a tangent of thought with a new, related figure and then ties the two together. One way of looking at a thing suggests a new way of looking at another thing, and that suggests yet another new way to understand something else altogether.

On a Deschutes County Road in Winter

Crossing that open country where mountains row up
like chorus girls, they each stood large on my road

this one sheer, the next cragged, the next slim bottomed, another
broad faced, another red topped, an elegant plump. With each

5 curve I traversed, skirting the troublesome faces and giving
wide berth to knife edges, admiring wild legs and canyons,

the wind shifted. Cloud boas dangled from fir shoulders, then
    fluttered off,
feather white. And I was twelve again, stiff with the prospect

10 of the slow dance and the cold sweat that accompanied
palms at basement parties cupped around a bony waist.

Revelation happens like that, in burlesque moments,
a grope for contact we want but are afraid to touch.

Then I knew it like my Ford pickup's ripped upholstery,
15 how, as night dropped its black negligee, somewhere

in the distance another would queue up, waiting to dance.

David Melville, 2016

The poem starts with the figure of speech it carries forward and returns to: "mountains row up / like chorus girls. . . ." Here are the two things, one being explained by comparing it to the other. The tenor is "the mountains," and the vehicle is "chorus girls." The poem explains the experience of seeing these mountains by comparing it to the experience of seeing a row of chorus girls.

In the second stanza, the poem attempts to describe the appearance of the various mountains by comparing them to the various dancers' bodies—slim-bottomed, broad-faced, red-topped, elegant[ly] plump.

In the third stanza, the speaker compares one negative and one positive characteristic of a mountain with a negative and positive attribute of a chorus girl: troublesome faces (to be skirted) and wild legs (to be admired).

In the fourth stanza, the comparison expands further, taking in not just the mountains themselves but the trees on them and especially the clouds hanging about them. The mountains have "fir shoulders," from which the "cloud boas," which are "feather white," "dangle," and then "flutter off."

Notice how the last four terms are vehicles for explaining not the mountains directly but the clouds. All of those comparisons depend on us understanding that the clouds are to the mountains as a feather boa is to a dancer. The main figure, "mountain is like dancer," determines the secondary figure "cloud is like feather boa."

The end of the fourth stanza and entire fifth stanza depart from the original figure. On a related tangent, the speaker's thoughts about dancers make him remember the awkward slow dance "at basement parties" in middle school.

The sixth stanza launches a new figure that joins the memory to the original proposition that mountains are like dancers: "Revelation happens like that, in burlesque moments, / a grope for contact we want but are afraid to touch." What's happening here?

"How revelation happens" is the new tenor, and the vehicle is "burlesque moments," like the cold sweaty palms cupped around a bony waist during slow dances at basement parties, "a grope for contact we want but are afraid to touch." The second part interprets that vehicle, as the speaker turns the thought over in his own mind and tries to make it more precise.

"Revelation" is more abstract than the appearance of mountains in winter. Perhaps the speaker means a psychological revelation, a flash of insight or understanding into the nature of the world, or the self, or other people. The poem says that seeing more deeply into the world's truth of how things are happens tentatively, clumsily. We seek but are afraid to find the answer, then it crashes in on us with the immediacy of physical contact.

The speaker's insight isn't directly related to the mountains. However, understanding the mountains as dancers leads the speaker to the memory of middle school dances. That memory leads to the insight about the nature of insights.

The final two stanzas tie these threads together. The speaker says, "then I knew it," and explains with a new figure of speech. The tenor is "how well the speaker knows this new truth," and the vehicle is "just as well as the speaker knows his Ford pickup's ripped upholstery." This implies that the speaker is pretty familiar with this truck, having lived with it and its torn seats a long time.

What did the speaker know then? The figure of the dancing girls returns: "as night dropped its black negligee, somewhere // in the distance another would queue up, waiting to dance." The first part of that line is an implied figure, indirectly comparing night to a burlesque dancer. When night drops its black negligee, the characteristics of a burlesque dancer are assigned directly to it. Just as a burlesque dancer ends the show by dropping her black negligee in a big reveal, so too night ends with darkness dropping away.

The end of night, of course, means the beginning of a new day, which may suggest the general passing of time. Dawn is a common symbol of the future. As one day ends, a new one awaits. As one dance ends, another begins. Perhaps the speaker's revelation is of how cyclical or endless time is. Perhaps night suggests the figurative darkness of depression or troubles. Perhaps the revelation is about revelations, that there is always another one waiting. We think we understand the world, but a deeper understanding always awaits us. Remember, he had just defined revelation as a dancer, and whatever comes next, whatever is "queuing up," is being defined as a dancer, too.

The point is not to figure out the "right" answer with a complex figure of speech like this. As always, just keep wondering what makes sense and how you might understand and appreciate the poem for what it actually says to you.

Conceits

Webs of linked and overlapping figures of speech can become intensely complicated. Such extended figures of speech are called **conceits**. Some poems make a sort of game out of trying to create the most complex web of interrelated figurative language possible. The pleasure, as in a riddle or a murder mystery, is in the intellectual exercise of unravelling the complexity. Readers enjoy untangling the web of figurative language and appreciating its cunning.

Conceits are common in sonnets and are often associated with seventeenth-century English poetry, especially the group called the Metaphysicals, but conceits appear in all sorts of poems and are certainly still in use today.

John Donne, the most well-known of the Metaphysical poets, is famous for the complexity and creativity of his conceits, as you will see in this next poem:

The Flea

Mark but this flea, and mark in this,
How little that which thou deniest me is;
It sucked me first, and now sucks thee,
And in this flea our two bloods mingled be;
5   Thou know'st that this cannot be said
A sin, nor shame, nor loss of maidenhead,

Yet this enjoys before it woo,
And pampered swells with one blood made of two,
And this, alas, is more than we would do.

10 Oh stay, three lives in one flea spare,
Where we almost, nay more than married are.
This flea is you and I, and this
Our marriage bed, and marriage temple is;
Though parents grudge, and you, w'are met,
15 And cloistered in these living walls of jet.
Though use make you apt to kill me,
Let not to that, self-murder added be,
And sacrilege, three sins in killing three.

Cruel and sudden, hast thou since
20 Purpled thy nail, in blood of innocence?
Wherein could this flea guilty be,
Except in that drop which it sucked from thee?
Yet thou triumph'st, and say'st that thou
Find'st not thy self, nor me the weaker now;
25 'Tis true; then learn how false, fears be:
Just so much honor, when thou yield'st to me,
Will waste, as this flea's death took life from thee.

John Donne, 1633

The speaker is attempting to convince the woman he's addressing to have sex with him by comparing a variety of aspects of their lives and their relationship to — wait for it — a flea.

The flea is the vehicle, and it's used to explain multiple tenors: having sex, being married, and the consequences of having premarital sex. The whole comparison rests on an understanding of human biology, common in Donne's time, that didn't really differentiate between various bodily fluids. For the speaker and his audience, the blood the flea sucked from them both would not have been understood to be different from the bodily fluids that mingle in sex. Indeed, the seventeenth-century understanding of conception was that it occurred from a "co-mingling of blood." If you keep that in mind, it makes the figure of speech much clearer—a little clearer, anyway.

In the first stanza, the speaker notices a flea on his lover's body. The speaker suggests that because their body fluids are already mingled in the flea that bit them both, and there is no harm or shame in that, then there can be no harm in mingling them by having sex either. The flea gets to enjoy the mingling of their blood without shame, which, "alas, is more than we would do."

In the second stanza, the speaker begins by begging the beloved not to kill the flea. She should not, he says, because they are joined by the mingling of their blood inside the flea. To the speaker, that means they are in fact married and are already living together in the flea! To kill the flea, then, would be murder because it kills him, suicide because it kills her, and sacrilege because it destroys the temple in which they were joined.

Finally, in the third stanza, the beloved has killed the flea. She points out, in triumph, that having killed the flea, she did not in fact harm either of them. She means this as a rebuttal to his figurative argument, but he quickly recovers and turns the argument on its head. It's true, he says, that you had nothing to fear from killing the flea; just so, it will harm you no more to have sex with me than it hurt you to kill the flea in which we were joined.

You may or may not find this very seductive, but it's certainly clever.

Final Thoughts

Descriptive language is not necessarily a part of every single poem, but imagery and figurative language are central to most poems. Imagery is direct description of facts that appeal to your physical senses—how something looks, sounds, feels, and so on. These details help the reader to imagine something.

Figurative language, also called figures of speech, describes something (the tenor) by comparing it to something else (the vehicle)—*this* is like *that*. Figures generally help the reader to understand something abstract or unfamiliar by comparing it with something concrete and familiar.

To finish off the chapter, here's a list of reminders, tips, and tricks to help you as you work with the descriptive language of poems:

- Even though in everyday use, "image" means "something seen," in talking about a poem, an "image" appeals to any of the body's senses, not just sight.

- Try going through a poem looking for images, sense by sense, rather than finding all the images in one line and then moving on to the next line. That is, read the poem and note every description that appeals to your sight. Then start over and note every description that appeals to your hearing. And so on.

- Understanding and analyzing figurative language can be difficult. Sometimes you will be challenged especially with complex, implied, and extended figures of speech. Just keep this basic model in mind: one thing is being explained in terms of another thing.

- Keep unraveling the knot of figurative language until you can identify tenor and vehicle—*this* is like *that*. Then ask yourself how. If "my love is like a red, red rose," how so? What qualities of a red, red rose does my love also have? How does thinking about a red, red rose help me understand love better, more fully, or in a new way?

- Figurative language usually depends on you knowing about or having direct experience of the vehicle, so don't shirk research if you need to find out more about the vehicle.

Remember, you use figurative language every day. Understanding one thing by comparing it to something else is built into your language and your brain. A figure of speech really intends to bring insight, understanding, and clarity. The poet hopes you'll grasp the comparison intuitively. You only need to break it down and figure it out when that intuitive apprehension fails you.

Exercises

This section gives you the chance to practice your understanding of descriptive language through guided readings of three poems and through focused creative writing exercises. Your teacher may or may not assign them, but they are designed to be completed independently if you wish.

For Readers

These three poems each provide a chance to practice understanding and appreciating imagery and figurative language. Unless you've already been given specific assignments by your professor, try doing this for each poem:

1. Complete the basic reading.

2. Jot down your own initial impressions. What did you understand to be happening on the literal level in this poem? Did you like it? Can you say how or why?

3. Try summarizing each poem in a written, formal way.

4. Highlight every image in each poem. Make margin notes that list what senses each image appeals to. Then list all the images in the three poems organized according to sense, and then sort the lists according to how rich or detailed the imagery is.

5. Go through the poems slowly and find all the figures of speech. Where is one thing being described in a way that doesn't literally make sense? Where is it being ascribed characteristics it doesn't literally have? Mark every single one.

6. Break down each figure into its constituent parts: tenor and vehicle. That pattern is always there. List out the ways each of those figures makes sense or is illuminating: How is X like Y? How does comparing X to Y help you understand X better?

Poem 1

Deciphering the situation in this next poem will help with understanding the figurative language. The double meaning of "to bear" in the title is important. A lot of readers find the first seven or eight lines a little disorienting; if that's the case for you, set them aside and move ahead, then come back to them. Line 20 is crucial.

Bearing a Child an Ocean Away

Between the devil and   and the (deep blue)
    Sea, this littlesweetness   this toy in a mouth
(books about how to do this. Too much advice) &
The random tadpole of chance, with its peach tail,
& the way kindness and betrayal both smell like cake —
there were seeds to sow, and some
evenings here were mornings.   There
    were deadlines to meet, & a fertility doctor
said, "Make me proud," so I sang softly   (to my,
      it turns out, empty womb in a Target store.)
So technically our first shopping trip as a mother/daughter
occurred   when you were not
    there & hadn't been born.
Time had plans for little

15   Shoppers.   (in erotic action
   across the ocean,   two mystery guests in a difficult
   situation
created their best accident): You,
      growing in her ocean: finger, finger, bone, bone, heart;
20 a muscle ripe as a rainy Valentine.
You would become a baby in China. I would
bear you like an imaginary friend I couldn't
      stop thinking of, wearing out the paperback of your
   love.
25 Meanwhile, in a secret alley,
            your lungs opened at first breath, & in Ohio,
your Grandmother ordered a quilt with your name on it. You,
   little water,
      evening river, fluting torrent, quiet spring.
30 (Your first lady disappears. You were left
      without the usual necessities).
   Know this: you did not enter alone.

Jan VanStavern, 2009

Poem 2

This second poem is also contemporary and uses language most people should understand at the literal level readily—although it does help to know a little about the life cycle of salmon. The heavy lifting of description, and of exploring and expressing ideas, is done by a series of fairly subtle and mostly implied figures of speech.

Sown

There are salmon who reach the spawning pool
but there are also those who lift
not in a leap from waterskin to water but from bear
hunger to dark and gorgeous digestion —
salmon on the riverbanks clawed through
or shat out, body-seeded
into tree and meadow over years
of returning urge, years
of bear and water trail.

     *

Salmon are in the trees now, in leaves looking out,
flashing in the turning branch, their smallest silver scale
in the dirt, nosing the root-ends to tunnel the height of seed,
            falling in leaf and soft trunk, rising in wind.

     *

           This shape-shifting:
it is the prophecy anyway, the crumbling wick
under the press of its own light. Everything is this close.

     *

And the bear, the rumbling matted black bear,
is also carried piece by piece, busily unhinged
and parted, carried into rich stink and rot

more gently than you can guess, more gently
than when she took the salmon from the river,
but still like that too, glistening on fierce waters.

Annie Lighthart, 2013

Poem 3

There's no figurative language like Elizabethan figurative language. For modern readers, however, it can take a lot of work to first read the poem, then read to really understand it, and then finally to delight in Shakespeare's complex, internally knotted conceits. However, you have the tools you need, and—sincerely—it does get easier with practice, and it's so worth it.

[Sonnet 60]

Like as the waves make towards the pebbl'd shore,
So do our minutes hasten to their end;
Each changing place with that which goes before,
In sequent toil all forwards do contend.
5 Nativity, once in the main of light,
Crawls to maturity, wherewith being crown'd,
Crooked eclipses 'gainst his glory fight,
And Time that gave doth now his gift confound.
Time doth transfix the flourish set on youth
10 And delves the parallels in beauty's brow,
Feeds on the rarities of nature's truth,
And nothing stands but for his scythe to mow:
And yet to times in hope my verse shall stand,
Praising thy worth, despite his cruel hand.

William Shakespeare, 1609

For Writers

The following exercises help you get to better understand the concepts for imagery and figurative language so that you can then bring them into your own writing with greater enjoyment and understanding. They are not designed to produce whole, finished poems, though if any of these exercises inspires you to start a poem, that's great, too.

1. Spend five minutes roaming around outside. Make a list of three interesting objects that you encounter on your travels. Have a seat and write out a description of each. Make your description as detailed as you can, but do not use any figures of speech! Next, imagine that each object writes its own haiku in the first person, announcing to the world its own true essence. Write those three haikus.

2. Write ten concise images and then list the associations that each has for you. For example, a horse running in a field might make you think of your childhood and warm summer afternoons. Take the list of images to at least four other people and ask them what associations, if any, they might have with the same images.

3. Write one-sentence figures of speech that explain each of the following things: romantic love, brotherly love, unconditional divine love, death, desire, infidelity, courage, suffering, hypocrisy, loneliness, America, inner peace, paranoia, and grace.

4. Think of six people you know. Write a short prose description of one key characteristic of each person. Next, reduce that description to a single figure of speech. Make a second set of figures, but make the vehicle an animal for all six people. Finally, write one more set of figures and make the vehicle a machine.

5. Practice extending some figures of speech. Pick one from a poem you've already written. Find multiple aspects of the tenor that can be explained by multiple aspects of the vehicle. For example, if your love is a red, red rose, what part is defined by the thorns? What part is defined by the scent? What is defined by texture?

Chapter 8

Symbolic Language

Key terms: allusion, symbol

The last chapter examined the language that poems use to describe the world. Images are the literal, sensory- based descriptions of the world. Figurative descriptions are created by comparisons. Almost everything you need to understand those kinds of descriptions is contained in the poem itself. If you have a good dictionary, you're set. However, sometimes poems use less literal and less obvious forms of figurative language to describe the world.

Poems may reach outside of themselves to the wide world for meaning. Because people share not only language but experiences, one way to quickly communicate something is for poets to refer to something they and their audience both understand already—a person, place, or event, a song or video—that has some shared meaning. Poems may also use a single thing, often something simple and short, to serve as a link or doorway to a complex collection of facts, options, and emotions.

Noticing and sharing these references and understanding how they operate in poetry is a crucial step in understanding and appreciating the poems that make use of them. As you saw with descriptive language, you'll find that you already use these kinds of language all the time in your everyday life.

"'Out, Out —'" is used twice in this chapter so that you can take a careful look at its symbolic language. To make sure it's still fresh in your mind, take another look before you proceed.

Allusions

An **allusion** is a reference to something outside the poem that is meaningful within the poem. Allusions are not generally meant to be obscure, confusing, or difficult. In fact, they're meant to be just the opposite. Poets use allusions to communicate, to make connections, to clarify, and to be interesting and helpful. Most poets choose allusions that they assume will be well understood by their audience.

Allusions to historical events or people, places, and art, like painting or music, are common in poetry. Especially before the mid-twentieth century, poets frequently allude to Greek and Roman literature and the Bible. Pop culture, history, politics, and almost anything else can show up as an allusion, too.

The gap between what the poet assumes we're familiar with and what we're actually familiar with can cause pain for student readers. However, in the age of the smart phone, filling yourself in isn't usually too difficult. As long as there's at least one clue for you to grab, you can start searching. Especially when the allusion is a proper noun, and capitalization tells you that a specific place or person is being referenced, all you have to do is make the effort to look it up.

The Convergence of the Twain
(Lines on the loss of the "Titanic")

I

In a solitude of the sea
Deep from human vanity,
And the Pride of Life that planned her, stilly couches she.

II

Steel chambers, late the pyres
Of her salamandrine fires,
Cold currents thrid, and turn to rhythmic tidal lyres.

III

Over the mirrors meant
To glass the opulent
The sea-worm crawls — grotesque, slimed, dumb, indifferent.

IV

Jewels in joy designed
To ravish the sensuous mind
Lie lightless, all their sparkles bleared and black and blind.

V

Dim moon-eyed fishes near
Gaze at the gilded gear
And query: "What does this vaingloriousness down here?" . . .

VI

Well: while was fashioning
This creature of cleaving wing,
The Immanent Will that stirs and urges everything

VII

Prepared a sinister mate
For her — so gaily great —
A Shape of Ice, for the time far and dissociate.

VIII

And as the smart ship grew
In stature, grace, and hue,
In shadowy silent distance grew the Iceberg too.

IX

25 Alien they seemed to be;

No mortal eye could see

The intimate welding of their later history,

X

Or sign that they were bent

By paths coincident

30 On being anon twin halves of one august event,

XI

Till the Spinner of the Years

Said "Now!" And each one hears,

And consummation comes, and jars two hemispheres.

Thomas Hardy, 1912

In the epigraph, the poem identifies its own topic, "the loss of the 'Titanic.'" Notice the capitalized noun? That's your clue, the key word for you to use in an online search. What you will find is that the Titanic was a luxury liner that sunk by collision with an iceberg on its maiden voyage in 1912. It had been designed with many safety innovations, and its makers had famously declared that "God himself could not sink this ship." Many people found the disparity between the claims of the manufacturer and the fate of the ship suggested human pride and folly in general. That allusion is the master key to the whole poem.

Allusion in "'Out, Out—'"

This poem has just a single allusion, and it's in the title. Frost assumes that we are familiar enough with Shakespeare that if he quotes from one of Shakespeare's plays, we'll recognize the source and that the meaning of the allusion will be available to us. Frost gives one clue by placing the title in quotation marks, indicating that it's probably either a quote from somewhere or dialogue spoken by a character. By the time we get to the end of the poem, we can see it's not dialogue.

Hopefully you noticed the quotation marks. If not, slow down. Read more carefully. Listen more carefully to the poem. The second thing to make you look for the allusion is that the title seems out of place. What does it mean? What goes out, or is called out? Out of where? If you're really clever, you might make the connection that the boy's death might be thought of figuratively as a light going out.

Looking for "out out allusion" in any search engine will quickly inform you that it's a quote from *Macbeth*. It's in the middle of a very famous speech given by Macbeth right after his wife dies:

> To-morrow, and to-morrow, and to-morrow,
> Creeps in this petty pace from day to day,
> To the last syllable of recorded time;
> And all our yesterdays have lighted fools
> The way to dusty death. Out, out, brief candle!
> Life's but a walking shadow, a poor player
> That struts and frets his hour upon the stage
> And then is heard no more. It is a tale
> Told by an idiot, full of sound and fury
> Signifying nothing.

Most readers find that speech to be a pretty dark assessment of human life and death. Frost certainly colors his poem with particular ideas and feelings by titling it with an allusion to this bleak speech. Knowing this allusion might cause you to reassess your understanding of the poem's tone.

Recognizing Allusions

Some poems don't make it so easy to track down the allusion. Instead of referring directly by name to a person, place, or thing, the poems refer indirectly to its attributes or associations. The poet hopes we're familiar enough with the allusion to catch on, as we can see in this next poem:

Sestina: Like

With a nod to Jonah Winter

Now we're all "friends," there is no love but Like,
A semi-demi goddess, something like
A reality-TV star look-alike,
Named Simile or Me Two. So we like
5 In order to be liked. It isn't like
There's Love or Hate now. Even plain "dislike"

Is frowned on: there's no button for it. Like
Is something you can quantify: each "like"
You gather's almost something money-like,
10 Token of virtual support. "Please like
This page to stamp out hunger." And you'd like
To end hunger and climate change alike,

But it's unlikely Like does diddly. Like
Just twiddles its unopposing thumbs-ups, like-
15 Wise props up scarecrow silences. "I'm like,
So OVER him," I overhear. "But, like,
He doesn't get it. Like, you know? He's like
It's all OK. Like I don't even LIKE

Him anymore. Whatever. I'm all like . . ."
20   Take "like" out of our chat, we'd all alike
Flounder, agape, gesticulating like
A foreign film sans subtitles, fall like
Dumb phones to mooted desuetude. Unlike
With other crutches, um, when we use "like,"

25   We're not just buying time on credit: Like
Displaces other words; crowds, cuckoo-like,
Endangered hatchlings from the nest. (Click "like"
If you're against extinction!) Like is like
Invasive zebra mussels, or it's like
30   Those nutria-things, or kudzu, or belike

Redundant fast food franchises, each like
(More like) the next. Those poets who dislike
Inversions, archaisms, who just like
Plain English as she's spoke—why isn't "like"
35   Their (literally) every other word? I'd like
Us just to admit that's what real speech is like.

But as you like, my friend. Yes, we're alike,
How we pronounce, say, lichen, and dislike
Cancer and war. So like this page. Click Like.

A. E. Stallings, 2013

If you've never seen Facebook, this poem won't make a lot of sense. In a way, the poem is *about* Facebook. It's also *using* Facebook as a way to explore how people form relationships and react to the world around them. When the poet claims that "Like is like / Invasive zebra mussels," she's not talking about the "Like" button itself being literally a destructive invasive aquatic species that is ruining habitats. Instead, the "Like" button stands in for a whole way of thinking about and relating to the world and other people that is destructive but insidiously pervasive and apparently unstoppable.

The best advice for finding these subtler allusions is simply to be aware that they're out there. If you come across a poem and get the feeling that there's more to it than you understand, consider the possibility that it's making allusions that you're missing. Are there any phrases, words, or quotations that seem more important than their literal meaning allows? Is there a turn of phrase or diction that seems out of place with the voice of the rest of the poem? Look at the title, too. As you saw with Frost's poem, there's often a tipoff there.

Going even further, some poems make allusions that are almost private or only understood by a small audience. The allusions may be impossible to locate without specialized reference material, or they may be even flat-out impossible. These poems may be more difficult to decipher. Luckily, though, this sort of thing is not common, and the poem generally works on some other level even if you don't get the allusion, as may be the case in this next poem:

Ode to the Apple

It's ironic that you would be free:
toothsome, crunchy, cold, wet, ordinary
(how do I absorb the ordinary?),
no-guilt lollipop of a lighter life.

5   A girl I knew in college went to England
and lost half her body weight eating apples.
When asked why, and she said, "I couldn't afford
museums and food, so I ate apples."

Thirty years later, I do too.
10   Yes, I still love zucchini
and pears with olive oil, grill marks,
and salt, I can stare guiltlessly

at bacon (I just lost some readers),
delight in chicken in herbs,
15 and cook valiantly with
chopped onions and the tricky roux.

But you, sliced sweet globe,
are celebrated by science
and a calorie counter. You count as Zero.
20 Taken without limits, you make days full.

I can avoid wines and cheeses,
and that Devil, butter; the oil-bathed
lettuces and challenging temptations
in tacos, crepes, and buns—and find
25 you, bright crisp and ordinary.

My anytime late-night crunch,
you make me strong enough to say no.
You shrink my size as my age grows larger;
you let me pretend I can change.

30 Investing in nothing,
like everyone sometimes does,
I become a local, flawed,
slightly smaller, and somewhat hopeful Eve.

Jan VanStavern, 2019

This probably makes a reasonable amount of sense even if you don't get the allusion. The speaker praises the addressee, who is "the apple." Obviously, the apple is seen as a tool for weight loss, a reference the speaker makes numerous times, including in the story of her friend from college.

The allusion peeks out in the first line: The apple is "free." In lines 19–20, it comes on stronger: "You count as Zero, / Taken without limits." Notice how the "Zero" is capitalized. That's the poet throwing you a little hint. If you've been a member of Weight Watchers any time in the past ten years, you will instantly recognize the allusion here. In the Weight Watchers system, food is assigned point values, and you are expected to limit your intake to a certain number of points per day. In this system, fruits and vegetables—including the apple of this poem—are free and "cost" zero points.

Getting this allusion and knowing this about Weight Watchers isn't absolutely necessary to understand or appreciate this poem. However, it does make the poem more understandable and enjoyable. It also makes lines like "how do I absorb the ordinary?" or "Investing in nothing" more sensible and directly relevant.

Symbolism

Generally, a **symbol** is something that represents or stands for something else. In literature, a symbol is a concrete thing that refers to something abstract and transcendent. Symbols can be animals, objects, images, a time of year, or almost anything else we can imagine—even events or people.

A wedding ring is a symbol of a spouse's devotion. A flag is a symbol of a nation's history, hopes, and values. A police badge is a symbol of civil authority. A swastika is a symbol of evil—or good fortune in south and east Asia. George Washington symbolizes honest, effective government, if not America itself. Judas Iscariot, who betrayed Jesus in the New Testament, symbolizes treachery and betrayal.

Students are sometimes intimidated by symbolism in literature, especially in poetry. Some feel as if symbols are a secret language only accessible to initiates in the cult of poetry. Others feel the whole idea is a fraud perpetrated by English teachers to make their students feel dumb. Neither are true. Your everyday life is full of symbols, and you are perfectly comfortable with them. You understand that the word "dog," for example, is not a dog itself but a set of letters that represents a dog. You understand that the flowers you give your mother are not your actual affection and respect for her but a symbol that represents your affection and respect. Human consciousness is itself an unfolding process of creating and interpreting symbols that cannot be avoided.

Nonetheless, some readers see the symbols in a poem more easily than others. They gravitate towards more associative and symbolic thinking, seeing, and communicating. Others are more concrete and literal thinkers. They may have a hard time believing that nonconcrete, nonliteral communication is valuable, perceptible, or that it even exists.

And that's all fine. Thank heaven for human variability. If you tend to view the world more literally, take comfort in the idea that reading the symbols in literature is a skill that you can learn, even if it doesn't come easily. If you have a positive attitude and apply yourself to it, with practice you'll learn.

Symbolism in "'Out, Out —'"

Does anything in here suggest ideas, concepts, or feelings beyond the literal content of the poem? The allusion in the title certainly might make us think about the meaning of human life. This allusion in the title sets up the whole poem as a meditation on this big issue.

The literal story is small and sad. A rural tragedy strikes one family, one community. The people are nameless and faceless, almost generic. Does the boy's death, or the manner in which it occurs, suggest anything larger to you?

One of the most striking things about the poem is the vivid personification of the buzz saw. It is not a tool, but a cunning, wrathful, deadly monster waiting in the midst of the unsuspecting family. You might find it hard to use a modern power tool and not think of this poem afterwards.

The conclusion is also very memorable. The boy's death is shocking, and then that shock is compounded by the shocking response of the people around him.

The boy is the only character of real note other than the buzz saw. He's portrayed sweetly, almost pathetically. His one strength is to be able to see things as they are, even though he can't quite accept what he sees. He is an innocent who has been put into a situation that is far too dangerous for him to survive. He's up against a foe he can't handle.

The buzz saw is a powerful tool that the boy voluntarily uses. He *thinks* it makes his life better, and it is working for him. However, it is actually a malicious and murderous monster. The flesh of the boy, innocent and soft, is mangled by the relentless aggression of the machine. Does this seem analogous to any situations which are broader, more general? Are there other circumstances in which people invent something which they think they control, and is making their lives better, but turns out to have a great cost, to be dangerous and uncontrollable?

Many might see the buzz saw as being symbolic of the industrial world, the machine world, and the boy symbolic of all of us, humanity. The whole industrial economy of factories, dynamos, cars, which we created to serve us, turns out to be relentlessly mangling and killing us all.

Did Frost intend the poem to be about this broader idea, to be a critique of the destructive power of the machine age? That doesn't matter in the slightest. We're not trying to guess Frost's intentions in writing the poem. We're just asking ourselves what the poem Frost wrote might make us think of if we read it carefully.

Symbols as Allusions

There's nothing inherently "American" about the bald eagle. Benjamin Franklin made a strong argument that the national bird should be the wild turkey instead. However, it was decided in 1782 that this bird would be a symbol of the country, and thus it is true now. The eagle is such a pervasive symbol that you probably don't even remember learning what it meant, but somewhere along the way you were taught. It's a common, public symbol that the American culture shares.

If a poet puts a bald eagle in a poem and we understand it to symbolize America, we've recognized that symbol in the same way we might recognize an allusion to an historical event or a movie. Our full understanding and appreciation of the poem depends on us having knowledge about the world outside the poem. We know what a bald eagle symbolizes, not because of clues in the poem but because we learned it at some point in the past and we bring that knowledge to the poem.

Symbols and allusions that rely on your prior knowledge exist on a spectrum from extremely well-known to obscure. Because these kinds of symbols are dependent on a shared culture to be meaningful, they're especially easy to miss in poems from distant times or places.

The good news is that you can use the same techniques and tools that you used for finding and understanding allusions to notice and decipher these shared symbols, though you may need to be a little more careful in the sources you use. There are several scholarly dictionaries of symbols, usually accessible online through your college library's portal. There are also several free resources online that are easy to find with a quick internet search. Use the same precautions in choosing and using them as you would with doing any research online.

Here's an example of a poem that opens with an allusive symbol:

My Heart Leaps Up

My heart leaps up when I behold
A rainbow in the sky:
So was it when my life began;
So is it now I am a man;
So be it when I shall grow old,
Or let me die!
The Child is father of the Man;
And I could wish my days to be
Bound each to each by natural piety.

William Wordsworth, 1807

Rainbows are natural symbols. Beauty that appears in the sky mysteriously, unpredictably, born of rain, suggests some sort of cosmic goodness. Surely, there must be some basic cosmic goodness at work somewhere if rainbows exist? In Judeo-Christian culture, the rainbow is also an explicit and well-understood symbol of God's love of humanity and active presence in history, as explained aat the end of the story of Noah's Arc in Genesis 9:12-17

Here, the rainbow appears in the second line, and it is the only image in the whole poem. The speaker tells us that the sight of a rainbow powerfully affects him now, just as it did when he was a small child. He repeats how much it still impacts him and how he hopes it still has this effect on him when he's old—and if it doesn't, let him die!

The rainbow doesn't appear, or seem to be directly referenced, in the last three lines. The speaker makes an observation that "the Child is Father of the Man," and expresses his wish that his whole life he should feel a "natural piety"—piety meaning "the quality of being religious or reverent." The speaker wants his whole life to be pious. What does that have to do with the rainbow that dominated the first six lines of the poem?

Understanding that the rainbow symbolizes God's love for humanity helps us answer that question. The speaker wants to keep that knowledge of God's love in his heart and live accordingly for his whole life.

Symbols as Figures of Speech

Not all symbols come from a shared library of cultural symbols. Often, poets create and use symbols in their poems just as they do figures of speech. Symbols are suggestive, not absolute. Nonetheless, they perform the same basic job as figurative language. They tell us about one thing in terms of something else.

In conventional figures of speech, either the tenor or the vehicle may be implied, or both may be stated clearly on the page. In a symbol, the tenor is always absent and is always something abstract and generally transcendent, and the tenor may stand for a variety of things all at once.

There's no foolproof way to find this kind of symbol. Just remind yourself to be open to the idea that some things may take on greater significance than they would if you only understood them literally. Pay attention when something in the poem seems to get more attention or to play a larger role than necessary. Consider the way things in a poem may parallel or suggest some greater, abstract idea. Look for incongruous details or attributes in the poem. Ask yourself, "Does this remind me of anything bigger than itself?" Look for signs that it might.

For example, let's consider this poem:

The Grand Silos of the Sacramento

From a distance, at night, they seem to be
industries—all lit up but not on the map;
or, in this scientific age, they could be
installations for launching rocket ships—
5   so solid, and with such security, are they. . .
Ah, but up close, by the light of day,
we see, not "pads" but actual paddies—
for these are simply silos in ricefields,
structures to hold the harvested grain.
10   Still, they're the tallest things around,
and, by night or day, you'd have to say
they're ample for what they do: storage.
And, if you amble around from your car,
you can lean up against one in the sun,
15   feeling warmth on your cheek as you spread
out your arms, holding on to the whole world
around you, to the shores of other lands
where the laborers launched their lives
to arrive and plant and harvest this grain
20   of history—as you hold and look, look
up, up, up, and whisper: "Grandfather!"

Lawson Fusao Inada, 1997

Most of this poem is an extended image, a description of grain silos in rice paddies. The title even gives the silos the honorific title "The Grand Silos of the Sacramento." Unless it's sarcastic, the title is tipping us off that we've got some important silos here.

Evidence in the text makes it clear that the silos are more than just silos. When the speaker discusses how to relate to the silos, he suggests an embrace. Have you ever hugged a silo? This nonsensical suggestion is a clue that you're moving out of the realm of the simply literal. This embrace includes not just the silos but also the people who built them and the "shores of other lands" from which they came, which is again literally impossible.

In the last two lines, the speaker links "you" directly to the "laborers" who planted these fields and harvested "this grain of history," as "you" look up and whisper "grandfather!"

The silos invite you to think about something bigger. This is symbolism, and the silos are symbols. What do they symbolize? If the silos are the vehicle, what are the possible tenors? The poet spells this out for you. The silos represent the long history of immigrant farm labor, the people who are the speaker's own ancestors—and, he suggests, the audience's ancestors, too. All the complicated feelings and facts that are wrapped up in the history of immigrant farm labor, for the whole community and in particular for their descendants, are symbolized by the silos.

If that's so, what is this poem saying about all those ideas through their symbol, the silos? All the literal feelings and actions are transferred through the symbol of the silos to the tenor. You can transfer all those associations from the symbol to the tenors. The poem is heaping praise on the history of migrant labor, the people, the work they did, what they built. Through the use of this symbol, the speaker embodies his love and respect.

This is how a symbol works in a poem.

It's important to pause a moment to remember that the poem isn't a riddle. You're not trying to find the one true answer to anything. You're definitely not trying to figure out what the author meant. As always, you're simply describing what you see, what it makes you think, how it makes you feel, and how it works on the page and in your mind and heart. Let's take a look at a slightly less clear example:

The *Boston Evening Transcript*

The readers of the *Boston Evening Transcript*
Sway in the wind like a field of ripe corn.

When evening quickens faintly in the street,
Wakening the appetites of life in some
5   And to others bringing the *Boston Evening Transcript*,
I mount the steps and ring the bell, turning
Wearily, as one would turn to nod good-bye to Rochefoucauld,
If the street were time and he at the end of the street,
And I say, "Cousin Harriet, here is the *Boston Evening*
10   *Transcript.*"

T. S. Eliot, 1915

Literally, this poem describes a man coming to his cousin's house and handing her a newspaper.

Why might we think there is a symbol here? First, in a nine-line poem, the very long name of the newspaper, "The *Boston Evening Transcript*," is repeated three times. Second, the newspaper is also the title of the poem. Clearly, then, it's important. But why?

Interestingly, the poem doesn't tell us anything at all about the paper itself. We don't know what it looks like, what its editorial policy is, how long it is, how many Pulitzer Prizes it's won—*nothing*.

The newspaper is mentioned every couple of lines and provides the poem its title, but it is never described at all. That's odd. If you, for some reason, wanted to write a poem about a newspaper, don't you think you'd include some information about the newspaper? This is the kind of discrepancy that should make you think, "Hmmm. Maybe there's something going on here at more than the literal level."

Let's look at each place the newspaper is mentioned. In the first line, you are told its readers "sway in the wind like a field of ripe corn." Hopefully you recognize that as a figure of speech. The readers are not literally a field of corn, nor are they literally swaying in the wind. The readers are being *compared* with a field of corn, one that is about to get harvested. Comparing a crowd of people to a field of ripe grain or corn is a traditional way to emphasize their mortality and their proximity to death. Emphasizing the fact that they sway in the wind extends the figure. The readers are made to seem passive, pushed around by the wind blowing at that moment, and following its lead all together in a big crowd. It's not a favorable description.

The second appearance of the newspaper is even more brutal. The evening, according to lines 3–5, wakens the appetites of life in some people. Presumably, "the appetites of life" means the desire for fun stuff—eating dinner, drinking, socializing, dancing, sex—all the delightful ways people enjoy life once the workday is done and the sun goes down. However, this is not what the evening brings to *everyone*. People are divided into two types, apparently, those who have fun and live life in the evening, and those who get The *Boston Evening Transcript* delivered.

Finally, the speaker describes how unbelievably and depressingly weary he is as he brings the paper to his cousin, apparently visiting her. Thus, he links himself and his family to the subscribers to The *Boston Evening Transcript*, to people who are ripe and close to death. They lack individuality or initiative, follow the times and the crowd, and don't do anything fun or pursue any of life's appetites. He himself seems tired, listless, bored, and boring.

The *Boston Evening Transcript* seems intimately linked to a whole class of people and becomes a shorthand for their way of life. These are the people of The *Boston Evening Transcript*. The *Boston Evening Transcript* symbolizes this bored, boring, tired, exhausted, herd-like way of life, which is seemingly stripped of any joy and only one step from the grave. It stands in for a whole constellation of feelings, practices, habits, beliefs, institutions, customs, and more. It doesn't explain any of them, but it sums up and represents them all.

Final Thoughts

Symbolic language is strongly associated with poetry, but not every poem uses symbolic language. When it *is* used, understanding and appreciating it is a crucial key to understanding and appreciating the whole poem.

Symbolic language includes allusion and symbolism. Allusions are references to actual things outside the poem that are meaningful inside the poem. They depend on us being familiar with the person, place, work of art, event, or whatever that the poet refers to. Symbolism is the use of one thing to represent something else, or more often, a whole constellation of related something-elses. It's useful to understand that symbols generally function like extreme forms of either allusion or figurative language.

To finish off the chapter, here's a list of reminders, tips, and tricks to help you as you work with symbolic language:

- Remember that there's no easy way to find an allusion you're not familiar with. Just keeping in mind that there may be allusions in the poem is helpful.

- Be sure you understand any proper nouns in the poem. Almost any proper noun, by its very nature, functions as an allusion.

- Look for clues in the title — or epigraph, if there is one. Allusions are often pointed out in the title. Be sure you can explain the title.

- Don't get hung up on finding symbols as if they were Easter eggs on your grandmother's lawn. Just ask yourself whether what's going on literally, in the action of the poem, reminds you of anything else.

- You're looking for places where the meaning of the text seems to extend beyond its literal words to suggest some larger, more broadly applicable ideas. The evidence you need is in the text of the poem, not in your knowledge of the author's intentions.

- Consult reference works that catalogue and explain conventional symbols. These can help you understand unfamiliar symbols.

- Test your identification of a symbol. If you suspect something has symbolic value, ask if the symbol makes sense in relation to the rest of the poem. A symbol is not decorative. It is woven into the poem and works alongside whatever else is going on in the poem.

Finding symbolic meaning in a poem is as much an act of the imagination as anything else. When you're reading a poem, try asking yourself what it makes you think of and what it makes you wonder about. Who knows what you'll find? Symbols often impact you unconsciously, and being open to and following up these more free-floating associations and echoes is an important part of understanding and appreciating a poem.

Exercises

This section gives you the chance to practice your understanding of these elements through guided readings of three poems and through focused creative writing exercises. Your professor may or may not assign them, but they are designed to be completed independently if you wish.

For Readers

These three poems each present clear and interesting use of symbolic language. Practice understanding and appreciating the allusions and symbolism. If you're not given specific assignments by your professor, try doing this for each poem:

1. Complete the basic reading.

2. Jot down your own initial impressions: What did you understand to be happening on the literal level in this poem? Did you like it? Can you say how or why?

3. Secure your understanding of the situation, as you studied in Chapters 3–5.

4. Summarize and paraphrase each poem as described in Appendix B.

5. Go through the poems slowly and find all the proper nouns. Make sure you what each refers to, including any possible multiple meanings. Write them down!

6. Using the guidelines explained in this chapter, and considering the paraphrases you just wrote, review each poem searching for possible symbols. Does anything seem to suggest something more than its literal meaning? Try not to self-censor your inquiry, at least at this point — the main goal should be opening up possibilities, not foreclosing them. Mark or underline anything that seems to point to broader possible meanings.

7. For every possible symbol, ask yourself if it could be understood as an allusion — is there a shared, socially-constructed symbolism at work here? Don't be shy about doing some research; the internet makes it easy.

8. For those possible symbols which seem more figurative than allusive, try to explain them the same way you would a figure of speech: tenor and vehicle. Remember multiplicity and ambiguity are OK, but there should be that basic pattern: the symbol represents, stands in for, or suggests something else.

9. For every possible symbol of any sort, ask yourself if it makes sense in the context of the whole poem. Does the symbolic meaning make some sort of sense? Do the various symbols work together at the symbolic level? Symbols don't have to be rational or linear, but in most poems they do create some kind of coherent experience, emotional, intellectual, or aesthetic. Jot down a short description of the symbolic level or experience of each

poem. Describe how it works with, against, or independently of the literal experience of the poem.

Poem 1

Many things are being defined and explained in this second example, but the speaker is the ultimate subject. "A mandala built / to be / erased" is a very specific allusion. Make sure you understand what the speaker is talking about—the whole clause, not just "mandala."

Opened

I watch a snowflake
shape its notion of water
into symmetry.

My eyes open me.

5   I'm a mandala built
to be
erased,
a snowflake, a former crystal,

now

10   a water drop,

now

a memory.

A. Molotkov, 2015

Poem 2

This poem is built almost entirely out of allusions. Finding them all is a lot of fun, and YouTube makes it easy. The initial key is in the title, as is often the case. Once you figure out the dense network of allusions and other figures of speech, it's worth asking what you've learned about the speaker. He tells you this is his "credo," after all.

Prince Credo

I believe in the dearly beloveds,
in the temple of the power chord, and
    for years in the early 80s,
that Prince was Filipino.
I believe in acting my age and not
my shoe size. In never being
a weekend lover, and in the hard work
    of a voice stretched into a silk bag
    filling fast with silt.
I believe in paisley and purple.
    That a kerchief is manly.
    That sexy is in the word and
    in the way that every guitar
    has its own ghosts to love.
Believe that the interval between
the chorus and the solo is holy
and that darling Nikki would happen
one day in the ethereal dance of adolescence.
Forgive me if I go astray.
    Forgive me, but I believe
    in Apollonia, Apollonia,
    and Apollonia.
That the fastest way to heaven
was across a Graffiti covered Bridge
    into the neck of a Stratocaster.
Believe in the litany of amplifier.
    In the hiss of feedback.
    In the bite of the lower lip. Beloveds,

I believe in eyeliner.
30 In androgyny and in the sylph-like tease
of an upturned collar.
I believe in frills and crop tops.
In the hard jab of a note
between shoulder blades. I believe
35 in smoke and the cherry red
of the moon and trying
to be quiet when the parents are home.
I believe in the gospel of summer
and in the car parked sideways.
40 And goddamn, I believe in the party,
and that it was meant to last.

Oliver de la Paz, 2017

Poem 3

This poem is a fortress of symbolism brooding behind a moat of allusions. Work through the allusions first. There are a lot of references to Irish mythology and history here. Then look for traditional, allusive symbols. Then ask yourself if anything seems to take on symbolic meaning within the text. Finally, do some research into Yeats and his use of symbolism. You'll find that interesting.

To the Rose upon the Rood of Time

Red Rose, proud Rose, sad Rose of all my days!
Come near me, while I sing the ancient ways:
Cuchulain battling with the bitter tide;
The Druid, grey, wood-nurtured, quiet eyed,
5 Who cast round Fergus dreams, and ruin untold;
And thine own sadness, whereof stars, grown old
In dancing silver-sandalled on the sea,

Sing in their high and lonely melody.

Come near, that no more blinded by man's fate,

10 I find under the boughs of love and hate,

In all poor foolish things that live a day,

Eternal beauty wandering on her way.

Come near, come near, come near — Ah, leave me still

A little space for the rose-breath to fill!

15 Lest I no more hear common things that crave;

The weak worm hiding down in its small cave,

The field-mouse running by me in the grass,

And heavy mortal hopes that toil and pass;

But seek alone to hear the strange things said

20 By God to the bright hearts of those long dead,

And learn to chaunt a tongue men do not know

Come near; I would, before my time to go,

Sing of old Eire and the ancient ways:

Red Rose, proud Rose, sad Rose of all my days.

W. B. Yeats, 1893

For Writers

The following exercises help you get to know and practice the concepts related to the symbolic language of a poem. They're not designed to produce whole, finished poems but to help you experiment with these smaller elements so that you can use them more effectively to create poems in your own time.

1. Using Inada's "The Grand Silos of the Sacramento" as an example, create a symbol that represents and explains a group of people you admire. Try it again, but this second time, use a group that you loathe.

2. Without using any reference material, list as many conventional symbols — both the symbol and what you think it symbolizes — as

you can think of in five minutes. Stay at it the whole five minutes. Don't let up.

3. List ten events, ten works of art (pop songs, video games, TV shows are fine), and ten people who you think are sufficiently well-known by a general audience today to be usable as allusions in a poem. Then explain what each item in your lists could allude to.

4. Browse through Milton's *Paradise Lost* and pick five lines that you could use as titles of poems. Write pitches for each poem as you did in the Chapter 3 exercises, and as part of your pitch, explain how the allusion will relate to the poem. Try the same thing with lines from any of Shakespeare's plays. Then try it with lines from the *King James Bible*.

5. An "apostrophe" is an address to something that can't respond — usually an inanimate object, a dead person, or even an abstraction. As such, it's a subtle form of personification. Why else would you be talking to it? It traditionally begins with "O," as in "O death, where is thy sting? O grave, where is thy victory?" (1 Cor. 15:55). Draft an apostrophic poem of your own in which you address any of the following characters: the west wind, God, Earth, death, a deceased relative, a historical figure, an inanimate object in the room, or Love.

Chapter 9

Musical Language, Part 1

Key terms: schwa, refrain, syllable, stressed syllable, rhyme, end rhyme, internal rhyme, single rhyme, multiple rhymes, exact rhyme, slant rhyme, rhyme scheme

Counting-Out Rhyme

Silver bark of beech, and sallow
Bark of yellow birch and yellow
Twig of willow.

Stripe of green in moosewood maple,
Colour seen in leaf of apple,
Bark of popple.

Wood of popple pale as moonbeam,
Wood of oak for yoke and barn-beam,
Wood of hornbeam.

Silver bark of beech, and hollow
Stem of elder, tall and yellow
Twig of willow.

Edna St. Vincent Millay, 1928

Nothing *happens* in this little poem. There are no characters, no action, no setting, and no story. There are sentences, the vocabulary is accessible, and the syntax is conventional and readily understood. But that skeleton of sense is no more than the barest frame. The muscles, the heart, the pumping blood of the poem are all sound, all song.

This chapter starts with the most basic components—the sounds of letters and how they make a kind of music. You'll review the definition of a syllable and solidify your understanding of the difference between stressed and unstressed syllables. You will begin to explore the wide world of rhyme.

Throughout this chapter, you will refer back to "Counting-Out Rhyme," so be sure you put it through a careful basic reading before going any further.

The Basic Musicality of Language

Sounds have objective, physical reality. The sounds of words are created in your body with your lips, tongue, cheeks, lungs, nose, and throat. They need the physical medium of air to be born, to travel through, and to actualize in your ears. They are received in your body, which uses hair and bone and skin to turn them into perceptions before they can become thought. Sounds have qualities like pitch and tone and timbre that differentiate them physically. These are qualities we can measure objectively.

Everyone understands this about music—a fast song is different from a slow song, a guitar sounds different from a trombone, and a low note cannot be mistaken for a high note. The different sounds impact us differently on an immediate, physical level.

It's also true with language. Musicality is created in the sounds that make up the words and phrases. Some syllables are long and slow. Some are short and quick. Some are spoken with greater volume and clarity. Some are spoken more softly and indistinctly. Some vowel sounds are high-pitched and some are low-pitched. Some consonants hit us quickly but have a long decay, and others start slowly but cut off quickly. Some sounds merge and others clash.

Sound is part of hearing, but it's also part of speaking. Some sounds require us to open the mouth and nasal passages wide. Some require us to pinch them tight and click the teeth together. Some require us to stick out our tongues. Some "tongue twisters" literally are twisters of our tongues. The way the words affect our bodies colors our experience of them in all kinds of ways.

Consider two examples: "rock" vs. "stone" and "cease" vs. "quit." In each pair, the two words have the same denotation. However, try saying them out loud, and then have someone else say them to you. Listen closely. Do they feel any different to you? Is the experience of hearing them or reading them aloud any different?

Most find "rock" to be harsher than "stone." It conjures up images of something sharper, more jagged—and bigger. Can you imagine going "stone climbing" rather than "rock climbing"? The effect in "quit" versus "cease" seems even more pronounced. "Quit" seems more severe, direct, and aggressive while "cease" seems gentler. None of these are fixed or universal connotations, but they are common.

"Stone" and "cease" are longer syllables than "rock" and "quit." "Stone" and "cease" are also higher-pitched sounds than "rock" and "quit." They form different sorts of linkages with the words around them. Imagine "the poetry of Earth is quitting never" rather than "the poetry of Earth is ceasing never." Ugh!

Many consonants—like \k\, \t\, and \g\—are short, sharp, and somewhat explosive. Other consonants—like \m\, \n\, and \r\—hum and resonate in the mouth and can easily be extended into a long "mmmmm" or "grrrrr." Others are soft, drawn out, and "liquid," like \s\ and \l\. The hard vowels, such as the \ā\ in "cake" or the \ī\ as in "night," cause us to draw back our lips and mouth, making them higher pitched. Others, like \oo\ as in "moo," must be said with the mouth open. They have a lower pitch.

For now, the goal is just to start being aware of the sounds and musical qualities of the language you hear and recite. Notice it and ask how it affects you. Look for patterns in the sounds that make up the poems you read and hear.

Musicality in "Counting-Out Rhyme"

What can we discover about the musicality of the language in the poem that opened this chapter?

The first thing to notice is that there are relatively few short, sharp consonants like \t\ or \k\. Where they do occur, they're often paired with other consonants that soften them, such as the \tw\ combination in "twig" or \str\ combination in "stripe." The round, soft, slow \w\ sound is everywhere, as is the slow, liquid, gentle \l\ sound.

Most of the vowels are big, round, long, and open-mouthed. The \ō\ sound, as in "willow," dominates everything else. The very soft "uh" sound, like at the end of "popple," is also everywhere. The most common hard vowel sound is \ē\, which is very high pitched. It serves as a pleasing counterpoint to the low, gentle "oohs," "ohs," and "ahs." Without it, the poem might seem gloomy.

Many of the syllables are quite long. Try saying "moonbeam" out loud. Then say "tick-tock" out loud. Notice how much slower "moonbeam" is?

To many readers, all these sounds work together to create a poem that is calm, peaceful, gentle, and soft. Notice how the other non-sound elements work together and complement this impression. There is no action, no conflict, no characters, nothing ugly or distressing. It's just a description of plants in nature.

Musicality in "Cleaning Magazines"

Here's an example of a poem creating a very different kind of music with its basic sounds. As you read the next poem—out loud!—pay special attention to those sounds and your thoughts and feelings as you listen.

Cleaning Magazines

They lie like
carcasses, stiff
on a greasy rag field,
hollowed
5 out by guttural rage
and rusted by the hot
breath of whatever
is left after.

There are harder things
10 to clean than these
bullet wombs;
the rot rubs off,
easy. We lay one
down, oily, like new,
15 reach over and pick
up another.

Virginia Robinson, 2005

There's not much of a story here, either. Some ill-defined characters are doing *something*, but the action is very limited. That's not to say you should skip paying attention to the situation altogether.

As we start to examine the basic sounds, we hear that this poem has many short, sharp consonant sounds, like \t\, \g\, and \k\. These consonants require a burst of explosive air through pursed lips. They erupt and fade quickly. Almost every single line—and they are short lines, at most five or six syllables—has several of these sharp consonant sounds. This is especially pronounced in the first stanza. But even in the second stanza, where the consonant sounds are on average a bit softer and more liquid, they occur at least once per line.

The most common and frequent vowel sound is the so-called

schwa—the unstressed "uh" vowel sound represented by \ə\ in pronunciation guides. This is the vowel in "carcass̲e̲s̲," "g̲u̲ttur̲a̲l," and so on. The schwa is the most generic, unvoiced, background sort of vowel sound possible. Say it over and over again, and pay attention to how it sounds and feels. Most find it dull and unpleasant. It's often mixed in with the almost equally dull and unvoiced \ä\ in this poem—as in "c̲a̲rcasses," "the r̲o̲t rubs off," or "up a̲nother."

The vowel sounds are on average fairly short and fast. They work with the clipped consonants to create a staccato sound pattern. There are relatively few high, bright, distinct vowels or soft, long, open-mouthed vowels. Compare the vowel sounds with those in "Counting-Out Rhyme" if the difference doesn't seem at once apparent to you.

Sound and sense color and inform each other in this poem. This is an ugly-sounding poem about a dirty scene. Look at the words: "carcasses," "greasy," "rag," "hollow," "rage," "rust," rot," and "oily." The poem is about literal dirt and grease and chemical filth, the act of cleaning used, soiled machines that can be used to kill people. Sound and sense form a background of at least implicit, impersonal violence, if not actual wartime violence against human beings.

At the end, the tone brightens a little. As the task is being completed, the speaker allows that "there are harder things / to clean." Notice that's where some brighter sounds come in, too. There are more liquid, soft consonants and more bright, clear vowels.

At this point, students are often tempted to ask something like this: "Couldn't this just be coincidence? Was the author *really* trying to use sound in this way?" For the most part, the answers don't matter. Sounds and other patterns in the poem have an impact on the reader who notices them and often even on the reader who doesn't notice them consciously. It doesn't matter what the author intended or if it's a coincidence.

However, for the sake of argument, we might examine the following evidence on this question of whether poets ever use or think about sounds in this way. In a rare testament on the subject, Edgar Allen Poe wrote an essay ("The Philosophy of Composition," 1846) explaining how he wrote "The Raven." Fairly early on in the process, Poe decides that to achieve his desired result, he's going to need a **refrain**—a word or short phrase repeated in every stanza. That refrain, Poe decides, should be simply "nevermore."

Why does the raven say "nevermore," and nothing but "nevermore"? Because Poe knew that the raven needed to say something "sonorous and susceptible of protracted emphasis, [which] led me to the long o as the most sonorous vowel in connection with r as the most producible consonant." The basic musicality of the language was everything.

The Syllable

A syllable is a phenomenon of sound, so it's easier to understand in speech than in writing, but let's give it the old college try here. A **syllable** is a basic unit of speech and word formation that is made of a single vowel sound, with or without surrounding consonant sounds. It is an uninterrupted utterance, a single basic sound.

Words may consist of only a single syllable, such as "word," "pail," "cross," and "Bob," or of many syllables, such as "tower," "transient," "telescope," and "vertiginous." Again, a syllable is a sound unit, not a spelling unit, so syllables can be many letters or only one letter when written as part of a word. The syllables in a word are not always entirely fixed either. Some words, like "fire," "royal," "realtor," or "caramel," can be pronounced several different ways, resulting in different numbers of syllables.

If it's not obvious how a word is divided up into syllables, look in a dictionary. They divide words into syllables. Being able to identify syllables is useful and important for a variety of reasons in understanding and appreciating poetry. Using a dictionary is a great help when you can't tell for sure where the syllables break.

Stressed and Unstressed Syllables

One of the most important reasons to find the syllable divisions is that it helps us to recognize the different levels of stress or emphasis placed on different syllables. Spoken English naturally places greater stress on some syllables than others. A **stressed syllable** may be more fully vocalized, louder, or longer. The vowel sound may be distinct or it may be that schwa sound. Any bit of spoken English more than a few syllables long is going to present a pattern of stressed and unstressed syllables. This pattern of stressed and unstressed syllables is regular, meaningful, and aesthetic.

We experience this pattern on all these levels, even if we can't quite articulate what we're experiencing. Children understand that if they put the em • **pha** • sis on the wrong syl • **la** • ble, it sounds funny. Learning how to correctly stress words in speech is thus a perennial challenge for people studying spoken English as a foreign language. There are elaborate and detailed theories of how stress operates, but this basic understanding is enough for now.

Confusion over stress in pronunciation can produce real misunderstanding, as in the following word pairs:

> <u>re</u>fuse / re<u>**fuse**</u>
> <u>**pro**</u>duce / pro<u>**duce**</u>
> <u>**pre**</u>sent / pres<u>**ent**</u>
> <u>**sub**</u>ject / sub<u>**ject**</u>

The first word in those sets is a noun. The second is a verb. Getting the stress wrong as a speaker will confuse your listeners.

Sometimes, however, stress is a matter of conscious pronunciation:

> <u>**I**</u> gave it to him.
> I <u>**gave**</u> it to him.
> I gave <u>**it**</u> to him.
> I gave it to <u>**him**</u>.

These sentences have slightly different connotations. In such cases, the conscious emphasis can override the regular passive linguistic pattern, and the listener perceives the variation from normal as meaningful and important. Normally, the line would probably be stressed like this: "I **gave** it to **him**." Sentences 1 and 3 are thus the strongest departures from normal and grab the most attention from a listener.

Recognizing Stressed and Unstressed Syllables

This process is an art more than a science and is often open to interpretation. Nonetheless, it is a rational, orderly process, not magic. Anyone can find the stressed syllables. A good ear for the rhythm of speech is not necessary. These general principles and procedures will help you get started identifying stressed and unstressed syllables:

- **Pronunciation of stress in a poem should not be different from pronunciation in regular speech.** The point is to use the regular patterns in normal speech artfully, not to invent new patterns by pronouncing words in unusual ways.

- **All multisyllabic words have at least one stress**. In multisyllabic words formed from a monosyllabic root and prefixes or suffixes, the stress usually falls on the root word. To find the stress or stresses in a multisyllabic word, you can consult a dictionary.

- **English generally doesn't tolerate more than two unstressed syllables in a row.** Of any three normally unstressed syllables in sequence, one will often be "promoted" unconsciously assigned a stress relative to the other two. The promoted syllable is generally the middle one.

- **Content considerations can impact stress.** A normally unstressed syllable that takes on great importance in a line may be promoted. On the other hand, a normally stressed syllable that is de-emphasized or obscured by the content of the line may be "demoted."

- **Multisyllabic words exert influence over monosyllabic words.** Multisyllabic words are less likely to include promoted or demoted syllables. So start with the multisyllabic words and then move on to the monosyllabic words.

- **Single-syllable "content" words are stressed.** "Content" words are words that have meaning in and of themselves: nouns, main verbs, most modifiers, personal pronouns.

- **Single-syllable "function" words are not stressed.** Function words are words that serve to connect or assist content words. This includes conjunctions, articles, helping verbs, prepositions, demonstratives, and most pronouns.

- **When using one's ear, try testing the stress back and forth across the word.** Pronounce the word with the stress deliberately and artificially placed on one syllable, then the next, then back again. Listen for what sounds closest to natural speech, or least "wrong."

Stressed and Unstressed Syllables in "Counting Out Rhyme"

Most of the words in this poem have only one syllable. The few multisyllabic words have only two, and the divisions between syllables should be mostly easy to find. If they're not easy for you, however, the dictionary will show you exactly where the break occurs.

After you break the poem up into syllables, you need to distinguish which are stressed and unstressed. Use the techniques outlined above, starting with the multisyllabic words. The dictionary gives you the stressed syllables. Notice that "moonbeam," "barn-beam," and "hornbeam" are all two-syllable words in which both syllables take a stress.

After marking the multisyllabic words, you can proceed to the single syllable words, using the rules above for function versus content words. Again, the distinction is strong in this poem, making for a clear process.

All the unstressed single-syllable words are clearly less important function words—"of," "and," "in," "for." Having done just those two simple tasks, what do you see?

<u>Sil</u> • ver • **<u>bark</u>** • of • **<u>beech</u>**, • and • **<u>sall</u>** • ow
<u>Bark</u> • of • **<u>yell</u>** • ow • **<u>birch</u>** • and • **<u>yell</u>** • ow
<u>Twig</u> • of • **<u>will</u>** • ow.

<u>Stripe</u> • of • **<u>green</u>** • in • **<u>moose</u>** • wood • **<u>ma</u>** • ple,
<u>Col</u> • our • **<u>seen</u>** • in • **<u>leaf</u>** • of • **<u>ap</u>** • ple,
<u>Bark</u> • of • **<u>pop</u>** • ple.

<u>Wood</u> • of • **<u>pop</u>** • ple • **<u>pale</u>** • as • **<u>moon</u>** • **<u>beam</u>**,
<u>Wood</u> • of • **<u>oak</u>** • for • **<u>yoke</u>** • and • **<u>barn-</u>** • **<u>beam</u>**,
<u>Wood</u> • of • **<u>horn</u>** • **<u>beam</u>**.

<u>Sil</u> • ver • **<u>bark</u>** • of • **<u>beech</u>**, • and • **<u>holl</u>** • ow
<u>Stem</u> • of • **<u>el</u>** • der, • **<u>tall</u>** • and • **<u>yell</u>** • ow
<u>Twig</u> • of • **<u>will</u>** • ow.

Look at how regular the pattern of stressed and unstressed syllables is! Only the final words in the third stanza vary from the regular pattern of stress-unstress. Very few readers would notice that the pattern is so absolutely regular without taking the time and effort to actually analyze it.

Manipulating this naturally occurring feature of English has traditionally been one of the most important expressive tools of the poet. Here, the chaotic natural stress pattern of the language is ordered, through diction and syntax choices, to make an artificial and musical pattern that's far more regular and predictable than any normal spoken conversation or prose passage would be. This kind of purposeful arrangement of the stressed and unstressed syllables can be used to create all sorts of other music and be more complicated and interesting, as you will soon see.

Rhyme

Many people think of rhyme as inseparable from poetry. If it doesn't rhyme, is it really poetry? However, rhyme is only one of many elements that can define and create a poem. In many languages, there is no rhyme in poetry at all. English poetry copied rhyme from poetry in French and other romance languages in the early Middle Ages.

At the other extreme, there are also many people who think of nonrhyming poetry as "modern" and rhyming poetry as "traditional." This is also inaccurate. Old English poetry did not rhyme at all, nor did much poetry in Middle English. Unrhymed verse has been part of modern English right from the beginning. Seventeenth-century poet John Milton wrote a blistering attack on rhyme in his introduction to *Paradise Lost*, and Shakespeare wrote his plays in unrhymed verse.

The role and importance of rhyme in poetry was much debated and contested in Milton's time, and it still is today. Unrhymed poetry is more common, but rhyming poetry is alive and well. Rhyme is not omnipotent or omnipresent. Rhyme does not define "poem." However, it is a part of poetry, and it's here to stay.

Rhyme is one of those subjects for which the phrase "deceptively simple" was created. Most preschoolers recognize and can give examples of rhyming words. Most could easily recognize the rhymes in this list:

> bed / embed / said / read
> bay / weigh / astray / they
> wing / asking / unifying / testifying
> lady / bee / abbey / tabby

But what exactly makes these words "rhyming"? The entire ending syllable is not exactly the same in each one because the ending syllables may start with different consonant sounds. The spelling is certainly not the same in each one. However, the ending syllable after its initial consonant sound *is* the same. Notice that they don't have to have the same number of syllables, either, as long as that final syllable sound after its initial consonant is identical.

Rhyme is the repetition of the same vowel sound followed by the same consonant sound — if there is one — in the final syllable of two or more words and in close enough proximity that it creates an obvious pattern. That's the basic definition, but there is a lot of variation just under the surface of that definition that you should be aware of.

Varieties of Rhyme

Rhyme is such a rich subject that there are different varieties of rhyme.

First, rhymes can be either internal or end. **End rhyme** occurs at the ends of lines, and is the most common.

When people talk about rhyme, they usually mean end rhyme. **Internal rhyme**, on the other hand, is rhyme occurring in the middle of a line or lines. It might be within a single line or between multiple lines, and a word in the middle of a line might rhyme with the last word of one or more lines. That is, if a word from the middle of the line rhymes with the word at the end of the line, that is internal rhyme. When words from the middles of multiple lines rhyme with each other, that is also internal rhyme.

For some examples, let's look at the first six lines from Poe's "The Raven":

> Once upon a midnight dreary, while I pondered, weak and
>   weary,
> Over many a quaint and curious volume of forgotten lore,
> While I nodded, nearly napping, suddenly there came a
>   tapping,
> As of someone gently rapping, rapping at my chamber door.
> "'Tis some visitor," I muttered, "tapping at my chamber door;
>   Only this, and nothing more."

5

This poem has so much rhyme happening in so many places that it might make us dizzy. Lines 2 and 4–6 share an end rhyme. Internal rhymes link the middle of two lines to their ends—"dreary" rhymes with "weary" in line 1 and "napping" rhymes with "tapping" in line 3. Elsewhere, internal rhymes link the middle of one line to the end of another—"tapping" at the end of line 3 rhymes with "rapping" in the middle of line 4. Internal rhymes link words within the middle of the same line, as in the repetition of "rapping" in line 4, words within the middle of lines 3, 4, and 5: "napping," "rapping," and "tapping."

In addition to noticing *where* rhyming words occur, the number of syllables that match in each word creates different varieties of rhyme. Rhyme can also be single or multiple.

Look again at our excerpt from "The Raven:" the "lore" / "door" / "more" rhyming words all only have a single syllable—thus they are single rhymes. Also notice that "nearly" and "gently" each end on the same -ly sound. These are also single rhymes. Even though the words the rhyming syllables occur in have more than one syllable, the other syllables don't rhyme. Compare that to "dreary" and "weary" or "tapping" and "rapping." Both of those rhymes are double rhymes—the first syllables rhyme with each other and the second syllables rhyme with each other.

Multiple rhyme doesn't have to be confined to a single word. Words are sometimes strung together to create multiple rhymes. The rhyme pattern comes out of the pattern of sounds, not the pattern of words, as we see in the underlined words from these four lines of "Those Eyes," by Ben Jonson:

> For then their threats will k<u>ill me</u>; / ... / For then my hopes
> will sp<u>ill me</u>.
> For so will sorrow sl<u>ay me</u>; / ... / Mine own enough betr<u>ay me</u>.

Single rhymes are often called masculine, while multiple rhymes are often referred to as feminine. These terms don't have anything to do with human genders. They derive from French poetry jargon and ultimately from the grammar of Latin, in which words are classified according to gender as a linguistic concept. Feminine rhyme is used in some comic verse forms, such as the limerick, and some people think of it as inherently comical. However, plenty of poems that don't even crack a smile are written using feminine rhyme.

Some people use the terms "feminine rhyme" and "masculine rhyme" more restrictively, not only distinguishing number of rhyming syllables but the relationship between the rhyming syllables and whether or not they are stressed.

We don't need to worry about those, or the many other, labels given to other types and sub-types of rhyme, but it's worth considering how the interactions of stress and rhyme create variety and might impact how we hear and appreciate a poem. In the following rhyming word pairs, the stressed syllables are in **bold**, and the rhyming syllables are <u>underlined</u>:

Single Rhymes	**<u>bay</u>** / **<u>weigh</u>**—A stressed syllable is rhymed with a stressed syllable.
	la • <u>dy</u> / **tab** • <u>by</u>—An unstressed syllable is rhymed with an unstressed syllable.
	<u>wing</u> / **ask** • <u>ing</u>—A stressed syllable is rhymed with an unstressed syllable.
Double Rhyme	**<u>ab</u>** • <u>bey</u> / **<u>tab</u>** • <u>by</u>—The double rhyme starts with a stressed and ends with an unstressed syllable.
Triple Rhyme	**u** • <u>ni</u> • **<u>fy</u>** • <u>ing</u> / **tes** • <u>ti</u> • **<u>fy</u>** • <u>ing</u>—the triple rhyme starts and ends with an unstressed syllable; the stressed syllable is between them.

Most people find the rhymes in which a stressed syllable at the end of a word rhymes with a stressed syllable at the end of another word to be the "strongest"—clearest, most obvious. Rhymes like "lady / tabby," on the other hand, may not feel like "real" rhymes at all to some. Even though the final syllables have the exact same sound, the fact that the initial syllables don't, and those initial syllables are where the stress falls in each word, makes some people wonder if there is a "real" rhyme. In short, the answer is yes. These differences may not seem important or even evident to you, but keep them in mind when analyzing the rhyme scheme of a poem.

Everything discussed so far is a subcategory of exact rhyme, created when you hear the same vowel sound followed by the same consonant sound close enough to each other that a pattern is established. **Exact rhyme**, in most discussions, is the assumed default. However, it is not the only possibility!

Slant rhyme is created when only the ending consonant sound of a set of words are the same, or nearly the same, and the preceding vowel sounds are not. This is also known as "near," "off," "half," or "imperfect" rhyme. The following are all examples of slant rhyme:

cut / sat

picture / afar

gates / press

allocate / biscuit

sopped / leapt

Many poems drop a few instances of slant rhyme into an otherwise regularly rhymed poem for dramatic effect. What makes this a slant rhyme, as opposed to a coincidence of ending consonant sounds, is that it appears where we expect an exact rhyme to be.

The point of discussing and defining all these variations of rhyme is not to add complexity but to open possibility. It's not important to have a catalog of all the kinds of rhyme in a poem. All these distinctions and categories are not goals themselves but tools to help you reach a goal. Understanding and being able to recognize and talk about the different kinds of rhyme hopefully helps open your eyes—and ears—to where rhyme is in the poem and how it contributes to the overall effect of the poem.

Rhyme in "Counting Out Rhyme"

Each stanza of this poem rhymes all three of its lines. Those are all exact, masculine end rhymes. However, there's a lot of other rhyming going on in this poem. Every stanza has some internal rhyme. If nothing else, the preposition "of" is repeated inside every single line, creating a universal internal rhyme. In the first stanza, "bark" rhymes with "bark" in lines 1 and 2. "Yellow" in the middle of line 2 matches the end rhyme of every line, and makes a multiple rhyme with "yellow" at the end of line 2. "Green" in line 4 rhymes with "seen" in line five. "Popple" in the middle of line 7 picks up the end rhyme from stanza 2. "Oak" and "yoke" rhyme in the middle of line 8. And "wood" starts every line in stanza 3, meaning every line in stanza 3 has internal double rhyme with "wood" and "of."

Rhyme Scheme

Rhyme scheme refers to a particular method for noting and discussing the rhyming pattern in a poem. In short, we assign a letter to every line-ending sound, staring with "A" for the first line. If two lines rhyme, they share the same letter. The result is a string of letters that describe the rhyming sounds compactly. It's a quick and easy way to identify and talk about the pattern of rhymes in a poem.

Identifying the Rhyme Scheme in "Counting Out Rhyme"

Let's use St. Vincent Millay's poem as an example again. What are the line-ending sounds?

> Line 1: The ending sound is \ō\. You assign "A."
> Line 2: The ending sound is also \ō\, so it's another A
> Line 3: The ending sound is \ō\, so it is also A. The first stanza's rhyme scheme is thus AAA.
>
> Line 4: The ending sound is \uhl\. The \uhl\ sound is a new sound, so you use "B."
> Line 5: The ending sound is \uhl\. B.
> Line 6: The ending sound is \uhl\. B. The second stanza's rhyme scheme is BBB.
>
> Line 7: The ending sound is \eem\. The \eem\ sound is a new sound, so you use "C."
> Line 8: The ending sound is \eem\. C.
> Line 9: It's another \eem\, so it's a C. The third stanza's rhyme scheme is CCC.
>
> Line 10: The ending sound is \ō\, which is a not new sound. The first stanza was also \ō\ and was designated as "A." You'll use "A" here as well.
> Line 11: The ending sound is \ō\. A.
> Line 12: The ending sound is \ō\. Another A. The fourth stanza's rhyme scheme is AAA.

That makes the rhyme scheme of the poem AAA / BBB / CCC / AAA, with the slash marks showing the division between stanzas.

Rhyme schemes are an analytical or descriptive tool. It's something to use as you work toward understanding the song elements in a poem. Making these notes in a poem's margins is a great exercise even when you don't think there is a rhyme scheme. Writing it down is really the only way to be sure. The pattern often only emerges in the process of noting it.

Rhyme schemes are also commonly used prescriptively, too, as part of describing a received form. For example, the Shakespearian sonnet is partially defined by conforming to the rhyme scheme ABAB / CDCD / EFEF / GG.

Final Thoughts

Many poems tell interesting stories, but all poems are at least a little bit like a song. The musicality of language itself is the heart and soul of many poems. Hearing that music is central to understanding and appreciating them. The variety of sounds that words make can create a subtle music all by itself.

The syllable is a basic unit of language, generally defined as the sound of a vowel and the consonants around it. In English, syllables can be accented or unaccented, and this basic feature of the language is something that poems can fashion into musical patterns. Rhyme, most broadly, is the repetition of ending sounds in words, usually at the ends of lines. Rhyme is fundamentally simple but also exists in many variations and can be created, manipulated, and mixed with other song elements in many ways.

To finish off the chapter, here's a list of reminders, tips, and tricks to help you as you work with musical language:

- In dealing with any song element, read out loud, read out loud, read out loud. Then have someone read to you and listen with the poem in front of you and a pencil in your hand. There is no substitute for feeling the poem in your mouth and hearing it in another voice. Get help from a real human being, in person, if you can. This isn't the easiest material to learn from the silent page.

- Scribble all over the poems. It's hard to keep track of all the individual pieces in your head while you try to figure out what kind of pattern they make. Making notes as you find the sounds allows the pattern to emerge naturally.

- When analyzing syllables, use the dictionary to locate the syllable breaks and the stress patterns in multisyllabic words.

- When listening for rhyme specifically, try reading, at least at first, only the last syllable of each line out loud. "Close enough" generally counts in rhyme. If you can reasonably imagine a word rhyming, let it rhyme.

- Remember that pronunciation changes over time. Even a reasonably good dictionary is not going to consistently indicate those changes in pronunciation. In fact, we don't always exactly know how words were pronounced in the past.

- Make sure there's really a pattern if you think you're seeing rhyme. Especially with common word endings like "-ing" or "-ed," there can be random repetitions that don't really constitute rhyme. If you see rhyme in several lines, or in between several lines, that's the kind of pattern you're looking for.

The most important thing is to cultivate a new habit of mind. Remind yourself to be aware of and attentive to sound in the poem prior to and underlying meaning. Be open to it even when it doesn't seem to fit into any of the categories discussed in this book. That basic shift in attitude and awareness is more important than a technical understanding of any particular element or concept.

Exercises

This section gives you the chance to practice your understanding of these elements through a structured reading of three poems and through focused creative writing prompts. Your professor may or may not assign them. If not, they can completed independently if you wish.

For Readers

These three poems each present a clear and interesting situation in which to practice understanding and appreciating rhyme and the basic musicality of language. If you're not given specific assignments by your teacher, try doing this for each poem:

1. Complete the basic reading.

2. Jot down your own initial impressions: What did you understand to be happening on the literal level in this poem? Did you like it? Can you say how or why?

3. Using the examples at the start of the chapter as a model, write out an analysis of any patterns in the basic sounds of the poem.

4. Write out the rhyme scheme for each poem. Expand on that by writing an extended analysis of the rhyme, including a description of the differing types and locations of rhymes you find.

5. Divide the entire poem up into syllables and mark the accented or stressed syllables. Write out a short description of any patterns you find.

Poem 1

This is a sixteenth-century poem, predating Shakespeare, in an eleventh-century stanza form. You may need to look into changing pronunciations to help you analyze the sounds in the poem, especially the rhyme, but otherwise the poem is startlingly contemporary and easy to read at the literal level.

[They flee from me]

They flee from me that sometime did me seek
With naked foot, stalking within my chamber.
Once have I seen them gentle, tame, and meek,

That now are wild and do once not remember

5   That sometime they have put themselves in danger

To take bread at my hand; and now they range,

Busily seeking in continual change.

Thanked be fortune it hath been otherwise

Twenty times better; but once especial,

10   In thin array after a pleasant guise,

When her loose gown from her shoulders did fall,

And she me caught in her arms long and small;

And therewithall so sweetly did me kiss

And softly said, "Dear heart, how like you this?"

15   It was no dream, for I lay broad awaking.

But all is turned through my gentleness

Into a strong fashion of forsaking;

And I have leave to part of her goodness,

And she likewise to use newfangleness.

20   But since that I so gently am served

What think you by this that she hath deserved?

Sir Thomas Wyatt, 1557

Poem 2

This next poem is not only a tour de force of musical language but a wild admixture of neologism and allusion, high culture and low. Have fun!

"Bugle"

Joshua said to all the Neophytes,

"Come here and listen to the words of Tod.

This is how you will know that the Living Tod

is among you and that he will certainly drive out before you the

5   Canaanites,

Hittites, Hivites, Perizzites, Girgashites, Amarites, and
    Jebusites,
the Light Brites, stalactites, East Bound Red Eye Flights,
bedbugs, chiggers, ticks, and mites,

10   the toddler at day care who bites,
the naked meth freak in your yard last night,
men on bicycles wearing spandex tights, cover bands who play
    'Afternoon Delight,'
people who moon about geese mating for life, dogs whose

15   barks exceed their bites,
these three words together: macht, frei, arbeit."
So said Joshua, son of Nun, just before Jericho to the
    Neophytes.

Tod Marshall, 2014

Poem 3

After the intensity of those two, this next poem may seem simple. It is clear and modern, but it's also sophisticated and interesting musically. Pay attention to any possible correspondence to received forms.

Weekend Swim with Wedding Band

To let the workday failures go, I float the gold-
leaf surface of the lake; not graced like Christ
but plain like lily pads with tendrils cold

and swaying to the frozen depths. The sky is iced

5   with smog, with light, with formlessness. I tip
my head, arch back, and disappear; zeitgeist

of late, late-modern times, thick limbs at rest. I slip,
a muscled curve and then I cannot feel
or breathe. Clear, void, and numb except where gripped

10   by metal, caging circle, tiny keel
        that rocks between my knuckles trapped by bone
        for now, what's kept of promises, what's real.
        For you I rise. I could not rise alone.

Caitlin Scott, 2019

For Writers

The following exercises help you get to know and practice the concepts related to the music of a poem. They're not designed to produce finished poems but to help you experiment with these important elements so that you can use them more effectively to create poems in your own time.

1. Look online or in your local library for "The Owl and the Pussycat" by Edward Lear and "Jabberwocky" by Lewis Carroll—both the written texts and recordings of them. Thus inspired, write a "nonsense" poem of your own. Make it about sixteen to twenty-four lines long and make each line seven to eleven syllables long. As you do this, pay attention to the sounds above all. When you're finished, write a paragraph discussing the choices you made and why. Describe the sounds your poem generates.

2. Write ten rhyming couplets made up of ten-syllable lines and ten ballad stanzas, which follow a rhyme scheme of ABCB and are made up of eight-syllable lines. Then try revising the rhymes into slant rhymes. Then try revising to add one internal rhyme into each stanza.

3. Look online or in your local library for a copy of Marianne Moore's "The Fish." Write out a brief description / analysis of the syllabic pattern. Pick a different animal and write a close imitation that follows the same syllabic pattern.

4. Try writing twenty lines that each have a total of ten syllables and

five accented syllables. Then try writing twenty lines that each have four accented syllables, regardless of how many total syllables there are. The lines don't have to make sense together, but if you want to take it to the next level, make them work together as a whole poem.

5. Create ten pairs of rhyming multisyllabic words that are only single perfect end rhymes — no double or triple rhymes. Good luck.

6. Consider the following rhyme scheme, which is called *terza rima*: ABA / BCB / DED / EFE / FGF / GHG / HH. Write out five sets of twenty words that match this rhyme scheme. You don't need whole lines — just lists of individual rhyming words in that pattern. Pick your favorite list and then try to turn it into a poem by working backward from the rhyming words.

Chapter 10

Musical Language, Part 2

Key terms: alliteration, Anglo-Saxon form, consonance, assonance, onomatopoeia

In the last chapter, you learned about some of the most basic musical elements of language, including the fundamentals of rhythm and an introduction to rhyme. Those musical tools are enough to make any poem sing, but they're only the beginning of the many ways words make music in poetry.

One way to understand rhyme is that it is a patterned repetition of specific sounds in a specific place in the line. In this chapter, we will look at three other kinds of patterned repetition that repeat different kinds of sounds in different places in the line. We will also examine a very different kind of musical effect that's created when the words a poem uses mimic a sound directly.

We will use "Counting-Out Rhyme" from the start of Chapter 9 as an example several times this chapter, so please go back and review it before you proceed.

Alliteration

Alliteration is the repetition of sounds at the beginning of words, generally the initial consonant sound. Some people consider the repetition of initial stressed vowel sounds to constitute alliteration as well. Here are a few examples of alliteration, in **bold**:

- **s**ound / **s**illy

- **g**ore / **g**uts

- **t**emperament / **t**iny

For our purposes, "salad" and "slide" and "great" and "galloping" alliterate as well, even though "slide" and "great" start with two-consonant combinations of "sl" and "gr." For now, that's close enough.

As with rhyme, when we talk about alliteration as a working element of a poem, we're looking for a pattern of alliterating words. Instances of alliteration need to be close enough together, or arranged with such parallelism, that the echoing relationship between the sounds asserts itself and creates music.

Let's see if we can find that kind of pattern in "Counting-Out Rhyme."

Alliteration in "Counting-Out Rhyme"

"Counting-Out Rhyme" is almost as full of alliteration as rhyme. Let's take a close look at just the first stanza:

> Silver bark of beech, and sallow
> Bark of yellow birch and yellow
> Twig of willow.

The \b\ of "bark," "beech," and "birch" ties together lines 1–2. The \s\ in "silver" and "sallow" pulls the start and end of line 1 together. Line 4 contains an \m\ alliteration with "moosewood" and "maple," and begins with \s\ in "stripe" that's echoed in "seen." Listen to the way it also picks up the \s\ sound from line 1.

Moving on to stanza 3, we hear even more alliteration.

> Wood of popple pale as moonbeam,
> Wood of oak for yoke and barn-beam,
> Wood of hornbeam.

The repetition of "wood" in stanza 3 creates initial \w\ alliteration in every line. Line 7 has \p\ in "popple" and "pale," which also then pulls in the "popple" from line 6. The \b\ sound in "barn-beam" might not be considered alliteration by some people, since the second \b\ occurs inside a compound word. However, the fact that the second syllable takes a stress and that "beam" in "moonbeam" and "hornbeam" also both take stresses and rhyme as well as alliterate, creates a very strongly pronounced and heard pattern. It doesn't feel—or sound—like it's buried inside a word.

The ending stanza repeats many of the words of the first stanza, though with variation. As a result, there are considerable alliterative effects within it and between the two stanzas.

> Silver bark of beech, and hollow
> Stem of elder, tall and yellow
> Twig of willow.

This final stanza alliterates \s\ in "silver" and "stem," \b\ in "bark" and "beech," and \t\ in "tall" and "twig."

Notice how the rhyme and stress pattern in the poem interacts with this new musical effect of alliteration. You can think of each "sound effect" as an instrument in a band. Each makes its own music, but they're also working together to create something greater.

Strong Alliteration and Anglo-Saxon Form

Alliteration was especially important in Old English, or Anglo-Saxon, poetry. This language is very different from modern English and much closer to German. Various incarnations of **Anglo-Saxon form** abound, but the basic features are that it has four stressed syllables per line, each line is divided by a strong caesura and three of the stressed syllables also alliterate. The number of unstressed syllables per line is variable.

The following poem is an example of a modern English poem that fully inhabits this ancient form. Even though this faithfulness isn't common, this old form does cast a long shadow, and you should keep an eye out for subtler, less-complete incarnations of it.

Junk

Huru Welandes
worc ne geswiceð?
monna ænigum
ðara ðe Mimming can
heardne gehealdan.

— Waldere

An axe angles
               from my neighbor's ashcan;
It is hell's handiwork,
               the wood not hickory,
5   The flow of the grain
               not faithfully followed.
The shivered shaft
               rises from a shellheap
Of plastic playthings,
10   paper plates,

And the sheer shards
          of shattered tumblers
That were not annealed
          for the time needful.
15   At the same curbside,
          a cast-off cabinet
Of wavily warped
          unseasoned wood
Waits to be trundled
20   in the trash-man's truck.
Haul them off! Hide them!
          The heart winces
For junk and gimcrack,
          for jerrybuilt things
25   And the men who make them
          for a little money,
Bartering pride
          like the bought boxer
Who pulls his punches,
30   or the paid-off jockey
Who in the home stretch
          holds in his horse.
Yet the things themselves
          in thoughtless honor
35   Have kept composure,
          like captives who would not
Talk under torture.
          Tossed from a tailgate
Where the dump displays
40   its random dolmens,
Its black barrows
          and blazing valleys,

They shall waste in the weather

                                   toward what they were.

45   The sun shall glory

                           in the glitter of glass-chips,

Foreseeing the salvage

                       of the prisoned sand,

And the blistering paint

50   peel off in patches,

That the good grain

                    be discovered again.

Then burnt, bulldozed,

                      they shall all be buried

55   To the depth of diamonds,

                       in the making dark

Where halt Hephaestus

                    keeps his hammer

And Wayland's work

60   is worn away.

Richard Wilbur, 1961

Besides being a fantastic example of alliteration, this poem is another example of a poem with almost no story. It's an almost purely descriptive piece, a collection of images. It has no action, but it does have a lot of music.

Wilbur translates the epigraph, which is from a fragment of a tenth-century poem entitled "Waldere," as "Truly, Wayland's handiwork—the sword Mimming that he made—will never fail any man who knows how to use it bravely." The reference to a swordsmith named "Wayland" recurs at the end of the poem: "And Wayland's work / is worn away."

To help you see the pattern, the poem is reprinted below, broken up into syllables rather than words. The following elements are marked: syllable breaks (•), stressed syllables (<u>underlined</u>), alliterating sounds (in

bold), and caesura with the double vertical line (||). This version eliminates punctuation so you can focus on the pauses created by diction, syntax, and sound. Anglo-Saxon poetry was originally an oral performance in preliterate societies. When it was first written down in the Dark Ages, it was just one giant undifferentiated mass of letters with no punctuation, capital letters, or spaces between words.

As you saw with rhyme, it is the sound that alliterates, not the spelling. There are only a very few places where this poem deviates from the formal requirements at all — can you find them?

An • **axe** • **ang** • les || from • my • **neigh** • bor's **ash** • can
It • is • **hell's** • **han** • di • **work** || the • **wood** • not • **hic** • ko • ry
The • **flow** • of • the • **grain** || not • **faith** • ful • ly • **fol** • lowed
The • **shiv** • ered • **shaft** || **ris** • es • from • a • **shell** • heap
Of • **plas** • tic • **play** • things || **pa** • per • **plates**
And • the • **sheer** • **shards** || of • **sha** • ttered • **tum** • blers
That • were • **not** • an • **nealed** || for • the • **time** • **need** • ful
At • the • **same** • **curb** • side || a • **cast-** • off • **cab** • i • net
Of • **wa** • vi • ly • **warped** || **un** • sea • soned • **wood**
Waits • to • be • **trun** • dled || in • the • **trash** • -man's • **truck**
Haul • them • off • **Hide** • them || The • **heart** • **win** • ces
For • **junk** • and • **gim** • crack || for • **jer** • ry • **built** • **things**
And • the • **men** • who • **make** • them || for • a • **lit** • tle • **mo** • ney
Bar • ter • ing • **pride** || like • the • **bought** • **box** • er
Who • **pulls** • his • **pun** • ches || or • the • **paid-** • off • **jo** • ckey
Who • in • the • **home** • **stretch** || **holds** • in • his • **horse**
Yet • the • **things** • **them** • selves || in • **thought** • less • **ho** • nor
Have • **kept** • **com** • po • sure || like • **cap** • tives • who •
    would • not
Talk • **un** • der • **tor** • ture || **Tossed** • from • a • **tail** • gate
Where • the • **dump** • **dis** • plays || its • **ran** • dom • **dol** • mens
Its • **black** • **bar** • rows || and • **bla** • zing • **val** • leys
They • shall • **waste** • in • the • **wea** • ther || **tow** • ard • **what** •

they • <u>were</u>

The • <u>sun</u> • shall • **<u>glo</u>** • ry || in • the • **<u>gli</u>** • tter • of • **glass-** • chips

Fore • <u>see</u> • ing • the • <u>sal</u> • vage || of • the • <u>pri</u> • soned • <u>sand</u>

And • the • <u>blis</u> • ter • ing • **paint** || **peel** • off • in • **patch** • es

That • the • **good** • **grain** || be • dis • <u>cov</u> • ered • a • **gain**

Then • **burnt** • **bull** • **dozed** || they • shall • **all** • be • **bur** • ied

To • the • **depth** • of • **dia** • monds || in • the • <u>mak</u> • ing • **dark**

Where • **halt** • He • **phaes** • tus || <u>keeps</u> • his • **ham** • mer

And • **Way** • land's • **work** || is • **worn** • a • **way**

Consonance and Assonance

Consonance and assonance are capable of creating strong musical effects, but they also tend to fade into the background compared to rhyme, rhythm, and even alliteration. Consonance and assonance are less likely to give a strong structure to a poem or define the characteristics of a form. Instead, these devices of sound are generally elaborations or flourishes that complement and offset the other musical effects.

Consonance

Consonance is a pattern of repeating consonant sounds in the middle of words. The pattern may include, but cannot be made up solely of, consonant sounds in the middle of words echoing consonants at the start or end of words as well. Like rhyme and alliteration, consonance is more noticeable when it occurs in stressed syllables.

The concept of consonance can be fuzzy. Some sources use consonance to mean slant rhyme, alliteration, or some version of them. It's useful, though, to think of consonance as its own phenomenon. To get a handle on those differences, consider these three examples:

Wet Willie whistles wetly.

Through the throw the cat began to mew.

However sweetly you ask, none cower in sewers.

The first is an example of both alliteration, with \w\ sounds, and of consonance, with \l\ sounds. The second is an example of internal slant rhyme, with \w\ sounds, and of alliteration, with \th\ sounds. There is no consonance. The third is an example of consonance only with \w\ sounds.

Assonance

Assonance is a pattern of repeating vowel sounds. Here are a few examples of assonance with the repeated vowel sound in bold followed by its pronunciation:

> be**a**m, fl**ee**t, Ar**a**bian \ē\
> m**ou**ntain, s**ow** \ou\
> J**a**ne, fl**ai**l, d**ei**gn \ā\
> **I**, cry**i**ng, s**igh**, **eye** \ī\
> **oa**f, s**o**re, d**ough** \ō\

Like consonance, assonance is defined variably and can be folded into other terms, but it's useful to count and think about it about separately.

It's common to be confused about the difference between rhyme, especially internal rhyme, and assonance. Two things separate assonance from rhyme. The first is that rhyme comes only at the end of words rather than sometimes in the middle of them, as assonance can. The second is that rhyme has a matching ending consonant sound, and assonance does not. This example should help make the distinction clearer:

> Wet Willie feels a bit silly while whistling at the filly.

This sentence has both internal rhyme and assonance. Sometimes they link up with each other. Let's identify the rhyme first (underlined):

> Wet • <u>Wil</u> • lie • feels • a • bit • <u>sil</u> • <u>ly</u> • while • whist • ling •
> at • the • <u>fil</u> • <u>ly</u>.

"Willy," "silly," and "filly" are all double rhymes. These three words rhyme with each other. This line has strong internal rhyme. What about assonance? The assonance is in bold:

> Wet • <u>Wil</u> • <u>**lie**</u> • feels • a • bit • <u>sil</u> • <u>**ly**</u> • while • whist • ling •
> at • the • <u>fil</u> • <u>**ly**</u>.

The long \ē\ sound that forms the second part of those rhymes also creates assonance with the long \ē\ sound in "feels" and "whistling." Those two words don't rhyme with the other three, but they do create a pattern of assonance. There's a second pattern of assonance, too, which is indicated with italics:

> Wet • <u>W*i*l</u> • <u>lie</u> • feels • a • b*i*t • <u>s*i*l</u> • <u>ly</u> • while • wh*i*st • ling •
> at • the • <u>f*i*l</u> • <u>ly</u>.

The short \i\ sound that forms the first part of the double rhyme ("Willie," "silly," "filly") also creates a pattern of assonance with "bit" and "whistling."

It's worth reminding you that when you're thinking about assonance as an element in a poem, you're looking for a pattern, working with or against other elements, not just the random reoccurrence of vowel noises. English only has so many vowel sounds; it's inevitable that they'll repeat in most poems or even stanzas or lines.

Consonance and Assonance in "Counting-Out Rhyme"

Let's examine these devices of sound in St, Vincent Millay's poem, one stanza at a time. Take a careful look at the first stanza again. The rhyming words "sallow," "yellow," and "willow" create a pattern of consonance through their middle \l\ sound. They also bring "silver" into their orbit with its central \l\ sound.

> Si_l_ver bark of beech, and sa_ll_ow
> Bark of ye_ll_ow birch and ye_ll_ow
> Twig of wi_ll_ow.

What other repeating consonant sounds can you hear? The \r\ sound in "silver," "bark," and "birch" also creates consonance in lines 1 and 2.

> Silve_r_ ba_r_k of beech, and sallow
> Ba_r_k of yellow bi_r_ch and yellow
> Twig of willow.

The \w\ sound in "twig," twice in "willow," and at the end of "sallow" and "yellow" creates consonance tying together all three lines. Notice that the ending /w/ in "sallow" and "yellow" does double duty here. It's part of a rhyme pattern when we only consider those two words, but it also attaches to the other closely repeated /w/ sounds in line three and a consonance pattern is created as well. It's not one or the other, in this case: it's both at the same time.

> Silver bark of beech, and sallo_w_
> Bark of yello_w_ birch and yello_w_
> T_w_ig of _w_illo_w_.

What about assonance? In the first two lines, the /a/ sound occurs in both "and" and "sallow." Again, it's the fact that the sound is at the start of some words but the middle of others that makes this assonance, not alliteration. Contrast that with /ō/, which occurs only at the end of "sallow," "willow," and "yellow," which is what makes it rhyme, not assonance.

> Silver bark of beech, _a_nd s_a_llow
> Bark of yellow birch _a_nd yellow
> Twig of willow.

Assonance is also in the first and final lines, with the /i/ sound in the middle of "silver," "twig," and "willow."

> Silver bark of beech, and sallow
> Bark of yellow birch and yellow
> Twig of willow.

The second stanza features a close interplay between rhyme and consonance. The rhyming words "maple," "apple," and "popple" create consonance through that middle \p\ sound. They also pull in "stripe" with its ending \p\ sound.

> Stripe of green in moosewood maple,
> Colour seen in leaf of apple,
> Bark of popple.

However, this stanza goes further than the first and doubles that pattern! The final \l\ sound that finishes the rhyme in those three words also pulls in the middle \l\ sound in "colour" and the initial \l\ sound in "leaf."

> Stripe of green in moosewood maple,
> Colour seen in leaf of apple,
> Bark of popple.

"Stripe," "green," "colour," and "bark" also create consonance across all three lines with their internal \r\ sound.

> Stripe of green in moosewood maple,
> Colour seen in leaf of apple,
> Bark of popple.

For contrast, notice that the ending /f/ sounds in "of" and "leaf" are slant rhyme, not consonance, because the sound occurs solely at the end of words.

What about assonance? The strong, stressed \ē\ sound creating internal rhyme between "green" and "seen" connects to the same sound in "leaf."

> Stripe of **gree**n in moosewood maple,
> Colour s**ee**n in l**ea**f of apple,
> Bark of popple.

There's a second assonance in the last line, created by the soft \a\ sounds in "bark" and "popple."

> Stripe of green in moosewood maple,
> Colour seen in leaf of apple,
> B**a**rk of p**o**pple.

The third stanza breaks the patterns the last two established. Hopefully you're noticing by now that this stanza seems to go its own way in many musical regards. It doesn't use consonant sounds within the rhyming words to link to consonant sounds in other words. However, consonance *is* created between the three rhyming words with the center \n\ and \b\ sounds.

> Wood of popple pale as moo**n** • **b**eam,
> Wood of oak for yoke and bar**n**-**b**eam,
> Wood of hor**n** • **b**eam.

It also uses consonance to link to the previous stanza. The \p\ in the first line's "popple" and "pale" link up to the five \p\ sounds in the previous stanza.

> Stri**p**e of green in moosewood ma**p**le,
> Colour seen in leaf of a**pp**le,
> Bark of **p**o**pp**le.
>
> Wood of **p**o**pp**le **p**ale as moonbeam,
> Wood of oak for yoke and barn-beam,
> Wood of hornbeam.

What about assonance? In the second line, assonance occurs in three words in a row, with the long \ō\ sound in the internal rhyme pair ("oak" and "yoke") also matching "for" and linking to the third line's "hornbeam."

> Wood of popple pale as moonbeam,
> Wood of **oa**k f**o**r y**o**ke and barn-beam,
> Wood of h**o**rnbeam.

It continues the soft \a\ assonance from the previous stanza as well, repeating it in "popple" then drawing in "barn-beam."

> Stripe of green in moosewood maple,
> Colour seen in leaf of apple,
> B**a**rk of p**o**pple.

> Wood of p**o**pple pale as moonbeam,
> Wood of oak for yoke and b**a**rn-beam,
> Wood of hornbeam.

Finally, the long \ē\ sound that creates the end rhymes also creates assonance with the long \ē\ sounds in lines 1 and 2 of the previous stanza.

> Stripe of gr**ee**n in moosewood maple,
> Colour s**ee**n in l**ea**f of apple,
> Bark of popple.

> Wood of popple pale as moonb**ea**m,
> Wood of oak for yoke and barn-b**ea**m,
> Wood of hornb**ea**m.

The final stanza is rich in consonance. Every line has at least one \l\ sound: "silver" and "hollow" in line 1, "elder," "tall," and "yellow" in line 2, and "willow" in line 3.

> Si**l**ver bark of beech, and ho**ll**ow
> Stem of e**l**der, ta**ll** and ye**ll**ow
> Twig of wi**ll**ow.

Just as in the first stanza—from where the entire line is repeated—the
\w\ sound in "twig" and "willow" and at the end of "hollow" and "yellow"
creates consonance tying together all three lines.

> Silver bark of beech, and hollo**w**
> Stem of elder, tall and yello**w**
> T**w**ig of **w**illo**w**.

And finally, the \r\ sound in "silver," bark," and "elder" ties together
lines 1 and 2 and echoes the same sound pattern in the first stanza.

> Silve**r** ba**r**k of beech, and hollow
> Stem of elde**r**, tall and yellow
> Twig of willow.

The soft \a\ assonance that began in the second stanza carries through
the fourth stanza, animating "bark" and "hollow" in the first line and
"tall" in the second.

> Stripe of green in moosewood maple,
> Colour seen in leaf of apple,
> B**a**rk of p**o**pple.

> Wood of p**o**pple pale as moonbeam,
> Wood of oak for yoke and b**a**rn-beam,
> Wood of hornbeam.

> Silver b**a**rk of beech, and h**o**llow
> Stem of elder, t**a**ll and yellow
> Twig of willow.

The long \ē\ assonance that started in the second stanza makes its
final appearance here as well with "beech" in the first line.

> Stripe of gr**ee**n in moosewood maple,
> Colour s**ee**n in l**ea**f of apple,
> Bark of popple.

Wood of popple pale as moonb<u>ea</u>m,
Wood of oak for yoke and barn-b<u>ea</u>m,
Wood of hornb<u>ea</u>m.

Silver bark of b<u>ee</u>ch, and hollow
Stem of elder, tall and yellow
Twig of willow.

Because this stanza repeats the first part of the first line and the entire third line of the first stanza, it, of course, repeats the assonance created by the soft \i\ that ties together "silver" in line one with "twig" and "willow" in line three.

S<u>i</u>lver bark of beech, and hollow
Stem of elder, tall and yellow
Tw<u>ig</u> of w<u>i</u>llow.

It also brings in a fourth assonance with the /e/ sound connecting "stem," "elder," and "yellow" in line 2.

Silver bark of beech, and hollow
St<u>e</u>m of <u>e</u>lder, tall and y<u>e</u>llow
Twig of willow.

This poem, which has an unusually high amount of repetition, also has more assonance and consonance in tighter patterns than you'll find in many other poems. Most readers find it pleasant to the ear, and it rolls easily off the tongue. The patterns of assonance and consonance that tie it together under the surface help to explain why.

Onomatopoeia

Onomatopoeia is the use or creation of words to mimic natural sounds directly. A lot of sources classify onomatopoeia as a figure of speech, but in this book, we use "figure of speech" in a more limited way.

We can distinguish two sorts of onomatopoeia. The first and simplest is the use of words that don't mean anything other than the sound they mimic. "Pow," "hiss," "meow," "ding-dong," and "snap" are all examples of direct onomatopoeia. The first line of this couplet from Langston Hughes's "The Weary Blues" shows a straightforward onomatopoeia in action:

> **Thump**, **thump**, **thump**, went his foot on the floor.
> He played a few chords then he sang some more —

In poetry, though, onomatopoeia is usually subtler. For example, a poet might use words that suggest the actual sounds of things being described or happening in the poem. Consider this excerpt from "Cynthia in the Snow" by Gwendolyn Brooks, which describes the falling snow:

> It hushes
> It shushes
> It flitter-twitters;
> and whitely whirs away

Every word in this excerpt means something. No words are simple and pure onomatopoeia. However, the poem uses a lot of quiet, soft, open-mouthed sounds, like \sh\ and \wh\, \u\ and \w\. These words both imitate and suggest the quiet of the falling snow.

Moreover, the first two verbs that describe what "it," the snow, is doing have both literal and figurative meanings that relate sound to sense. On one level, snow doesn't "hush" or "shush" — those are human actions, right? Your mother is the one who hushes and shushes you. In that sense, then, these words are implied figures of speech. In another sense, however, these are literal descriptions because snowfall, especially a heavy snowfall, with accumulation, actually does hush and shush the world quieter by absorbing sound.

Sometimes a poet uses a variety of other devices of sound, such as rhythm or alliteration, to create an overall onomatopoeic effect in which the whole exceeds the sum of the parts. Often the meaning and context are necessary to provide the suggestion the mind needs to hear the sound the poet wants to create. The sounds the words make don't have to relay a fixed thing, but in the right context they can. For example, consider just the first stanza from this next poem that's all about the onomatopoeia.

from "The Bells"

I.

Hear the sledges with the bells —
Silver bells!
What a world of merriment their melody foretells!
How they tinkle, tinkle, tinkle,
In the icy air of night!
While the stars that oversprinkle
All the heavens, seem to twinkle
With a crystalline delight;
Keeping time, time, time,
In a sort of Runic rhyme,
To the tintinnabulation that so musically wells
From the bells, bells, bells, bells,
Bells, bells, bells —
From the jingling and the tinkling of the bells.

Edgar Allen Poe, 1849

In the first stanza of this longer poem, Poe evokes and replicates the sound of ringing bells on horse-drawn sleighs, the same sound, by the way, that's described in the Christmas carol "Jingle Bells." You might consider which is more effective. Before you reread or think any more about the poem, though, try to imagine the sound of horse-bells, or search for a recording of them.

Someone might describe the sound of horse bells as fast, high, sharp, and repetitive. But chaotic? It's a full, constant tapestry of sound, at least if the horses are on the move. However, there's not a lot of variety. The sounds that the bells make are narrow, so the sound of the bells is fairly repetitive.

If you read the poem out loud, you'll hear a music that can be described similarly. There's a great density of repetition. There are six rhyme sounds that recur in the stanza. Sometimes they repeat densely and quickly, and sometimes, they're more spaced out. There's a free intermix of internal and end rhyme. A lot of the rhyme comes from repetition of whole words. There's lots and lots of rhyme but no dominant pattern ever emerges. All are short syllables, quick to utter.

Similar dense, chaotic patterns of other devices of sound are found here, too: alliteration, assonance, and consonance, all layered on top of each other. It even has a very uncommon word, "tintinnabulation," which means "the sound of ringing bells." Many people say the word sounds like bells ringing, for the same reasons we've been talking about here. Do these *have to* remind us of bells? Is there anything in these particular sounds that demands "I am the sound of a bell"? No. But, they extend that possibility. Given the subject and content of the poem, a pattern of sound is created that can remind us of and act out the sound of those bells ringing, ringing, ringing.

Final Thoughts

Rhyme is only the first of many kinds of patterns that poets make by repeating sounds within and between lines. Alliteration is a pattern of repeated initial word sounds. Repetition of consonant and vowel sounds within words—as opposed to at the beginning or end of words—are known as consonance and assonance. Onomatopoeia is the use of words that sound like what they describe. Being aware of, and developing the habit of looking systematically for, other patterns of repetition is a vital tool in understanding and appreciating the music of poetry.

To finish off the chapter, here's a list of reminders, tips, and tricks to help you as you work with the musical language of poems:

- Read out loud, listen to others read, and annotate the poem as you listen. Be sure to take notes as you go, as the pattern may not emerge at first. Finding alliteration is not a lot different than finding rhyme.

- Be more attentive to syllables than to words. Alliteration is strongly linked to the pattern of stressed syllables.

- Remember to listen to sounds instead of looking for spelling. Look up words if you're not sure how to pronounce them. You don't have to and shouldn't guess.

- It can be tough to isolate vowel and consonant sounds from each other and thus to hear assonance or consonance. In addition to patience, your best friend is the dictionary, which includes a pronunciation guide for every word.

- Notice how much of the consonance and assonance in "Counting-Out Rhyme" is tied into the rhymes. Assonance and consonance tend to get drowned out in isolation, but they are accented and highlighted when used in conjunction with other musical effects.

- Onomatopoeia is more than "words that don't mean anything but the sound they seem to make." Anytime the poet uses letters and words to create sounds that mimic or evoke natural sounds, we're in the world of onomatopoeia.

- Be attentive to the overall pattern of sounds in the poem and the effects they create. There's no secret Poets-Only Onomatopoeia Decoder Ring that indicates "word sound X = sound from life Y."

It would be cool, though, if there was.

It can be easy to overthink this. Is this internal rhyme or assonance? Is this consonance in this line but alliteration over here? It often depends on how you look at or pronounce it. If this starts to feel maddening, take a deep breath and step away from the poem for a minute. The point of learning to recognize these musical elements is only to help you better understand and appreciate the poems. So take your time to listen and appreciate, but don't drive yourself crazy.

Exercises

This section gives you the chance to practice your understanding of these sound devices through a structured reading of four poems and through focused creative writing prompts. If your professor doesn't assign them, they can still be completed independently if you wish.

For Readers

These four poems each present interesting music and give you a chance to practice understanding and appreciating the other musical elements. If you're not given specific assignments by your professor, try doing this for each poem:

1. Complete the basic reading.

2. Write down your own initial impressions: What did you understand to be happening on the literal level in this poem? Did you like it? Can you say how or why?

3. Get some scratch paper and then highlighters, colored pencils, or whatever works for you for annotating sounds. You'll find it easier to work these things out, especially at first, by scribbling all over the poems and using color coding to make the sound patterns visual. Play around with different tools or systems for annotating the sound. It's less important to learn someone else's

method than to work out one that you like. Ask your professor for help if it feels too overwhelming.

4. Remember that you need to both read these out loud and listen to someone else reading them—repeatedly. Make notes as you do.

5. Be systematic. Take one sound element at a time and find all the ways that element plays out in the poem. Mark the poem up. Create a different, marked up copy for each element.

6. Write a paragraph or two summarizing each element at work in the poem. Explain how it connects to the content of the poem, if you see a connection. If you don't see any connection, explain that.

7. Don't force anything. It's only a test in the sense of it being a test of your powers of observation. There's no secret code to unlock. Just pay attention and record what you notice.

Poem 1

The song elements at work in this next poem are subtle enough that you might miss them if you don't pay attention or at least follow something like the process suggested above. Look for alliteration, assonance, and consonance. Remember, it's the *pattern* of sounds that makes the effect.

Young Couple Marries in July

On their wedding day: white pellet rain of rice and clear light.
Her cheeks fruited, his smile guileless as bread.
Some life before them the celebrants could taste:
lavender and plum and a third element unnamed.

5   The community bore gifts in colored bowls and gleaming foil.
The elders fanned flies.
The children gamboled, sugar-fed,

and threw their shoes into the elm-shade and ran
away with shrieks of celebration.

10   Bride and groom waltzed on a floor laid across summer grass.
Between them, beneath white froth,
beneath pretty girl-fat and viscera,
a spoonful of baby sat at the center.

It was all for her: rice and light, flower and foil,
15   flies and shrieks and limitless wonder across the grass.

Dawn Diez Willis, 2013

Poem 2

As you read through this next poem, ask yourself if an overall onomato-
poetic effect of any sort is being created. Ask yourself how the overall
sound seems to work—or not—with the overall sense. This means you
need to make sure you have a good overall understanding of the sense.
Make sure you look up all the proper nouns!

Watershed

Come, Clearwater. River of my birth. Come
snowmelt high and wild from canyons, Lochsa, Selway,
fork your cold fire through the narrows. Eddy around granite,
spill wide in summer light. Flash those ruby shallows.
5   Lift my heart on your whitewater riffles.

Come to me in dreams, in memory, come April
and flaming October, ice floes, dropoffs, all your deep
green holes. Float by Syringa, sumac, mica sand, dried
hellgrammites, blue heron. Minnow flicker. Summer-smell.
10   Slide between palisades, rimrock, that tall basalt,
obsidian. Pour through me like blood.

Bear me beyond the swallowing monster's heart,
past Coyote's fishnet and the rattlesnake
on toward the confluence. Take me to sea.

Bette Lynch Husted, 2013

Poem 3

The poem that follows has some straightforward onomatopoeia, as well
as our other song elements. Pay attention to the patterns the poet creates
with repetition. Notice how these patterns are based on and extend out
from the repetition of entire words and phrases.

Invitation to Mr. W.

Before the birds find their breakfast, before the clack of wooden
clogs advise me of my neighbor striding to her coop,
another woman turning on the sprinklers with a swoooshhhhhh.

5   Before I'm awake enough to call and question you again, before you
navigate with enigmatic answers and dead ends,
please come flying —

Over the Willamette that wends itself into town in a V,
over the Masonic cemetery replete with street lights, verses,
dear, please come flying —

10   In this summer of my 40th year, in this season of blackberries,
cherries, and inexplicably sweet pears, won't you
just come flying —

Forget your double life, your despairing heart, and other minor
irrelevancies. Come with your old blue van, come with your kayak
15   but do come flying —

Over the Cascade mountains, over Allan Brothers, and Black Sun,

we'll rise above the university and be back in time for tea, so
>get ready

>>to come flying —

Come out with me to Fall Creek, to the place where the islands part,
20 where we scaled rock and scree to find who we might have been
>>flying —

Come with your intense, your insistent gaze, come with silver
hair, and your body lithe and inspiring. The time is right, the
>landing

>>clear, come now!

25 Leave bright caution and computers and your excuses
in the wind. Today, before we're gone—
>>do come flying —

after Elizabeth Bishop's "Invitation to Miss Marianne Moore"

Susan Rich, 2006

Poem 4

The final poem makes extensive use of alliteration, and it's interesting
to see how the alliteration is working in conjunction with the pattern
of stressed syllables. Both the sense of this poem and the sound of this
poem are based on an allusion. Be sure you figure out who Captain
Haddock is!

Captain Haddock vs. the PTA

Bewildered Saint of the curse, bulbous
& profane, I invoke you against this *Nest*
Of Lice & Vipers: O volcanic Captain, I implore you, pour
Your scorn upon these *Borgias*; before these *Braggarts*
5 Unfurl your thick invective, show your bullet head

5 Whiskey-pickled, weathered & pupilless, sweating
 In a bantam rage, your sad-fish face a fist;
 Ostrogothic versus the matrons
 Voluble against the *Vampire's* slander
 Because I would never say *Vivisectionist* to her face
10 While you old Captain Fatstock, Hopscotch, Havoc
 Denouncer of *Bullies, Knitters & Bandits*
 Live to make the air around you frantic
 To spill your black lake of *Cannibal* ink.

Amy Beeder, 2009

For Writers

These exercises help you get to know and practice these musical elements in your own writing. They help you experiment so that you can later use these patterns to create poems in your own time. The main thing is to have fun playing around with these devices of sound.

1. If you wrote a nonsense poem in Chapter 9, go back and revise it to add in some of these new devices of sound. Don't go over or under the syllable count per line that you've already established. Try creating three different versions with three different goals. Your goal might be to have two alliterating words in every line, for example.

2. Find five onomatopoeia that you like and use each as part of a title for a future poem. Then invent five onomatopoeia that English seems to be lacking but really needs, and use each of *them* as part of a title for a future poem.

3. Write twenty lines of Anglo-Saxon meter. It's more fun than it sounds.

4. Write a description of an unpleasant event, place, person—or all of them together—that uses purposefully unpleasant-sounding lan-

guage to create and reinforce the mood.

5. Pick out a couple of your own poems, either clearly in progress or "done," if there is such a thing. Revise each to either add a pattern of assonance or consonance that reinforces and extends a different pattern that's already in the poem.

Chapter 11

Rhythmic Language

Key terms: rhythm, accentual rhythm, meter, accentual-syllabic rhythm, foot, iamb, trochee, anapest, dactyl, spondee, pyrrhic, minor ionic, foot, monometer, dimeter, trimeter, tetrameter, pentameter, hexameter, heptameter, octameter, scansion

From the Middle Ages until the middle of the twentieth century, no one would have dreamed of teaching or even discussing English-language poetry without a central focus on rhythm. The rhythm of the language was an English-language poem's central feature for more than a thousand years!

However, this is no longer true. In fact, it is common now to go through an entire introduction to poetry class—or even an entire English degree—with little more than a passing mention of rhythm. This is tragic and foolish. Studying poetry without learning about rhythm is like studying automotive repair without learning about motors. Rhythm is what powers the whole machine.

We will not make this all-too-common mistake. Although you may find it challenging at first, the basic study of rhythm in poetry was once nearly universal in grade schools, so you can handle it. As you'll see, it's no different than studying rhyme or any other element. To begin, all you need to do is get comfortable with a couple of basic concepts and learn some new terminology.

This chapter builds on the "The Syllable" section from Chapter 9, so it might be a good idea to review that now. While you're there, reread "Counting-Out Rhyme" again. We'll take another look at that poem and how rhythm powers it.

Rhythm Basics

Rhythm refers to any recognizable pattern of repetition and variation in sound or movement. You need both parts — repetition and variation — to create rhythm. Even a very simple rhythm like your heartbeat includes both repetition and variation. Put your hand over your heart and you will feel the rhythm of your own body. There are two different beats — lub/dub, expand/contract — that are repeated against a backdrop of silent rest.

In poetry, as in all spoken or written language, rhythm can be established or recognized in any of the devices of sound. Patterns of rhyme or alliteration are "rhythmic" at this basic level. However, talking about rhythm in poetry as a specific element usually means **accentual rhythm**: the rhythmic pattern created by the variable accent levels of syllables. This chapter is based on understanding the difference between accented and unaccented (also called stressed and unstressed) syllables and being able to distinguish them in a poem.

Accentual Rhythm in "Counting-Out Rhyme"

"Counting-Out Rhyme" is reproduced here with syllables divided by a dot (•) and bold and underlined when they are stressed. See if you can find any kind of pattern.

> **<u>Sil</u>** • ver • **<u>bark</u>** • of • **<u>beech</u>**, • and • **<u>sall</u>** • ow
> **<u>Bark</u>** • of • **<u>yell</u>** • ow • **<u>birch</u>** • and • **<u>yell</u>** • ow
> **<u>Twig</u>** • of • **<u>will</u>** • ow.
>
> **<u>Stripe</u>** • of • **<u>green</u>** • in • **<u>moose</u>** • wood • **<u>ma</u>** • ple,
> **<u>Col</u>** • our • **<u>seen</u>** • in • **<u>leaf</u>** • of • **<u>ap</u>** • ple,
> **<u>Bark</u>** • of • **<u>pop</u>** • ple.

Wood • of • **pop** • ple • **pale** • as • **moon** • **beam**,
Wood • of • **oak** • for • **yoke** • and • **barn**- • **beam**,
Wood • of • **horn** • **beam**.

Sil • ver • **bark** • of • **beech**, • and • **holl** • ow
Stem • of • **el** • der, • **tall** • and • **yell** • ow
Twig • of • **will** • ow.

Can you put what's revealed through this markup into words? One thing you can describe is the size of the stanzas and the syllable and stress content of the lines. Each stanza has three lines. The first two lines of each have eight syllables, while the third line has four syllables. Every single line begins with a stressed syllable.

In stanzas 1, 2, and 4, the first two lines have four stresses, and the third line has two, while each of the lines end with unstressed syllables. However, stanza 3 breaks the pattern by adding an extra stress at the end of every line. That results in lines 7 and 8 having five stresses each and line 9 having three. The alternation of stressed and unstressed syllables is extremely regular. Stressed syllables alternate with unstressed syllables every time, except for those last syllables in the third stanza.

This calm rhythmic pattern seems to go along with the calm content and gentle music of the whole poem. There are very few surprises. The pattern established in the first few lines mostly holds throughout. This is a basic description of the accentual rhythm of this poem, without any special jargon or concepts. However, we can go deeper!

When annotating a poem by hand, the way, the more-or-less traditional system for noting English-language accentual rhythm is to put an accent (´) over the stressed syllables and a breve (˘) over the unstressed syllables. That's easier than underlining or other forms of highlighting because you can change your mind so easily by just erasing one mark and replacing it with another.

Meter

Rhythm is a broad term and is useful on its own. However, in discussing rhythm in poetry, we often want and need to analyze what's called the "meter" of the poem. **Meter** means a regular pattern and identifiable structure of stress in a line of verse. Like "form," it can be used multiple ways, both descriptively and prescriptively.

A Brief History of English Meter

The ideas about meter and the terminology used are alien for most of us at first. However, understanding a little about the history of English and about rhythm's evolving place in English-language poetry will help you understand how and why these terms are used and give you a context for what follows.

The first thing to understand is that not all languages have a meaningful pattern of stressed and unstressed syllables. Japanese, for example, does not strictly or formally differentiate between stress levels in spoken syllables. To an English speaker, spoken Japanese may sound clipped, flat, or expressionless. Likewise, an English speaker learning Japanese must overcome the natural tendency to vary stresses in pronunciation. Native English speakers learning Japanese often sound bizarrely sing-song or chantlike to native Japanese speakers.

On the other hand, in some languages, the role of stress is even stronger, and the rules governing stress are more regular. Stress is a central feature of German languages, which English inherited from its German roots. Stress patterns were the dominant organizing principle in Old English poetry, too, along with alliteration. A line of Old English poetry is primarily defined by the number of stressed syllables it contains, regardless of the total number of syllables.

Modern English, born from Old English and Middle French, came into existence more or less during the Renaissance. This was a time when classical literature and philosophy were being rediscovered and exerting a dominant influence on almost every area of the cultures of Europe. The impact of classical poetry and literary study on modern English literary theory and practice was very strong.

Stress is not an important part of Greek or Latin. However, syllables in these languages are of fixed and defined length—long or short. The interplay of long and short syllables is important in spoken Latin and Greek and crucial in Latin and Greek poetry. Classical literary criticism identified a fixed number of strictly defined lines, in which there are two defining criteria: 1) number of syllables and 2) the pattern of long and short syllables.

Poetry written during the early development of modern English, before the Renaissance, often used both Old English and French lines or varying combinations of them. The Old English lines were accentual, defined by number of stresses per line. French poetry is primarily defined by the number of syllables it contains, however, and other organizing principles, such as end rhyme. The French lines were thus syllabic, defined by the number of syllables per line.

Renaissance English writers and literary critics attempted to create theories and models to regularize this situation. To create an English metrical system, they imported the strictly defined lines of classical poetry. English does not have long and short syllables, but it does have stressed and unstressed syllables. Thus, "stressed" was substituted for "long" syllables and "unstressed" for "short" syllables. Because of the French heritage, it also considers the number of syllables total in every line to be of critical importance.

Therefore, a rhythmic system that organized lines according both to number of syllables per line and not just the number of stressed syllables, but the pattern of stressed and unstressed syllables, was born. Known as **accentual-syllabic rhythm**, it dominated English poetry from the Renaissance until the twentieth century, and it remains important in the work of many contemporary poets.

The traditional study of meter, and the traditional meters you will learn to identify, as well as the system for categorizing them, are all based on accentual-syllabic rhythm.

Meter as Formal Pattern

As you remember from Chapter 2, "form" can be a general description of the shape and structure of a poem. Form also has a specific meaning in poetry, referring to an established set of rules that define a poem's patterns. Meter is one of the most important criteria that define traditional forms. Just as a sonnet has to conform to a certain rhyme scheme, for example, it's also expected to conform to a certain rhythmic pattern, or meter.

There are a variety of ways to talk about meters as formal patterns. You might say a poem "is a sonnet." You might say, "this poem is in a traditional meter" or "this poem is metrical." You might describe how "this poem follows the metrical rules for a sonnet" or "this line is in a fixed meter." More commonly, you might name the specific meter of a poem or line based on the established traditional form.

Just like some traditional forms have special names, such as "sonnet" or "villanelle," regularly occurring and common meters have traditional names that are constructed using a system of special terminology. Even though the terminology takes some getting used to—be patient!—you will see that it's actually a great tool. These terms make it easy to communicate quickly and accurately about a complicated subject. The name of a meter always describes two things:

1. The dominant pattern of stressed and unstressed syllables

2. The number of syllables in a line—its length

You may, for example, have heard the term "iambic pentameter" used to describe the lines in Shakespeare's plays. That is the name of a meter in those plays.

The first term, "iambic," refers to the dominant pattern of stressed and unstressed syllables. Each common combination of stressed and unstressed syllables has its own special name. The pattern that dominates in Shakespeare's plays is named the "iamb."

The second term, "pentameter," refers to the length of a line. A single unit of any common pattern is called, weirdly, a "foot." Line length is determined by the number of feet in a line. In Shakespeare's plays, each line has five feet. "Penta" means five.

When you put these two classifications together, you get a two-word description of the rhythm in the line, which you call its meter. "Iambic pentameter" thus describes a line made up of five iambic feet, or just iambs.

The Foot

When talking about rhythm in poetry, the **foot** is a unit for measuring meter. It is a set pattern of stressed and unstressed syllables that is repeated throughout the line.

Think about all the other things you commonly measure—time, distance, or weight. "Time," for example, is an abstract concept. It doesn't come with the labels we put on it. It just flows, ever forward, into eternity. However, we can still observe cycles or patterns in time. The sun, for example, rises and sets in a regular pattern over time. The days get longer and shorter in a regular pattern of time. We use those patterns to help us divide this limitless thing called time into units—day, week, month, season—and then use those units to measure it.

We do the same thing with sound in poetry. The sound of a poem just flows on like time, especially when we're listening to it. However, there are patterns in the sound, so we can name those patterns and then use them to divide and measure the sound.

You already know the name of the smallest unit—the syllable. Syllables are the building blocks of feet, just like minutes make up hours. Because a foot is a unit of sound, it is independent of spelling and words just as other sound devices are. One foot can contain multiple words, and one word can be broken into multiple feet. The word is a unit of story. The foot is a unit of song.

English feet have either two or three syllables and at least one stressed syllable. We define each one by how many syllables are in it and by the pattern of stressed and unstressed syllables within it. The names for feet are Greek names that just have to be learned. They're archaic and bizarre—but not any harder to learn than terms in biology or math or auto repair. You can handle it.

There are four major and two minor feet, and you'll examine each in detail now.

The Iamb

The first major foot is the **iamb**: a two-syllable, or **duple**, foot, sequenced thus: first unstressed, then stressed (˘ ´). The adjective is "iambic," so you would say, "iambic foot," "iambic word," "iambic line," "iambic pentameter," and so on. Here are some iambic words, with the stressed syllables in bold and underlined:

> per • **chance**
> ad • **mit**

These iambs are created out of two words:

> a • **crow**
> be • **good**

These lines are taken from poems in which sequences of iambs are created out of mixing and splitting words. In addition to highlighting the stressed syllables, a single vertical line separates each foot, which is another standard practice:

> I • **found** | a • **dimp** | led • **spi** | der, • **fat** | and • **white**
> Did • **gyre** | and • **gim** | ble • **in** | the • **wabe**
> We • **romped** | un • **til** | the • **pans**

The Trochee

The second common foot is the trochee. The **trochee** is another duple foot, and the sequence is first stressed, then unstressed (´ ˘). This is the reverse of an iamb. The adjective is "trochaic," so you would say, "trochaic foot," "trochaic word," "trochaic line," "trochaic pentameter," and so on.

The dominant foot in "Counting-Out Rhyme" is the trochee. Here are some trochaic words with the stressed syllables highlighted:

lov • er

stap • le

These trochees are created out of two words:

laid • to

close • the

These lines are taken from poems in which sequences of trochees are created out of mixing and splitting words:

Once • up | **on** • a | **mid** • night | **drear** • y, | **while** • I | **pond** • ered, | **weak** • and | **wear** • y

Dou • ble, | **dou** • ble, | **toil** • and | **trou** • ble

Should • you | **ask** • me, | **whence** • these | **stor** • ies?

The Anapest

The third major foot is the anapest. The **anapest** is a three-syllable, or **treble**, foot, and the sequence is unstressed, then another unstressed, and then stressed (˘ ˘ ´). The adjective is "anapestic," so you would say, "anapestic foot," "anapestic word," "anapestic line," "anapestic pentameter," and so on. Here are some anapestic words with the stressed syllables highlighted:

un • der • **foot**

con • tra • **dict**

These anapests are created out of multiple words:

on • the • **lam**

who • de • **cides**

These lines are taken from poems in which sequences of anapests are created out of mixing and splitting words:

> The • As • **<u>syr</u>** | ian • came • **<u>down</u>** | like • a • **<u>wolf</u>** | on • the •
> **<u>fold</u>**
> 'Twas • the • **<u>night</u>** | be • fore • **<u>Christ</u>** | mas • and • **<u>all</u>** |
> through • the • **<u>house</u>**
> The • im • **<u>mor</u>** | tal • de • **<u>sire</u>** | of • im • **<u>mor</u>** | tals • we •
> **<u>saw</u>** | in • their • **<u>face</u>** | es • and • **<u>sighed</u>**.

The Dactyl

The fourth major foot is the dactyl. The **dactyl** is another treble foot, and the sequence is first stressed, then unstressed, then another unstressed (´ ˘ ˘). The adjective is "dactylic," so you would say, "dactylic foot," "dactylic word," "dactylic line," "dactylic pentameter," and so on. Here are some dactylic words with the stressed syllables in bold and underlined:

> **<u>po</u>** • et • ry
> **<u>mus</u>** • ic • al

These dactyls are created out of multiple words:

> **<u>out</u>** • of • the
> **<u>snap</u>** • ping • his

These lines are taken from poems in which sequences of dactyls are created out of mixing and splitting words:

> **<u>This</u>** • is • the | **<u>for</u>**est • pri | **<u>me</u>**val. • The | **<u>mur</u>**muring |
> **<u>pines</u>** • and • the
> **<u>Can</u>** • non • to | **<u>right</u>** • of • them
> **<u>Just</u>** • for • a | **<u>hand</u>** • ful • of | **<u>sil</u>** • ver • he

Beyond these four major feet, there are two minor feet, the spondee and the pyrrhic. They're "minor" because they don't really stand on their own.

You will never find a whole line of these. Instead, they substitute for one or two other feet in a line, thus creating variation and surprise.

The Spondee

The **spondee** is two stressed syllables in a row (′ ′). Here are a couple of lines that include a spondee, indicated with italics:

> With • **swift**, | *slow*, • *sweet*, | **so** • ur; | a • **daz** | zle, • **dim**
> When • **A** | jax • **strives** | some • **rock's** | *vast* • *weight* | to •
> **throw**,

The Pyrrhic

The **pyrrhic** is two unstressed syllables in a row (˘ ˘). Here are a couple of lines that include a pyrrhic or two, italicized:

> "*It* • *is* | the • **star** | to • **ev**' | ry • **wan** | d'ring • **bark**
> "My • **way** | *is* • *to* | be • **gin** | *with* • *the* | be • **gin** | ning."

It's very uncommon—some would say impossible—to have two pyrrhic feet in a row. Two spondees in a row is also uncommon. If you remember our discussion of the syllable, after two, or at most three, unstressed syllables in a line, one syllable gets promoted or demoted to create variation. The same happens in reverse, too, with a demotion of a nominally stressed syllable in the midst of a string of stressed syllables.

The Minor Ionic

One other term worth knowing is the **minor ionic**, which is a foot-pair, a pyrrhic followed by a spondee (˘ ˘ ′ ′). It's sometimes called the **double iamb** because it doubles the pattern of an iamb. Here are a couple of lines made of minor ionics with the stressed syllables in bold and underlined:

- "To • a | **green** • **thought** | in • a | **green** • **shade**"
- "When • the | **blood** • **creeps** | and • the | **nerves** • **prick**"

Minor ionics are especially common in iambic lines because most listeners find they complement and extend the existing rhythm, providing variation without clashing.

Metrical Feet in "Metrical Feet"

This funny little poem was written as a lesson for the poet's son to teach him to recognize the metrical feet by showing them in action. If you read it out loud, it does give you good examples of how the different rhythms sound. The poet uses classical terminology here, referring to stressed syllables as "long" and unstressed as "short."

from "Metrical Feet"

Trochee trips from long to short;
From long to long in solemn sort
Slow Spondee stalks, strong foot!, yet ill able
Ever to come up with Dactyl's trisyllable.
Iambics march from short to long.
With a leap and a bound the swift Anapests throng.

Samuel Taylor Coleridge, 1806

Let's break it down into its constituent syllables and feet with the same highlighting we've been using. A vertical line separates each foot:

Tro • chee | **trips** • from | **long** • to | **short**;
From • **long** | to • **long** | in • **sol** | emn • **sort**
Slow • **Spon** | dee • **stalks**, | **strong** • **foot**!, | yet • **ill** | **a** • ble
Ev • er • to | **come** • up • with | **Dac** • tyl's • tri | **syll** • a • ble.
I • **am** | bics • **march** | from • **short** | to • **long**.
With • a • **leap** | and • a • **bound** | the • swift • **An** | a • pests •
   throng.

Isn't that clever? Every line describes the kind of foot it is exclusively made out of.

The Line

Each line name is itself two parts. The second half of each is always "meter," sensibly enough. The first half is the Greek word for a number:

Monometer is a line of one foot.

Dimeter is a line of two feet.

Trimeter is a line of three feet.

Tetrameter is a line of four feet.

Pentameter is a line of five feet.

Hexameter is a line of six feet.

Heptameter is a line of seven feet.

Octameter is a line of eight feet.

People who think too hard about these categories disagree about whether or not a line longer than octameter is possible. At any rate, attempts at longer metrical lines are rare. It doesn't happen in any traditional meters or forms. The most common lines in English are tetrameter and pentameter.

As you saw earlier with "iambic pentameter," the names of the meters are just combinations of these two terms, foot and line length. If you are told that a sonnet should be written in iambic pentameter, you know that means that each line is composed of five unstressed-stressed syllable pairs—iambs. Likewise, if, in reading Poe's "The Raven," you notice that most of the lines are made up mostly of stressed-unstressed syllable pairs and that they tend to be sixteen syllables long, you can succinctly describe it as being "in trochaic octameter."

Should you have the chance to demonstrate an actual understanding of these concepts and terms at a party, the effect on your audience can hardly be exaggerated.

Scansion

The process of examining a line or a poem in order to discover and analyze its meter is called **scansion**. The verb is "to scan." Sometimes the verb "to scan" is also used to mean "composed using a regular metrical pattern." For example, once these terms become part of your vocabulary, you might ask, "Does this line scan?" That means, "If I scanned it, would I find a basically regular pattern?"

Scansion can help you identify a poem as a received form. It can also help you judge whether a poet's attempt to write in a received form is fully successful. Other elements of a poem may also be easier to understand or appreciate once the poem's meter has been made explicit and consciously examined through scansion.

Especially if you don't have much experience reading metrical poetry, scansion will help you fully appreciate the artistry of a poem. Reading a metrical poem without awareness of its metrical structure is like watching television with the sound off—you're missing one of the main elements of the artist's work. Scansion reveals that dimension of the work. It allows you to understand effects you perceived but couldn't explain.

Scansion is also the first step in a rhythmic analysis of a poem. This kind of close reading analyzes the meter of the poem, either as a central element to developing an overall understanding and appreciation of the poem or as an end in itself. Many poems begin their lives as metrical experiments or formal exercises, which makes the content completely secondary to the author's original purpose. A rhythmic analysis may bring you much closer to the core of such a poem's being than anything else you can do.

Recognizing the Feet

Once you have divided a poem into syllables and tentatively identified which syllables are stressed and unstressed, the next step in scanning it is to group the syllables into feet and identify what kind of feet they are. Then you move on to the line lengths.

Dividing the line into feet is not necessarily complicated, but admittedly, it is even less of a science than identifying the stressed and unstressed syllables. Perfectly regular lines composed entirely of the same feet make for dull listening and don't give the poet much chance to use meter expressively. Therefore, even in "metrically regular" poetry like Shakespeare's iambic pentameter, substitution or variation within lines is fairly common. The practice of adding or dropping the occasional syllable at the end or beginning of a line is also common.

Often the division of lines into feet is clear enough, but in a complex poem with lots of variation, it can be difficult to identify a dominant foot. **Dominant foot** means the most common foot in a line. A five-foot line in which three of the feet are iambic would be called an "iambic line," for example, even though there are two non-iambs in the line.

Luckily, there is a system to follow that will help you. Work your way through these steps, refer to the examples and the definitions here, and be patient. It's worth it—and it gets very much easier with practice.

1. **Start at the end of the line and work backward.** Variation most commonly occurs toward the beginning of lines, but it can occur anywhere.

2. **Be open to altering your identification of syllables as stressed or unstressed as the work continues.** It's a normal part of the process to make initial identifications and then go back and revise.

3. **Don't forget to consider how content may impact which syllables take a stress.**

4. **Be willing to leave thorny lines undivided and move on to a new line.** Look for a pattern to emerge over the poem as a whole.

5. **Be aware that ambiguity is normal and resolvable**. A trochaic line with an extra unstressed syllable at the beginning or that has dropped an initial stressed syllable is essentially impossible to differentiate from an iambic line—and vice versa. The same goes for anapestic or trochaic lines with strange starting feet or tacked-on syllables. Don't forget your negative capability!

6. **Remember that iambic lines that begin with trochees or spondees, especially at the start of a stanza, are fairly common**. The minor ionic is also common in iambic poems. Don't let these common substitutions throw you off. Keep your eye on the overall pattern, not the individual variations.

7. **When stuck, assume that a line is iambic.** The iamb has always been the dominant foot in English poetry, so much so that some argue it is the natural "foot" of English prose and speech. Even if your assumption is wrong, sometimes working outward from that assumption and correcting it gives you a place to start.

Recognizing the Meter

Once you identify the dominant foot in a given line, just count the number of feet in that line. It should now be easy to assign a two-word name to the line, such as trochaic trimeter or whatever it is. Once all this is done, you have identified the line.

You need to do this for every line. Keep an open mind by looking for patterns of different line lengths. A shorter line at the end of each stanza, for example, is not at all uncommon. Some poems have alternating line lengths. Once you've gone through all the lines a couple of times and your identification of each is feeling fairly settled, it's usually clear if the whole poem has a dominant meter. If most of the poem's lines are five feet long, for example, and if most of the feet in each line are iambs, then you can say that the meter of the poem is iambic pentameter. Even if every sixth line is a dimeter line, you still say the poem is iambic pentameter.

Sometimes a poem is more or less evenly divided between two meters. Sometimes no dominant pattern emerges, even though most of the lines scan. Both cases are perfectly normal and believable. When you describe the rhythm of the poem, just describe it exactly as you find it. Having done so, you are, at least provisionally, done. You have scanned the poem.

Scanning "Counting-Out Rhyme"

Try this out with "Counting-Out Rhyme." You already have it divided into syllables, and you've identified the stressed and unstressed ones. That's most of the work of scansion! Start where you left off:

Sil • ver • **bark** • of • **beech**, • and • **sall** • ow
Bark • of • **yell** • ow • **birch** • and • **yell** • ow
Twig • of • **will** • ow.

Stripe • of • **green** • in • **moose** • wood • **ma** • ple,
Col • our • **seen** • in • **leaf** • of • **ap** • ple,
Bark • of • **pop** • ple.

Wood • of • **pop** • ple • **pale** • as • **moon** • **beam**,
Wood • of • **oak** • for • **yoke** • and • **barn-** • **beam**,
Wood • of • **horn** • **beam**.

Sil • ver • **bark** • of • **beech**, • and • **holl** • ow
Stem • of • **el** • der, • **tall** • and • **yell** • ow
Twig • of • **will** • ow.

Luckily the meter in this poem is clear and straightforward. Look at how regular it is! Of the four main feet you've learned, do any appear here?

You've also observed that every line starts with a stressed syllable. Nine out of twelve end with an unstressed syllable. Every line has an even number of syllables, either eight or four, which is not divisible by three. That suggests you are looking at lines of two-syllable feet rather than three-syllable feet. What is the two-syllable foot moving from stressed to unstressed? The trochee. If you try to divide this into trochees, how does it go? Remember, start at the back and work forward, at least at first. A single vertical line separates each foot:

<u>**Sil**</u> • ver | <u>**bark**</u> • of | <u>**beech,**</u> • and | <u>**sall**</u> • ow
<u>**Bark**</u> • of | <u>**yell**</u> • ow | <u>**birch**</u> • and | <u>**yell**</u> • ow
<u>**Twig**</u> • of | <u>**will**</u> • ow.

<u>**Stripe**</u> • of | <u>**green**</u> • in | <u>**moose**</u> • wood | <u>**ma**</u> • ple,
<u>**Col**</u> • our | <u>**seen**</u> • in | <u>**leaf**</u> • of | <u>**ap**</u> • ple,
<u>**Bark**</u> • of | <u>**pop**</u> • ple.

<u>**Wood**</u> • of | <u>**pop**</u> • ple | <u>**pale**</u> • as | <u>**moon**</u> • <u>**beam,**</u>
<u>**Wood**</u> • of | <u>**oak**</u> • for | <u>**yoke**</u> • and | <u>**barn-**</u> • <u>**beam,**</u>
<u>**Wood**</u> • of | <u>**horn**</u> • <u>**beam**</u>.

<u>**Sil**</u> • ver | <u>**bark**</u> • of | <u>**beech,**</u> • and | <u>**holl**</u> • ow
<u>**Stem**</u> • of | <u>**el**</u> • der, | <u>**tall**</u> • and | <u>**yell**</u> • ow
<u>**Twig**</u> • of | <u>**will**</u> • ow.

Perfect! The lines divide consistently into trochees. The only exceptions are in lines 7–9, where the final foot of each line is a spondee. Even with this variation, the majority of feet in each line and in the poem overall are trochees. You can tentatively identify the dominant foot as the trochee.

How long are the lines? Count the feet. Most are four feet, and some are two. Because the majority are four feet long, the meter should be called trochaic tetrameter—"trochaic" because the dominant foot is the trochee and "tetrameter" because the most common line length is four feet.

A full description of the meter of the poem would require a little more information, though. It would go something like this: "This poem is mostly in perfectly regular trochaic tetrameter, though every tercet ends with a dimeter line and every line in the third tercet ends with a spondee."

This poem has a very regular and straightforward meter, so it's a good starting point for you. A lot of the fun to be had and insight to be gained, however, comes from scanning poems that use more complex patterns to create more varied, interesting, and sophisticated rhythms.

Final Thoughts

Rhythm in poetry can refer to any pattern of repetition and variation, but it usually refers to the rhythm created by the pattern of variation of accented and unaccented syllables. This rhythm is more specifically called "accentual rhythm." Regular patterns in accentual rhythm, combined with regular patterns in the syllabic length of lines, work together to create "accentual-syllabic rhythm."

Scansion is the method and process of making obvious the accentual rhythm of a poem, and, especially, finding and identifying the meter in a poem. Meter refers both to particular traditional patterns of accentual-syllabic rhythm and to the rhythmic pattern of a poem generally. Scanning a poem is a systematic process that anyone can succeed at. It doesn't require a special "ear" or "sense" for rhythm, just careful, close reading and a good dictionary.

To finish off the chapter, here is a list of reminders, tips, and tricks to help you as you work with rhythm:

- Open your ears and eyes and mind to rhythm's presence and importance. This is probably the biggest trick to understanding and appreciating the rhythmic structure of a poem.

- Look for the interplay between the poem's rhythm and its content. Remember that what you're exploring is a relationship that invites possibilities. It does not determine outcomes.

- Don't forget that understanding meter depends completely on identifying syllables and differentiating stressed and unstressed syllables. If you're struggling, go back and reread Chapter 9.

- Scansion is not a process of finding what was hidden. It is a process of translating something you understand unconsciously into conscious thought that you can reflect upon and analyze.

- Scan poems in cycles or drafts. As you learn more, you'll see more. The units create the pattern, but the pattern informs the units, too.

- Don't neglect the basics you've been learning so far—read out loud, use a dictionary, and scribble all over a printed copy of the poem as you work.

The discomfort you may feel with rhythm comes from the newness of the ideas and the vocabulary. Stick with it! Familiarity with both will come with practice. However, the silent, written page is not the best way to learn this stuff. Get live help from a human being who understands meter, if at all possible. Lacking that, watch or listen to some discussions with examples.

This is just the surface of the study of rhythm in poetry. But it's a good beginning. If you can master these concepts and skills, you're well-positioned to understand and appreciate most of the significant and impactful effects of rhythm in a poem—and you're well-positioned to go further into the topic if it strikes your interest.

Exercises

This section gives you the chance to practice your understanding of meter through guided readings of three poems and through focused creative writing exercises. Your professor may or may not assign them, but they are also designed to be completed independently if you wish.

For Readers

These three poems each present clear and interesting opportunities to practice understanding and appreciating rhythm. If you're not given specific assignments by your professor, try doing this for each poem:

1. Complete the basic reading.

2. Jot down your initial impressions: What did you think was happening on the literal level? Did you like it? Can you say how or why?

3. Look for anything other than accentual-syllabic forms of rhythm. Mark patterns of repeated words or phrases.

4. Scan every poem.

5. Write out a short summary that describes the rhythm of the poem. If it has a regular meter, describe that.

Poem 1

This free verse poem doesn't follow a traditional meter, but it is nonetheless rhythmically sophisticated and interesting. Think about how content impacts the stress of syllables. This poem is a great example of how rhythm is a bigger concept than just traditional meter.

Once You've Thought About It

The triumph of the day: that the old dog
made it 12 hours without peeing in the house,
success in her success at staying asleep,
certainly no success in the 12 hours 'til I made it home,
5   because work, because work, because work,
work which kept me late and made me cry,
or nearly, because I can't tell what should or shouldn't
make me mad, what is or isn't mine
to question, am I right, am I right to have said it,
10   she stayed asleep and didn't wake to notice
that she had to pee, once you've thought about it you can't
stop thinking about it, but if you haven't
you can just dream, dream of running,
of finding the squirrel, of barking away
15   some old raccoon, of bringing home a stick,
a great big chewy stick, of getting to keep it.

Catherine Bull, 2015

Poem 2

This poem announces that sound is its subject right in the title, and continues to use musical vocabulary and concepts in its text. You may need to look up some of that vocabulary, in fact, as it's rather specialized. More that that, though, the language itself is musical. Look and listen carefully for all the musical elements the poet employs here. Don't lose track of the situation, either. Figure out what's going on, and how it relates to how the poem sounds.

Sound of Waves

Four shushes spaced to a 4/4 beat
two quarter notes, two eighth notes
and a rest at each measure's end
my wife repeats again and again
to lull our swaddled son to sleep.
Supposedly the rhythm's akin
to the original heart that swayed him
with its ocean thump, that ebb
and flood he emerged from unmoored
in both time and space. That seaward scrape!
By which, I mean, I too am now rocked
and reminded that though the heart works
unbidden, there is meaning in each beat
and in the choice we make to exhale
our warming breaths as prayer to place,
praise song to becoming.

Stephen Siperstein, 2017

Poem 3

This poem will definitely send you to your dictionary, but once you work out the meanings, the situation isn't complicated at all. "Fathers-forth" in line 10 is a neologism that means "creates," an interesting attempt to express the idea of "gives birth to" in the masculine. The inflection marks over "áll trádes" indicate that those words should both be read with a strong stress. This is an old-fashioned notation for making the content stress obvious.

Pied Beauty

Glory be to God for dappled things —

For skies of couple-colour as a brinded cow;
For rose-moles all in stipple upon trout that swim;
Fresh-firecoal chestnut-falls; finches' wings;
Landscape plotted and pieced — fold, fallow, and plough;
And áll trádes, their gear and tackle and trim.

All things counter, original, spare, strange;
Whatever is fickle, freckled (who knows how?)
With swift, slow; sweet, sour; adazzle, dim;
He fathers-forth whose beauty is past change:
Praise him.

Gerard Manley Hopkins, 1918

For Writers

The following exercises help you get to know and practice the concepts related to the rhythm of a poem. They are not designed to produce whole, finished poems but to help you experiment with these smaller elements so that you can use them more effectively to create poems in your own time.

1. Pick out three or four passages of ten to twenty lines from Milton's *Paradise Lost* and practice scanning them. Write a description of the meter as well as the enjambment. After that, try your hand at scanning two of Shakespeare's sonnets. Without worrying about rhyming, see if you can write a fourteen-line poem that uses the same meter.

2. Find some long-lined free verse poems. You might consider Walt Whitman or Allen Ginsberg as starting points. Then find some short-lined free verse—try William Carlos Williams or H. D. Look for and try to describe rhythmic patterns in both sets of work. Explain how they are creating or managing rhythm outside of the constraints of regular meter.

3. Choose any four of the traditional types of poetic lines described in this chapter, including iambic pentameter, trochaic tetrameter, dactylic trimeter, and iambic hexameter. If you don't want to pick for yourself, use these four. Write two example lines in each of these meters for a total of eight lines. The lines don't have to make any sense together. Each line can be self-contained. When you're done, write a brief paragraph reflecting on the exercise. Was it easy or difficult? Why or how? Discuss the experience and the topic.

4. Pick out a couple of your own poems that aren't yet done or that could be improved by revision. Summarize the basic topic, subject, or theme of each in one sentence. Search online for poems written before 1920 on the same subject or theme. Revise your poems to mimic, as closely as possible, the meter or other rhythmic structure of an older poem on the same subject.

Chapter 12

Visual Elements

Key terms: arrangement, typography, concrete poetry

[l(a]

l(a

le

af

fa

ll

s)

one

l

iness

E. E. Cummings, 1958

Most of this book is about the ways that poems are like stories and songs. However, a poem is also like a picture when it's presented on the page or any other visual medium, which has usually been the case for the past several hundred years.

Poetry's conscious use of visual elements is often thought of as a twentieth-century phenomenon. However, poets have experimented with and made use of appearance on the page since at least classical times. Every aspect of a poem can become an outlet for the creativity of poets. The visual elements interact with the story and song elements

267

and function as another way for the poet to create beauty and meaning.

We'll explore two major ways poems are like pictures—first, through their use of arrangement of text and white space on the page and second, through the manipulation of typography. These visual elements help to differentiate poetry from other literary forms and cannot be reduced or folded into any other elements.

Finally, we'll take a brief look at a special case in the use of picture elements, the concrete poem, in which the arrangement and typography work together to create an image with text.

Arrangement

By **arrangement**, we mean the placement of words on the page relative to each other and to the surrounding white space. All poems have arrangement, but in most poems, the arrangement follows a fairly standard convention:

- The poem is left-justified.

- The punctuation and spaces between lines and words is the same as with prose.

- An extra line of white space separates stanzas.

A poem's length and line endings are a consequence of the form and the other elements. In traditional verse, for example, a poem's length and line endings are defined by the metrical requirement of the form and the location of rhymes. In free verse, a poem's length and line endings might be guided by the poet's use of tension between syntax and line breaks. If a line extends beyond the right margin of the page, it is carried over onto the next line. A hanging indentation is normally used to show the line break. It is not part of the poem's design but a consequence of the printing process. These conventions are remarkably stable, and they've been followed since the early days of the printing press.

Deviation from this conventional pattern means the poet is using arrangement to create some new effect in the poem. This deliberate use of arrangement visually suggests, amplifies, substitutes, complements, or creates tension with conventional syntax, punctuation, or breaks in lines and stanzas. That is, the arrangement is a meaningful and expressive part of the poem.

If the poem describes something moving very slowly, for example, the poet may arrange the letters and words to suggest slowness and maybe even slow down the actual reading. Arrangement may also be used instead of punctuation to indicate how words and groups of words are related to each other. These are just a few possibilities. Usually, the connections between arrangement and content are imprecise, suggestive, and ambiguous. They are not usually clearly representational or definitive.

Paying attention to the arrangement of a poem opens up new avenues of appreciation and understanding. At the simplest level, line and stanza breaks draw our attention to song elements like end rhyme and metrical patterns. Arrangement may be used to draw attention to story cues like changes in speaker or setting. Arrangement may substitute for or supplement conventional language elements like punctuation. Noticing the pattern of substitution may make something that was difficult to read on the literal level clearer.

Arrangement in "l(a"

Let's consider the arrangement in our opening poem. The gap between conventional arrangement and this poem's arrangement is pretty wide. What do we notice about it? It's tall and thin, with a bunch of lines made up of only a couple of characters. Many readers don't even realize that there are conventional words in a conventional sentence here. At first, it might just look like random letters, except for the noticeable word "one" in line 7. If we remove all the line breaks and rewrite the poem, we get:

l(aleaffalls)oneliness

Adding in missing spaces to separate what are now-much-easier-to-spot individual words, we get:

l (a leaf falls) oneliness

The sentence "a leaf falls" has been stuck in the middle of the word "loneliness." That creates a neologism "oneliness," which seems like a synonym of loneliness, and splits the initial "l" off by itself. Lonely, like. If we get rid of that interruption, we end up with:

loneliness (a leaf falls)

This poem breaks up just four words into nine lines! That's enjambment beyond enjambment. Rewritten into a single line, the literal meaning is pretty straightforward. Loneliness is described or defined as a leaf falling — or, a leaf falling is described or defined as loneliness. What else can we notice about the arrangement?

The way the words are broken apart into constituent letters brings to mind isolated people in a crowd — in one place but not together, lacking the connections that make them meaningful.

The poem looks like a column — elongated, thin, vertical. The verticality might suggest movement up and down, like a leaf falling. It might suggest a solitary denuded tree. It creates an image that echoes the numeral "1" — a little longer at the top, with three characters, then broadening out to a wide base.

Remember, the idea here is not that the arrangement has to be reduced to "being" or representing any of these things. It may suggest any and all of them, or it may suggest something else even less clearly representational.

Arrangement in "Why I Don't Know Home"

Sometimes simple but unconventional arrangement can create multiple meanings by bringing together or separating text in unexpected ways. Let's take a look at this example, which makes unusual use of white space and line shifts:

Why I Don't Know Home

My parents sold the house	my brother and I tumbled in
Someone else's boots are at the door	from a romp in the snowplow's piles
The driveway's now a three-car garage and mudroom	with pails, soggy boots, shovels
Leaning on a tree, our marble slab kitchen counter	forgotten for something better
In the former kitchen, a dining room, chairs scattered	in a rush to play with our hand-drawn zoo
Half-played board games and toys	not allowed, ever, in the living room
Leftover pretzels on the coffee table	Mom said *The living room is for special occasions, guests*
A giant flat-screen tv glows	except those five days after a hurricane blew
Blankets on the floor	through we slept by the blue slate fireplace
The stairs repositioned, and the fireplace	holding onto the cold outside
A modern cook's kitchen in place of rhododendrons	my father's plants barren in winter
Hanging copper pots my mother never owned	crowded our dining room and porch
Our front door is now the back porch	screened-in, no mosquitoes
A u-shaped drive carves the old backyard	where we watched robins in old-growth trees
Cleared, maples and oaks	that we climbed on, swung from
I'm too old to jump on the king-of-the-mountain boulder	in the yard where Dad's grass never grew
Someone else is watching	his crocuses break snow each spring.

Heidi Schulman Greenwald, 2019

What we notice about this poem's arrangement right away is that there's a wide empty column that runs down the center of it. The lines to the left of the column are right justified, and the lines to the right are left justified. The column is even and regular in appearance whereas both sides of the poem are ragged. This creates the impression that the poem is centered on the column. It looks like a book open on the table, as if the column is the spine.

Conventionally, poems are left-justified. So, the left margin of this poem—the start of our visual experience—is automatically strange looking. Poems are occasionally centered on the page, but the empty space in the center here is unusual. In fact, this poem isn't actually centered. The space of the white column begins and ends with the ends and beginnings of words rather than in the true center of the line. Depending on where that word break falls, each line is a little off center.

At any rate, what do we make of this arrangement? How do we read this poem? Let's ignore the odd spacing and imagine the poem uses conventional line breaks while keeping the text centered:

My parents sold the house my brother and I tumbled in
Someone else's boots are at the door from a romp in the snowplow's piles
The driveway's now a three-car garage and mudroom with pails, soggy boots, shovels
Leaning on a tree, our marble slab kitchen counter forgotten for something better
In the former kitchen, a dining room, chairs scattered in a rush to play with our hand-drawn zoo
Half-played board games and toys not allowed, ever, in the living room
Leftover pretzels on the coffee table Mom said The living room is for special occasions, guests
A giant flat-screen tv glows except those five days after a hurricane blew
Blankets on the floor through we slept by the blue slate fireplace
The stairs repositioned, and the fireplace holding onto the cold outside
A modern cook's kitchen in place of rhododendrons my father's plants barren in winter
Hanging copper pots my mother never owned crowded our dining room and porch
Our front door is now the back porch screened-in, no mosquitoes
A u-shaped drive carves the old backyard where we watched robins in old-growth trees
Cleared, maples and oaks that we climbed on, swung from
I'm too old to jump on the king-of-the-mountain boulder in the yard where Dad's grass never grew
Someone else is watching his crocuses break snow each spring.

These lines mostly make sense. Some are kind of odd, though. In line 4, for example, why would a marble countertop be left leaning against a tree in the yard? Line 9 is definitely strange: "Blankets on the floor through we slept . . ." The syntax of that line is a little nonsensical. Likewise, in line 11, someone put a kitchen in place of the rhododendrons? Maybe they built an extension onto the house?

So, if this is how we read it, two questions come to mind. What do we make of some of these odd, nonsensical lines? And why bother with that big empty column in the middle of the poem? However, there is a completely different way to read the poem. What if the arrangement suggests two totally different stanzas? That is, what if each column is read as a stanza of its own, as in a two-column page arrangement in a textbook?

My parents sold the house
Someone else's boots are at the door
The driveway's now a three-car garage and mudroom
Leaning on a tree, our marble slab kitchen counter
In the former kitchen, a dining room, chairs scattered
Half-played board games and toys
Leftover pretzels on the coffee table
A giant flat-screen tv glows
Blankets on the floor
The stairs repositioned, and the fireplace
A modern cook's kitchen in place of rhododendrons
Hanging copper pots my mother never owned
Our front door is now the back porch
A u-shaped drive carves the old backyard
Cleared, maples and oaks
I'm too old to jump on the king-of-the-mountain boulder
Someone else is watching

my brother and I tumbled in
from a romp in the snowplow's piles
with pails, soggy boots, shovels
forgotten for something better
in a rush to play with our hand-drawn zoo
not allowed, ever, in the living room
Mom said The living room is for special occasions, guests
except those five days after a hurricane blew

through we slept by the blue slate fireplace
holding onto the cold outside
my father's plants barren in winter
crowded our dining room and porch
screened-in, no mosquitoes
where we watched robins in old-growth trees
that we climbed on, swung from
in the yard where Dad's grass never grew
his crocuses break snow each spring.

This also makes total sense, but it tells quite a different story. Words and phrases take on different importance and even meaning when the lines are broken apart and reassembled in this way. The first "stanza" is now all about what the old house is currently like. The second "stanza" is all about the speaker's memories of the house.

Some of the lines that didn't make sense in the first version make much more sense now—a different kind of sense. For example, instead of the rather strange "Blankets on the floor through we slept" in line 9 of our previous version, we get "A giant flat-screen tv glows / Blankets on the floor" in the first stanza and "except those five days after a hurricane blew / through we slept by the blue slate fireplace," both of which make a lot more sense.

On the other hand, there are some oddities in this version, too. The fist stanza starts with all capital letters while the second stanza has no initial caps. There are almost no complete sentences in the first stanza. It's basically just a long list of noun phrases. The transition from the first to second stanza doesn't really make any sense.

Neither of these two translations of the arrangement is "correct" —instead, they present two different readings of this unconventional arrangement. In fact, this arrangement makes us read it three ways—first one way, then the other way, then both ways at the same time. That's the amazing thing that arrangement creates here. We have multiple poems inhabiting the same space, overlapping, complementing, and working against each other simultaneously.

Notice, too, how the arrangement relates to the content. There's a gulf, a divide in the center of the poem, that creates a disjointed experience. It's not unlike visiting an old childhood home or other place once familiar that is now much changed. We may feel like we're in two places or times at once. We're conscious of a division from our own experience, and even from our understanding of ourselves, by the interrupting gulf of time.

Arrangement's Subtler Effects

Let's take a look at a poem in which the use of arrangement is subtler — but still important. Diction is important in this poem as well. There are probably words you don't know and some that might not mean what you think. Get out that dictionary!

Psychopomp

The heron landed at the crest of the driveway
the day John died. Pale bittern, bright blinkless eyes,
                  waterbound wing span.
                         The friend arrived,
following the heron after driving lost in the dark narrowed roads
5   around Larch Mountain. Small miracles, we believed,
                even those who didn't believe
                    talked about it over cigarettes
huddled outside around the chimenea, the brick patio sloped
to a knot of weeds and empty terracotta pots.
10   Especially those who saw him days before,
                 standing at the top of the staircase,
              naked,
pissing right to left, blind with meds, tattoos climbing his legs
plumed, chalybeous, the wobble at the tread
15   of the flight. The unbalance.
                The slow deep wingbeat.

Lisa Oliver, 2017

This poem might seem like it has four stanzas at first glance, but when you take a second look, you realize it's not divided into separate stanzas at all. There's an initial feeling of division, which turns out to mask a tenuous sort of unity. White space cuts deep into every other two lines from the left margin. The right margin looks like a zigzag, as the line endings zig their way farther right then zag back to the left before restarting the same cycle. Every fourth line is quite short, and then the line length widens out dramatically for two lines. And repeat.

If you imagine these lines are physical elements creating a structure of some sort, it doesn't seem like a very strong structure.

What effect does this arrangement have? How does it shape our experience of the poem? There aren't objective answers to these questions, of course. It's important to slow down and notice the arrangement and to ask yourself if it impacts your experience of the poem in any way.

The structure seems weak, wobbly, and off-balance. The poem appears divided at first but turns out to be unified. The arrangement meanders. It can even be seen as circular. Though the poem doesn't actually look like a circle, it does go out and come back, moving in a circular or cyclical way.

You might also ask if the arrangement seems in concert with the content. The poem is about driving dark narrow roads up a mountain, about a large bird with a "slow deep wingbeat," about the death of a friend who was "wobbling" and "unbalanced," "blind with meds," "pissing right to left," and "naked at the top of the staircase" before he died. There seems to be a correspondence between those things and the arrangement — swaying back and forth, wings opening and closing, car rounding the mountain on a road, up and up.

Could this same arrangement be used in a different poem with different content? Of course. Could this same content be presented in a different arrangement? Of course. Nonetheless, the two work together and influence our appreciation and understanding of the poem subtly and unconsciously at first.

Typography

Typography refers to both the typefaces or fonts used and choices within the typeface such as size, capitalization, bolding, color, and so on. Using conventional characters like letters or punctuation marks in unconventional ways—such as :-) to indicate a happy face—is an example of making use of typography, and it's a much older practice than you might expect.

In most published poetry, typographical choices are made by the publisher, according to its design considerations, rather than by the poet. For example, you may have noticed that in this book all the poems are in the same font as the rest of the text. That font choice was made by the textbook design team, not any of the poets. In many cases, typography is totally independent of the creative or compositional process of the poet. You might read a lot of poems and never encounter creative, purposeful use of typography, but it's worth a quick discussion.

When we stop ourselves from assuming that all typography is conventional and pay attention to how a poem uses typography and where it might stray from the purely conventional, we open ourselves to yet another layer in the complexity of the poem. Even if the poem isn't making any interesting use of typography, looking at the typography is still one more way for us to slow down and pay attention to everything.

Typography in "l(a"

Arrangement is more important in the opening poem than typography, but a neat use of typography echoes the subject of the poem. Notice how four of the lines begin with the lowercase letter "l." The character for the letter "l" is identical to the character for the numeral "1" in many typefaces, including the one in which we display it here and the one in which the poem originally appeared.

That means four of the lines appear to begin with the number "one," echoing the subject of loneliness. This couldn't be achieved with a typeface that didn't reuse the same character in this way. It's a typographical effect.

Expressive Typography

Let's take a look at a poem that uses typography to subtly establish the situation:

Yr Appt: *10:30 Thursday*

A looming orange guy
with a long split tail
edged in silver,
emperor of other fish
5 —too quick or by god he'd eat them—
turns, returns,
scorns the little scuba diver
discovering the treasure chest
again and again.
10 Tail flashes as he turns
drifts
rises in idle levitation
travels east/west along the smudged glass
a cobalt eye takes in fray of carpet,
15 exhaustion of faded purple
chairs, reliquary issues of *Allure*, of *Better Homes*,
of *Country Living*, of *Sunset*,
their corners drooping on the rack
beside the nurses' station.
20 If he takes in my presence,
my panic, he gives no sign.

Walt Schaefer, 2019

How does this poem use typography? We might notice the words in italics in lines 16 and 17, but that's conventional—those words are the titles of magazines. Is anything else out of the ordinary? Hopefully you noticed the title. The time and day are in a handwriting font over a heavy line. What in the world is that all about? The use of typography creates an allusion. You're either going to understand this, because you've witnessed it in your life, or not.

Many doctor's offices give out "Your Appointment" cards with a blank line for the receptionist to write a reminder of your next appointment time. The handwriting font replicates the look of this card and makes it clear that, if we get the allusion, this poem relates to an appointment at a doctor's office.

Unconventional Typography

This next poem uses typography in an entirely different way:

Fog
and the cranes resting over unfinished houses
and the houses, the lights left on in them, the river, all
drift off like the signature completing a suicide note.

~~Dear~~
~~those who will love me more in my absence,~~

Dear you who will forget what I looked like,

~~*Last night I was a drawbridge,*~~

~~*Last night I was the fog swallowing*~~
~~*a drawbridge*~~

For the first time, this morning I could see you
through the fog as a drawbridge sees the ship
that breaks it in two.

10   Into the silence, jackhammers and invisible grinding.
Voices within voices. Even without light I know dawn
is running through the city and the larger city beneath it.

If destruction hinges on what is beautiful
in making, let ~~my soul~~ my body collapse
15   *into roots something foundational.*

Now that I'm awake, it's time to carve up the day
into hour and progress. Into dig and follow. It doesn't matter
that I can't see what I know to be there.

Only after the body is gone do words come freely.
20   *I am sorry and you are sorry and ~~I think~~ I love*
that we don't know what for.

It's as if through cloudy glass three stories above the rooftops
the sky and city alloy. Ghost ships pass through the cathedrals.
Skyscrapers bellow for the bridge to part.
25   There are still things that need

to be said.

John Sibley Williams, 2014

Nonstandard typography can be seen right off the bat with the italicized stanzas and the strike-through text within those stanzas. What are those typographical choices doing in the poem? We need to dig into that a little bit to understand how they're working in close concert with the poem's content.

The poem seems to have two speakers. One describes a city coming to life at dawn, and another speaker writes a suicide note. At the end of the first stanza, the first speaker introduces the idea of "the signature at the end of a suicide note." This signature is the vehicle in a figure of speech that describes the tenor, the way "the cranes resting over unfinished houses, the houses, the lights left on in them, the river all drift off."

Then the second stanza picks up the imagined suicide note. The voice of the second speaker is consistently separated not only into its own stanzas but also through indented arrangement and italicized typography.

The strike-through text might mimic a crossed-out handwritten draft. This technique emphasizes the identity of the second speaker as a note-writer and reinforces the impression that we are reading a note. More than that, it shows the thought process of the speaker at work, giving us a record of compositional choices made. It reveals the speaker's character and thoughts as he gropes his way toward this final statement. Also, each crossed-out word or phrase opens up an alternate possible meaning of the sentence and passage it's in. None of that would have been possible without the use of typography.

The visual elements in a poem may complement or contrast the story and song elements, or they may do some of each at the same time. Tension, originality, beauty, surprise, complexity, curiosity, and delight are all created when the eye, the ear, and the mind work together on multiple levels simultaneously.

Concrete Poetry

Concrete poetry is a term used to describe a poem in which the visual elements do more than add a visual component to the text. They turn the text into a visual representation of the poem's content. As with many things in the world of poetry, there is no bright line that divides concrete poetry from other poems. Many might argue that our opening poem is a concrete poem because the image on the page suggests a lonely branch or a leaf falling through the air. However, most people reserve the term to refer to a poem that creates such a strong representational image that its meaning can be understood at least on some level even if the audience doesn't read the language the poem is composed in.

Concrete poetry is very, very old. We have some surviving example of Greek "picture poems" in the shape of pan pipes, a hatchet, and an egg from the fourth century BCE. The production of tiny images made entirely of verses written in highly stylized letters, is a tradition in Hebrew and Arabic dating back to at least the ninth century BCE. This is of interest not only as an example of concrete poetry but of the use of visual poetry to circumvent social and religious proscriptions against representing living beings in images.

[Figurative Calligraphy in the Shape of a Stork]

Ismâîl Zühdü, c. 1799

There are no known surviving examples of concrete poetry in the West through the Dark Ages, but beginning in the High Middle Ages, we find examples of poems using visual design carved into church woodwork, as the example on the next page, which comes from Germany in the early 1500s.

[Gerechtigkeitsspirale (Spiral of Justice)]

Anonymous, executed by Erhart Falckener, 1510

After the invention of the printing press, poets began almost immediately to experiment with visual elements. Poets used typography and white space to create an image of what the words described in what seemed like an innovation. This was certainly the first time that concrete poetry reached large audiences. Here is an excellent early example:

Easter Wings

Lord, who createdst man in wealth and store,
Though foolishly he lost the same,
Decaying more and more,
Till he became
Most poore:
With thee
O let me rise
As larks, harmoniously,
And sing this day thy victories:

10   Then shall the fall further the flight in me.

My tender age in sorrow did beginne
And still with sicknesses and shame.
Thou didst so punish sinne,
That I became
15   Most thinne.
With thee
Let me combine,
And feel thy victorie:
For, if I imp my wing on thine,
20   Affliction shall advance the flight in me.

George Herbert, 1633

The variable indentation creates two stanzas that each look, just a bit, like outspread wings—the subject of the poem.

Concrete poetry continues to appear from time to time, generally as a small eddy in an avant-garde stream, or as an occasional experiment by a poet working mostly in more conventional modes. Here's a contemporary example, perhaps a bit less obvious than Herbert's. Be sure to put it through the basic reading, and figure out the situation before you think about how the image reflects the content.

What the Old Mole Said

Well said, old mole! Canst work in the earth so fast.
A worthy pioneer.
— Hamlet (*Hamlet*, Act I, Scene V)

in our day
        tunnel vision, son.
                that's how we pushed
                        the grubby ground—

18-feet per hour—

record time.

we did not lunch behind

raspberries or catch

our breath beneath

a hosta leaf.

indeed, we mounded

incidental casualties

above our underground—

a stretch of woolly thyme,

a blatant columbine,

a pansy in the way—

but gave no heed

to squirrels' nuts

or squawking stellar jays.

we drilled through clay

and stoney clotted dirt.

no sissy flower beds

for us or fluffed-up strips

of red bark dust.

here and everywhere

we sneered at sonic blasts,

snubbed stinky-bomb attacks,

steered clear of poisoned traps.

we got to laugh the last.

now quit your whine

and show me what you're worth.

slough off your antic self

and pump those flat forelimbs.

slick back your velvet fur

and swear you won't procrastinate

to mine the grub-filled earth.

to eat or not to eat,
you're on your own, my son.

Carolyn Martin, 2014

What's being portrayed here? The title tips us off to the most important elements of the situation. The speaker is "the old mole," and in the second line the addressee is made clear—his son. What does the old mole discuss? Tunneling, digging through the earth, a mole's work. The use of indentation and short, short lines creates a concrete image to match: a tunnel running through the page like the mole's tunnel runs through the earth.

Final Thoughts

If a poem comes to you in any visual medium, on a screen or on a page, you need to pay attention to the fact that it is like a picture, in some ways, just as it's like a story and a song in some ways.

Poems make use of two main elements to achieve visual effects —arrangement and typography. Arrangement describes everything the poet does to place the words and punctuation in space, including the use of white space between lines or stanzas, indentation, margin spacing, alignment, and everything else. Typography refers to both the typefaces and choices within them, such as size, capitalization, italics, and so on. Concrete poems use these visual elements to create actual images that portray the content of the poem in some way.

To finish off the chapter, here is a list of reminders, tips, and tricks to help you as you work with the visual elements in a poem:

- When analyzing arrangement, try rewriting the poem using more conventional arrangement or translating arrangement effects into more conventional ways of achieving those effects, as we did when working with difficult syntax.

- Consider typography any time you see text that differs from conventional prose. When you feel the typography jump out of the background and make itself known, you're dealing with a poem in which this effect needs attention and analytical thought.

- Always look for patterns. Do patterns of syntax or diction consistently occur in conjunction with a certain typographical choice? Do typographical effects occur at consistent places in the syntax of the sentences, suggesting missing punctuation? Do they coincide with song elements, like a caesura or a change in meter? Do capitalized words seem to take on extra importance in the context of the story?

As you analyze the poem's visual elements, remember that you're not playing a game in which the goal is to ferret out the hidden "true meaning" of the poet's intentions. By now, you should know that you're just noticing what's on the page and what it makes you think and feel. No rules say this or that sort of arrangement automatically corresponds to this or that intended effect in the reader's mind. All you need to do is be attentive to the text and to yourself.

At the same time, keep in mind that these are choices the author made. They're not mistakes. The author wanted to do something that couldn't be better achieved through other arrangement choices. They are an attempt to communicate, to add beauty or meaning, so pay attention to them.

Exercises

This section gives you the chance to practice your understanding of these visual elements through guided readings of three poems and through focused creative writing exercises. Your professor may or may not assign them, but they are also designed to be completed independently.

For Readers

These poems each present clear and interesting opportunities to practice understanding and appreciating typography and arrangement. If you're not given specific assignments by your professor, try this for each poem:

1. Complete the basic reading.

2. Jot down your own initial impressions: What did you understand to be happening on the literal level in this poem? Did you like it? Can you say how or why?

3. Write a list or paragraph-length description of the arrangement in each poem.

4. Use a highlighter or a pencil—or something—to physically mark on the printed page any place that the typography seems unusual. Write out a list or description of what you find.

5. Think about anything the appearance of the poem on the page reminds you of visually. Does it create any sort of quasi-representative image? Write down anything you see.

6. Think about any way the poem on the page suggests something through images, even if it doesn't actually represent them directly. Write down those associations.

7. Brainstorm a list of any ways the appearance seems to correspond to, add to, or play against the content. This is a great activity to do in a group or with a partner.

Poem 1

This poem opens with an allusion, so be sure to look it up. Because it's an older poem, be prepared to work through slightly less accessible syntax and diction. As you're reading, notice how many elements the poem engages other than the picture elements. For example, did you notice the rhyme?

COLOSSIANS III.3

OUR LIFE IS HID WITH CHRIST IN GOD.

MY words and thoughts do both express this notion,
That **LIFE** hath with the sun a double motion.
The first **IS** straight, and our diurnal friend:
The other **HID**, and doth obliquely bend.
One life is wrapt **IN** flesh, and tends to earth;
The other winds t'wards **HIM** whose happy birth
Taught me to live here so **THAT** still one eye
Should aim and shoot at that which **IS** on high —
Quitting with daily labour all **MY** pleasure,
To gain at harvest an eternal **TREASURE**.

George Herbert, 1633

Poem 2

This poem's visual elements are both subtle and important. Keep working through it until you're sure you've found them all; there might be more than you expect at first. The epigraph also provides a sort of allusive reference to the upcoming poem's visual elements. Look up some of Merwin's poetry, and you'll see how.

Humans

a brief and strange species
— *W. S. Merwin*

the day begins in disarray *you ought you should you must*
you must you must you must   the bees will not

be stilled   what stitches mind to body   who cues the unraveling
if it's true we're infused with something not found in doorknob bird or bee

5 why am I confused about all the important things   crows
trampoline the power lines from house to house   they don't care

who runs the world   I gape at the sky   color of sunflower
color of blood   the world is not as I have believed it to be

I find no vantage   no long view across even the surface
10 peristalsis propels the worm into darkness   electricity

animates the lamp   the leaf drinks at the top of the tree
I understand none of the beautiful things   the sparrow bathes

in dirt   I don't know why   the birds do not ask themselves
or each other how are we to live   they do not ask us to love them

Elizabeth Austen, 2009

Poem 3

This next poem also starts with an allusion in the title, and it's not the only one. Be sure you've looked it up and understood it. This poem is contemporary, but the diction might still be challenging for some readers. Take your time and use that dictionary!

The poet described this poem as "exploded." Do you agree? Thinking about that might be a good departure point for you, but don't stop there.

Kali Yuga

    Cesium sun
     down: the Pacific ROLLS, CRACKles blue-lavender

on

stacks

5 of axles   carricle for freighted thoughts

of roiling sea-mind, ever-churning,

               whipping

its semen spittle, weeping

     milky pools

10 Uranus's testes still POTENT, three   millennia   on

may the isotopes not likewise linger   engender so much

Or should we welcome the MONSTER APHRODITE en-Birthing

             a Kali of a goddess, FIERCE, devOUring,
              bare waist belted

15   by   industrious   hands   cut   off the button mid-press

          strung-together-give-peace-a-chance-in-death-as-never-in-life

     necklaced by skulls   denuded   of rapacious, brutish thoughts

needing only one of Her   INFINITE   hands to hold the latest head

another to collect the dripping

20   blood in the compost bowl

                 nothing must be wasted, and nothing ever is
but it circles and feeds
           living on the dead
               dead on the living

25   lightning in the volcano
                       amino acids from the plume
                       amoeba's secret assignations
                       breed a strange future in the mud
               clay baby arises
30   to kiss these chemicals and find its dread mate

Or perhaps we will remain unified next time
TheSkitteringOneWillNotDivideButAgglomerate
LockOnEachToEachAndGrowTogetherIntoTheGreatestMind
ThisWorldHasYetSeenUndifferentiatedFromHeart
35 HornedTogetherAtLastAPerfectReflectionOfTheCosmos

               looking suspiciously like this sheet of moving water
           this living   breathing   earth of clanking stones
                  whatever will be
                  has been and
40   is now
                      ha

Jennifer Kemnitz, 2015

For Writers

The following exercises help you get to know and practice the concepts related to arrangement and typography. They are not designed to produce finished poems but to help you experiment with these elements so that you can use them more effectively to create poems in your own time.

1. Try your hand at a concrete poem. Write one from scratch, or, looking at your body of finished work, revise a poem that currently makes no particular use of visual elements into a new poem that does.

2. Assign a value or meaning to a typographical element. For example, you might make every adjective bold, make words of dialogue ital-

icized, make all nouns capitalized, or perhaps put everything that makes you sad into blue-colored lower case letters and blue. The only limit is your imagination. Apply your typography "rules" to a couple of your own poems and see how it turns out.

3. Revise some existing poems by removing all the typographical distinctions—no capital letters, even—and all the punctuation. Try using white space to replace punctuation. Perhaps every time a sentence ends, for example, you start a new line, or you replace every comma with three spaces.

4. Create some random visual elements in a new or existing poem. For example, indent every third line or insert five spaces every ten words you insert five spaces. Make the column that the poem has to fit in no more than twenty-five characters wide. Start by playing around with these random changes and see how they feel. Then try tailoring changes to fit the poem.

5. Create a poem—but not a concrete poem—that can't effectively be read out loud. Think about that. How can you do that, and what effect will that have on the reader?

6. Write or revise a poem into two columns and see what kind of effects you can create with that format.

Chapter 13

Reading the Whole Poem

Why It Almost Never Ends with Stripping

You start out doing it for the bucks —
more than you'd ever imagined,
enough, at first, to make up for the rest
of the shit that comes along with the job —
the groping despite the "No Touching" sign,
the bastards who bring in straight girls to con-

vince them they're bi, the girls nervous and con-
tinously fidgeting, while cash —
sweat-stained tens — shake in their hands, signaling
you over to dance while they imagine
themselves anywhere but there. "It's a job,"
you tell yourself, you'll just hold out the rest

of the summer. But you realize the rest
of the girls said the same thing, and they've con-
templated quitting for years, give blowjobs
in the back for fucking crazy money.
You don't want to be them but imagine
living the way they do, see them signing

five-figure checks on shopping sprees, signing
feature dancer contracts at clubs. You wrest

with the fact that girls who have the image
of putting out make ten times more. Buy con-
doms. Keep them on you just in case. The sugar's
pouring in — you're only giving handjobs.

25   You hear what you can make at outside jobs
doing bachelor parties, you're signing
on for three most weekends, making it
hand over fist, stripping at clubs the rest
of the week. The girl who dances as Con-
30   suela Cummings says she can imagine

you being "the next big thing. Imagine
your picture on boxes — Not just a job,
a career!" You read over the contract —
mark Xs for things you'll do, or not, sign
35   on the line — $5k if you check the rest —
anal, gangbang, scat bring in the greenbacks.

These days you don't read contracts, you just sign
to compete with the rest of the gravy-
starved girls who try to imagine it's just a job.

Shaindel Beers, 2006

Most readers will find Beers's poem pretty intense. It expertly uses the elements we've discussed. It tells a powerful story in an original way. It uses vivid language, both literal and figurative. It sings a song with lots of interesting musical effects. Moreover, it does all this while maintaining a strict received form, including a regular meter. Not only does this poem contain all those elements, it transcends them. Its intensity comes from all those elements working together.

But something more is happening here. This poem is memorable not just because it's entertaining, not just because of the poet's impressive skill, and not just because it's beautiful. This poem is memorable because it reaches outside its self-created world and touches the world we live in. It applies itself to reality by asking questions, raising challenges, and making an argument.

Great poetry doesn't have to do any of these things. Great poetry can be a world unto itself. However, one of the amazing things a great poem *can* do is alter the arc of our lives, the shape of the world, by making us see that life—that world—a little differently.

We've spent most of this book taking poems apart, which is essentially what analysis means, but all that taking apart is meant to be a means to an end, not an end in itself. The final step of analysis is to put it back together again.

This chapter looks at two ways to bring the poem together and apprehend it as a whole. First, it's important to make sure you've accounted for all the pieces and asked how they work together as a whole. Second, it's critical to examine your emotional response to the poem. In the next chapter, we'll then take up the big questions of what a poem means, if anything, and why you do or don't appreciate it.

Reviewing All the Elements

Before we start to explore how a poem comes together to make a whole greater than the sum of its parts, it's important to make sure we've noticed *all* the elements at work in the poem and understood how each contributes. By doing so, we extend and deepen our conversation with the poem by forcing ourselves to review it systematically.

Often, we first notice and get carried away by an element that strikes us most profoundly—maybe the action, or the tone, or whatever—and that becomes the center of our attention. There's nothing wrong with that unless it closes our eyes to what else is going on in the poem. Sometimes we have to force ourselves to read the whole poem carefully and to pay attention to the story, song, and picture elements within it.

It's useful to record your thoughts in writing, even if you're not formally writing about the whole poem in this way. Taking some detailed informal notes will get the job done. Run through all the elements of a poem that we've identified in this book and ask yourself if and how each is present in the poem.

Form in "Why It Almost Never Ends with Stripping"

There are seven stanzas—six sextets, one tercet—in this poem, so there are thirty-nine lines. What else do you notice about the form? We can start by looking at the ends of the lines. If we chart out the rhyme scheme, we quickly find that there is some sort of pattern here, though it's messy. There are some rhymes, some slant rhymes, quite a few entirely repeated words, and some sets of words that are close to each other, but not quite repetitions, such as "imagined," "imagine," and "image." Every stanza also has one line-ending word, different in every stanza, which is a synonym for money—"bucks," "cash," "sugar," "greenbacks," and so on.

It's hard to describe the pattern exactly, but if we take the synonyms for money as repeated words, and if we take the nearly-the-same words as repeated words, we would have a pattern in which there are only six ending words being used in all six sestets. That's definitely something so artificial it can't be a coincidence. There must be a form—a recipe—being followed here. At this point, it's time to get help. Let's ask the internet. A web search for "poem form 39 lines six sextets repeat end words" returns this result:

> **Sestina:** A sestina is a fixed verse form consisting of six stanzas of six lines each, normally followed by a three-line envoi. The words that end each line of the first stanza are used as line endings in each of the following stanzas, rotated in a set pattern.

Thanks, *Wikipedia*! Of course, there's a lot more to know about sestinas, like what exactly the pattern of the repeating end words is. However, at least we now know that we're dealing with a fixed form or a variant on a fixed form. The poet substitutes synonyms for one word instead of repeating the word itself and uses a number of different semirepetitions, such as homophones ("wrest" instead of "rest") and different forms of the words ("imagined" instead of "imagine"). And then there's that first syllable ("con-") used as if it were a word. That's interesting. We'll come back to that.

What else can we learn about the form? All the lines are between nine and twelve syllables, and almost all come in right at ten. They all have four or five stressed syllables, mostly five, and if we scan the whole thing, we'll find it's roughly iambic, with a fair amount of substitution and variation. The poem is more or less metrically regular. Some definitions of the sestina call for it to be written in iambic pentameter. Others call for a ten-syllable line. Most say there's no particular metrical requirement. This poem's meter keeps it firmly in the sestina camp, even if we use the most restrictive of those definitions.

The degree of enjambment varies highly. Many lines are end-stopped, but others are strongly enjambed, including the every-stanza "super-enjambment" of the line breaking in the middle of a word beginning with "con-." Some stanzas end on an end-stopped line and others on an enjambed line.

Speaker, Point of View, and Tone

One striking thing about "Why It Almost Never Ends with Stripping" is that the point of view is second-person — "you." The speaker is not so much addressing you as an audience as describing you, your life, your decisions and state of mind. The reader is thus inserted directly into the action as a character. The speaker is apparently a nonparticipant, whose omniscience extends into the thoughts and feelings, hopes and fears, of the characters, including "you," the audience, addressee, and protagonist all in one.

The tone of the poem seems angry, disgusted, disappointed, maybe a little sympathetic in places. Is it judgmental? The anger shines through right from the first stanza: "the shit that comes along with the job," "the groping," "the bastards." All of the characters are described negatively: the men as groping bastards, the women in the audience as weak-minded captives, the other dancers and you the protagonist as somewhat hapless and certainly foolish, continually making worse and worse decisions.

No one in the poem encourages the protagonist to make better decisions or take better care of herself. The poem goes out of its way to point out that the protagonist knows better but keeps going anyway. The end has a sort of "I told you so" or "you've made your bed, now you have to sleep in it" feeling. On the other hand, clearly the poem wishes better things for the protagonist and all the "girls." We feel both the judgment and the sympathy.

Situation

This poem is set in a time and place that feel close—contemporary America. It's probably a city, someplace where stripping can seem like "just a job," where plenty of bachelor parties are held every weekend, somewhere not too far from where porn is filmed. Maybe it's pre-internet—no mention of the internet, but the porn comes in "boxes."

There are plenty of characters. There's "you," the protagonist of this little story. "Just for the summer" makes you seem like a student. There are the other dancers. There are the customers and the "girls" they bring in. There are the people who make the porn, and there are the other "gravy-starved" women willing to be in it.

The action is fairly clear. The protagonist takes a job as a stripper, just for the money, just for the summer. She makes plenty of money, even though it's unpleasant work, but she also notices how much more money the girls make who have the image of "putting out," and how much the girls make who actually do "put out" in whatever fashion. We don't have to imagine or project the fact that the protagonist doesn't want to have sex for money. The omniscient speaker tells us so directly. However, the lure of the money is too great, and she starts doing the same.

After encouragement to do so by another dancer, the protagonist then starts making porn videos. At first, she's somewhat selective as to what she'll do in the videos. But eventually, she'll do anything and doesn't even pay attention to what's asked of her before doing it. Competition from other women seems to be a significant pressure on the protagonist at the end.

Language

The poem is full of imagery, but it's not very descriptive or vivid. It references plenty of concrete things but leaves the details to the reader's imagination. The most closely and richly described scene is the "straight girls" brought in by "bastards" to "convince them they're bi."

The diction is striking—a lot of it would get beeped out on network TV. It's direct, blunt, vernacular, and some would say vulgar. Even setting aside the curse words and sexual slang, the diction is very accessible and colloquial. Most college students can probably read this without going to the dictionary.

Likewise, the syntax is generally straightforward. The poem replicates the directness and informality of spoken language or internal monologue in the places that the sentences are fragmented or run together.

There is little figurative language in the poem, maybe none, except those phrases that have passed into vernacular diction: "making it hand over fist," the various euphemisms for money and sexual acts, and so on. But mostly, the poem's language is very literal.

Music

The most musical element in the poem is the rhyme/repetition scheme that we already described when we identified the form. See how it all ties together? The lines are loosely iambic and almost uniformly pentameter. Looking closely, we might notice now that the rhythm impacts the syntax and diction somewhat. Some connecting words, such as conjunctions and prepositions that we'd expect in formal writing, are missing.

With closer reading, we might notice a light, uneven but consistent pattern of alliteration. Accented initial consonants often repeat two or three per line or two lines. Most probably wouldn't hear it on a first reading or listening, but there it is.

Even though careful examination definitely reveals song elements at work in the poem, most of us might, at first glance, describe the poem as conversational or even proselike. How exactly the poem's music functions or contributes to its overall effect is a question worth coming back to later.

Visual Elements

The line lengths are governed strictly by the meter, not visual considerations. The poem's length on the page, whatever it turns out to be, is a side effect of the rhythmic choices that make the line. We end up with lines of generally the same length. None, for instance, extends much beyond the length of the title or is less than two-thirds the length of the title, which gives the poem a loose, general uniformity.

The white space between stanzas complements the formal patterns of the sestina and reinforces the strong divisions between stanzas. The visual isolation and differentiation of the envoi, or final tercet, seems especially strong. Otherwise, though, the poem makes no particularly striking use of visual elements.

Summary

What most people notice immediately in this poem are the situation, the diction, and the tone. It's important to be attentive to the strong formal and musical elements as well, though, as we assemble as complete and deep an understanding of the poem as we can. We might not catch these elements if we concentrate on the more readily apparent elements. You might also miss some of the complexities of the point of view and tone if you don't slow down and consider them methodically.

How the Poem Makes You Feel

We've spent a lot of time in this book *thinking* about poetry, which is good and worthy. But thinking is only one way—and maybe not the most important way—we respond to art. Most art makes us feel something, and maybe lots of things. For many poets and readers of poetry, the emotional experience of the poem is the most important one.

Feeling is an essentially subjective experience. And one of the seemingly inescapable features of the academic approach to art is that it doesn't make room for discussing emotions. We feel what we feel—what is there to say about it? Feelings aren't going to be graded or assessed. We don't even have a great vocabulary or method for discussing feelings in English. How often have you tried to tell someone how you feel and found that the right words won't come, or the words you use end up not fully or accurately expressing your feelings?

In a college-level literature class, the object is not to discuss how a story or poem makes you feel. Instead, the course equips you with tools to better understand the poem and its various contexts. You learn the structures, patterns, and conventions that give the poem shape. The course ultimately provides you a vocabulary for talking about the poem with others. Learning to think more clearly about a poem doesn't prevent or replace the emotional experience—it just doesn't get into it because it focuses on the poem rather than you.

At the same time, articulating your feelings about a poem and trying to understand why they arise, even if only to yourself, deepens your intellectual understanding by drawing your attention to elements you might otherwise overlook. By realizing when and if your emotional reactions come from something other than the poem, you can set your reactions aside and listen to the poem more carefully.

An emotional response is a signal for you. A poem makes you sad? Why? Is there anything "objectively" sad in the situation? If not, where is the sadness coming from? Often your unconscious mind notices things that slip past the conscious awareness, at least at first. Trust the feeling, at first, and investigate. See if it leads you somewhere.

The non-story elements may create a feeling or contribute to a feeling. Diction, for example, often does this. A string of words with strong emotional connotations can conjure up an emotion under the radar of the conscious mind. Musical elements can do this, too. A poem may have a bouncy nursery-rhyme rhythm, for example, that lightens the mood or creates a warm nostalgia for you. Lots of harsh consonants might make a grating, irritating impression without you even noticing. Who knows? The point is, as ever, to be attentive and be curious.

An initial emotional response can be—and often is—not based on the poem but on some memory or condition from your own life that the poem reminds you of. Your response to some isolated part of the poem—or even to something you *think* the poem is saying—can overwhelm what the poem is actually trying to tell you.

Pay attention to how a poem makes you feel, but don't let your feelings get in the way of listening to a poem.

We all know people who, when you start to tell them about your day, respond with a story about their day instead of acknowledging or asking about anything you just said. You know other people who, when you start to explain something that you're worried about, interrupt you to defend themselves against some presumed attack that they imagine is part of whatever you started to say. You know the people who cut you off and say "no" before they've even heard the whole plan because they did something like that once and it turned out terribly, a story they're happy to tell you right now for your edification.

You don't like this kind of treatment, right? Poems don't like it, either.

Many students will see a line, a phrase, or a character and form an incomplete understanding of the whole poem based on that quick, initial, and partial reading. Others may misunderstand a difficult element within the poem because it has some personal resonance, and then they respond to that personal experience rather than to the poem itself. It's normal to be reminded of things in our own lives by art and to have emotions based on those memories and associations, but when incomplete understanding triggers an emotional response that overtakes your entire reaction to the poem, that's a problem.

This doesn't mean those reactions are bad, wrong, or need to be ignored or rejected. It just means you need to give the poem a chance to be itself. You need to listen to it instead of responding to yourself and whatever it is about yourself that the poem reminds you of. The poem can't help what you bring to the reading, so don't make it responsible for that baggage.

It's good to notice your emotional reactions, to put a name to them and ask where they come from. It's good to check to see whether your reaction comes from the poem itself or from something the poem reminds you of. However, once you've done that, it's time to set those feelings aside as you work through your reading of the poem. Once you have a solid understanding of the poem that is as complete and accurate as it can be, you can then revisit those feelings and ask whether the poem really supports or corresponds to them.

Final Thoughts

The goal of analysis is not simply to separate and examine the parts of a poem individually but to reach a deeper understanding and appreciation of the whole poem. The final step before trying to get to that holistic understanding, though, is a thorough re-examination of the parts, with an emphasis first on making sure you haven't missed anything and second on how they interact.

After double-checking your understanding of all the elements, but before moving on to examine the possible meanings of a poem and your appreciation of it, it's also important to fully explore how the poem makes you feel. A central element of that exploration is sorting out what's actually in the poem from what you are projecting into the poem based on what it triggers in your memory or experience.

To finish off the chapter, here is a list of reminders, tips, and tricks to help you as you work on reading the whole poem:

- Let the elements we've studied in this book provide a sort of checklist. You're not ready to move on to talk about the whole poem until you can explain how *each* element is functioning in it.

- Analyzing the elements is a recursive process. As you closely examine the form, for example, you might notice something you had missed about the diction. As you study the visual elements, that might help you see something new about the speaker. Be open to that back-and-forth process of thought.

- Pay attention to your own feelings as you read, and critically investigate where and why they arise.

- Don't let your feelings overwhelm what the poem is trying to say. Listen carefully to the poem's whole story before you respond.

Understanding and appreciating a poem can be a reflective, emotional, and sometimes even spiritual experience. The disciplined, intellectual approach cultivated in this book is meant to enable and deepen that experience, not replace or displace it.

Exercises

This section gives you the chance to practice reading—and writing—the whole poem through guided readings of three poems and through focused creative writing exercises. Your professor may or may not assign them, but they are also designed to be completed independently if you wish.

For Readers

Here are three poems that present clear and interesting situations to practice your understanding and appreciation of poetry. Unless your professor gives you other instructions, try doing this for each poem:

1. Complete the basic reading.

2. Jot down your own initial impressions: What did you understand to be happening on the literal level in this poem? Did you like it? Can you point to specific passages that you liked more or less? Make written notes or mark up the texts.

3. Do a deeper reading, and, using the list of elements from this textbook as a checklist, fully describe the poem. Then break it down element by element.

4. Write an explanation, informally and in the first person, but as honestly and subjectively as you can, of your own emotional experience of each poem. Capture the emotional journey you went through, whether it was intense and long or dull and brief, not just the end state you arrived at. This is about describing your mind at work as much as the poem.

Poem 1

This poem contains a fair number of allusions, so be sure to look them up as you work through it. Notice that the last three stanzas are a long, non-literal description of what "you'd see" if you "looked into [the speaker's] eyes right now." Also, this is very much a poem of place. The place might not be explicitly identified, but you should try to get a sense of where it's set anyway.

Pipeline

On the new calendar,
on a day no one cares about,
I wake with the taste
of galvanized nails in my mouth.

The fog tumbles off the bay,
and those who hunger
for a clean shave and fortune
prepare their strategies
for the pipeline
that will tear through our acreage,
a ninety-foot clear-cut swath,
hundreds of miles long,
suits and easy money.

A thin white noise hissing
at the back of everything—
even my boots carry the sound,
even the chimney caps,
a drawer full of bobbins,
a chipped pint glass
and its mineral-brown water.

During these last weeks of summer
I get shuffled
from one day to the next
like a tin bucket
passed along a fire line,
the water slopping out,
never quite reaching the barn
or the dusty horses.

I want the music of Eric Dolphy
to drift above the land surveyors
triangulating the west side
of our property, that brass tangle,
that shot glass full of eels.

I want Tarkovsky
35   to show them the apocalypse
in a pitcher of milk.

The summer's out there
crashing through its own trees,
breaking its spine.
40   the wheat growing near our fence
turns to long, ordinary grass.

If you looked into my eyes right now
you'd see the gray drone
of Ocean Avenue
45   and the white sails
the dead hoist.
You'd see the landscape
spinning like a compass needle
above the dirt of a new grave.

50   You'd see a group of men
huddled around a fire
discussing what they'll buy
with the checkbook they found
in an abandoned tract house—

55   the smoke rising into the air
as if something significant
were about to happen,
as if the day isn't being ground
to a fine powder
60   by the gears of an elegant pepper mill
resting on the glassy black table
of this new century.

Michael McGriff, 2012

Poem 2

The next poem includes a number of non-English words, and they're not incidental. Language and languages are one of the subjects of the poem. The poet has followed convention in italicizing non-English words, which makes them easy to find. There are some other words which might not be common even though they are English, so use the web to help you define all these terms.

Columbidaes

Your family stitched the *sagai* together just like that
and the pigeon couplet cooed pillowtalk at dawn.
I was taught how deep to bend, to whom to bow
and the art of brushing feet with hennaed hands.

5   My pigeons cooed sweet nothings in the pink
while my Gujarati ran dry, Hindi bled into high school Spanish
and the art of brushing your grandfather's feet
was a play at submission nobody believed.

My Gujarati dried up, Hindi bled into Tico Spanish
10   as your mother fed me eggless cake and *pani puri.*
We played at submission, everyone pretended
a *gori* was good enough for the eldest.

Maa fed me *pani puri* and eggless cake
the day I drowned in *chaniya choli* because
15   a *gori* was good enough for her eldest, so
your family stitched the *sagai* together just like that.

Jessica Mehta, 2017

Poem 3

The following poem rests in a nexus of allusions. One allusion is in the epigraph, a poem by W. H. Auden. The title is an allusion to another poem by Auden, "Funeral Blues." And then there's the central figure of the poem—Whitney. "Whitney" is an allusion, fully identified in the second stanza. If you're not familiar with "Whitney," learning about her will help open up the poem for you, and the title of the Auden poem given in the epigraph is itself an allusion—who is W. B. Yeats?

Funeral Blues for Whitney
(after Auden's "In Memory of W. B Yeats")

I.

On the day you found what we were missing
us skinny, hungry, thugged out
young boys
stopped dead in front of the boom-box.

5   Runs were froze. Crap Games almost deserted.
Hood niggas disfigured by public statutes
were transformed by the sound waves
of you back in the day.
On you and your instrument, we young thugs agreed

10   you were wonderful back in the day.
And far from our projects
little homies dreamed you in evergreen forests
ghetto nerds were transfixed by radio plays
scattered over a thousand stations

15   scattered—squared—to a thousand more affections
immediately and all at once,
immediately, every time
we heard you and called ourselves
       to be better than we were.

20 Immediately, as we dreamed to be
something grand if not grandiose
if only to win your heart.
If only then, we would scheme up some shit
to unearth the sword from our gravel stones
25 and win—win you—
and live happily in your kingdom
but the magic dust ate you alive.

II.
Earth, receive a troubled guest.
30 Whitney Houston is laid to rest.
Let this Newark vessel lie
emptied of our dreams.
For in the nightmare of the dark
all the masks we had of your majesty
35 ate your face, all our refusals
to look into your blackness
have blinded and scarred our eyes.
Have turned to brown ash
all our crystal strewn pedestals
40 in a parable of genius and dust.

And now you hang in memory over us
our lady of chemical and too human sorrows
trapped eternally in a crystal cage
only free in the shadow of Sirius,
45 only free in fleeting notes and electrons
of youth, love and limitless potential
before yours turned slow to a curse.

Robert Lashley, 2013

For Writers

In honor of the integrative focus of this chapter, this set of writer's exercises proposes ideas for ten whole poems. You've been practicing with all your tools. Now it's time to put them all together. You're ready—go for it!

1. Write a still life—a description of a place or scene, without narrative or character. Pick a room in your home or the view out a window. No characters or action! Keep it under twenty lines.

2. Write a dialogue: Imagine a conversation between your parents on the day of your birth in a single quartet. Give each two lines—call, response, call, response. Expand it by adding an opening couplet that consists of one line describing each parent physically.

3. Write a portrait: Describe a person you see frequently but don't know well. Try avoiding any evaluative modifiers, and only use sensory modifiers. Keep it under twelve lines.

4. Eavesdrop on conversations in a public place: Use juicy or odd bits of dialogue as kernels for poems. Write life histories for the people based on these few lines of conversation.

5. Write a love poem—without any figurative language at all. No metaphors, no similes, none of that.

6. Open the college-level dictionary that has become your best friend over the course of this book, and let your finger fall upon the page, and write a poem entitled with the random word your figure just chose. Do not reject what your finger chooses. Your finger knows the word you seek.

7. Can you read a language other than English well? Write a translation of an existing poem. Can't read a language other than English? Write an *imaginary* translation of a nonexistent poem or retell an existing poem in an older style of English. Rewrite a favorite passage from the Bible or Shakespeare.

8. Parody or imitate a famous poem.

9. Write twelve haiku, one that expresses the essence of each month in nature wherever you live.

10. Write a nursery rhyme. Try it out on a toddler.

Chapter 14

Meaning and Appreciation

Key terms: theme, interpretation, genre, lyric poetry

At long last, this chapter takes up the question of what a poem *means*, if it means anything at all. You'll learn three questions to ask about what the poem does designed to help you approach what it means. It will also give you some strategies for clarifying why you do or don't appreciate a given poem so you can share those reasons clearly with others.

This chapter refers back to Shaindel Beers's "Why It Almost Never Ends With Stripping" from Chapter 13, so make sure you have that poem fresh in your mind as you proceed.

Deepening Your Understanding

So far, we've avoided serious discussion of what a poem might mean, the question that students often want to start with. To be honest, it's a little risky bringing it up now, too. The question tends to be a shortcut for readers who want to solve the poem as if it were a problem. Even for students who know better, it can easily lead to tying the poem to a chair and beating it with a rubber hose. That's something we've tried to avoid.

We've instead focused on what the poem *says*—learning to listen to it carefully, learning to listen to all the elements it uses to reveal itself to us. Having learned to listen carefully, however, we're ready to delve deeper into understanding poems. This section presents questions that will help you do that. Just promise not to get carried away.

Does the Poem Ask Questions?

Some poems ask us questions—or they ask the world questions on our behalf. Sometimes a poem literally and directly asks these questions, as in this short excerpt from Langston Hughes's "Harlem:"

> What happens to a dream deferred?
> Does it dry up
> like a raisin in the sun?

By raising questions like this, a poem invites you directly into some issue that it is struggling with, and you automatically draw on your own life as you attempt to answer. As you listen to the Hughes poem, you may not know the speaker's dreams or why they were deferred. However, everyone has dreams that they have to wait to achieve or that are never fulfilled. After reading these questions, you go to your experiences—your dreams deferred—and thus the world of the poem reaches out and connects itself to your world. Next you begin to think about others and their unfulfilled dreams, and so the poem extends into the broader world of your experience and knowledge.

In many poems, the questions are implied. A poem may make an assertion that seems counterintuitive to you. Or a poet might use a pronoun with no antecedent, as Beers does with the pronoun "it" in the title of her poem. These are all ways to raise questions.

Questions in "Why It Almost Never Ends with Stripping"

Let's consider the questions raised by Beers's poem. The title starts with a question word—why. It tells us that the poem is going to answer a question. It's a sly way of asking, "Why does it never end with stripping?" And wait, what does "it" refer to, anyway? "It" must be something that begins with stripping but doesn't end there, something for which stripping is the first part. Whatever "it" is, that's what this poem is about.

The title's question entangles our world and the poem's world. Maybe stripping is something you can connect to your own life, or maybe not.

Maybe the question connects to something in your direct experience, or maybe not. However, we can all relate to starting something for one reason and having it turn out altogether differently. And if this isn't a world you've experienced, the poem has suddenly brought it to you.

As the poem becomes increasingly dark, the main character goes further down the path of sex work—even though she doesn't want to—because the money is so good. By implication, not directly, the poem poses a more direct question for the audience: What would you do for money? What compromises of your own dreams, values, morals, or even safety would you—or have you already—made for money?

The poem also implies bigger questions. What kind of society do we live in, or what kind of people are we, that economic needs and desires force us to answer questions like these? What kind of world have we made for ourselves in which women's bodies are commodified like this? Why do men and women have this sort of relationship? Maybe it's even asking something deeper about human nature—why do we never have enough?

This poem will ask a lot of questions if you sit and listen to it long enough.

Does the Poem Challenge You?

When a poem asks a question, it wants the reader to wonder about the world, to be curious, and to learn more. When a poem raises a challenge, it forces the reader to take sides—to join the poem in objecting to something in the world, or to talk back to the poem and defend the world as it is.

This short excerpt from a longer poem, "Whitey's on the Moon," by Gil Scott-Heron, directly challenges the common understanding of an event most Americans celebrated as a collective triumph for the nation, if not the human race—the Apollo landings on the moon in the late 1960s.

> A rat done bit my sister Nell.
> (with Whitey on the moon)
> Her face and arms began to swell.

> (and Whitey's on the moon)
> I can't pay no doctor bill.
> (but Whitey's on the moon)
> Ten years from now I'll be paying still.
> (while Whitey's on the moon)

How does this excerpt challenge the audience? By highlighting not only the injury and illness of the sister but the inability of the speaker to pay for the treatment she needed, the poem challenges the assumption that the Apollo program was money well spent. It suggests that maybe that money would have been better spent on housing, sanitation, and healthcare.

The poem goes further, though. The "Whitey's on the moon" refrain clearly makes this a challenge not only about public spending but also about race relations in America. The poem also says that the Apollo program is not just an example of ill-spent public funds but an example of racial injustice and the systematic oppression of nonwhites by whites. Nonwhites are excluded from the planning, the decision-making, the collective triumph, and whatever benefits it might bring.

You can agree or not, but the poem challenges you to take a side. It's not asking what you think about an issue as much as it's telling you what it thinks about an issue and then demanding you respond.

Challenges in "Why It Almost Never Ends with Stripping"

It may not take a clear position on every question it raises, but the poem definitely makes some challenges as well. This poem has some opinions.

The title is a challenge, right from the beginning. This poem challenges an assumption about what happens working as a stripper — that it can stay what it starts out as, just stripping. "No," the poem challenges, "you're kidding yourself if you think that." On one level, that's a challenge to anyone contemplating taking a job as an exotic dancer. However, you might see that it's really a bigger challenge.

As a society, we have made stripping legal. By challenging what stripping really is, by asserting that it almost always leads to a lot of other things, the poem is not just challenging someone thinking about it as job. It's challenging all of society to reconsider what sort of industry we're allowing to flourish. Perhaps the poem challenges anybody who patronizes strip clubs — maybe unthinkingly, maybe casually, maybe as part of a group — to be more reflective and consider what kind of industry they're feeding.

Noticing these challenges doesn't mean you have to agree with the position they stake out. The poet might not even agree with them. But the challenges are there, waiting for your response.

Does the Poem Make Arguments?

An argument may also be challenging, but what distinguishes it from a challenge is that it works to back that challenge up with reasons or evidence of some sort. Sometimes an argument isn't especially challenging, too. A poem can simply make an argument about the way the world is or was without challenging you to consider how it should be. An argument is any idea about the world we live that the poem tries to show us is true.

Poems persuade us in ways that essays can't or don't. They're less likely to quote expert opinions or reference statistics or survey data. They're *very* unlikely to cite sources. Instead, they may make up facts and ask us to believe them, then use these "facts" as evidence. More often, if a poem makes an argument, it's likely to support that argument with the elements of story, song, and picture.

A poem's argument is often called a **theme**. However, "theme" is also used more generally to mean the subject or topic of a poem, or any concept that appears in a poem. The particular kind of analysis that focuses on explaining the poem's argument — all of them or one of them — is described as **interpretation**. This book has tried to steer you away from this question, at least so far, but it is worth inquiring into whether the poem makes an argument — after you have a solid under-standing of what the poem is saying, and after you recognize all the elements and how they work together.

Here is an excerpt from a poem whose argument is fairly obvious and direct, Robert Herrick's "To the Virgins, to Make Much of Time:"

> Gather ye rosebuds while ye may,
> Old Time is still a-flying;
> And this same flower that smiles today
> To-morrow will be dying.

First, make sure you get "gather ye rosebuds." This is a figure of speech in which "gathering rosebuds" is the vehicle and the implied tenor is "enjoying your youth." It is also an allusion to various biblical, classical, and other uses of the rosebud as a symbol of being young, especially the physical pleasures of a young, healthy body.

As long as that is clear, the argument should appear immediately. The first line presents the idea that the poem wants you to accept, believe, or do — its argument — and the next three lines give you reasons to agree with and accept that argument. The rest of the poem, by the way, continues in the same vein — enjoy your youth while you have the chance because time flies, and soon you'll be old and then dead.

Arguments in "Why It Almost Never Ends with Stripping"

Once again, the title is crucial. It proposes one central argument, that careers in stripping rarely end there. The rest of the poem tries to convince us that this idea is correct.

The first line explains why one starts stripping — for the money. In line 2, the poem develops the argument that the money is "more than you'd ever imagined." So, one starts stripping to make money, and it doesn't disappoint. The hoped-for money is there, even though the work is unpleasant.

The third stanza advances the argument further. We're introduced to others who have "con- / templated quitting for years," but instead "give blowjobs / in the back for fucking crazy money." Here's the first time the poem makes clear that stripping usually leads to prostitution. Why? *Lots* more money. It's hard to get out, too. The poem shows you other "girls" who keep saying they'll quit—but don't.

The end of the third stanza and the start of the fourth invite readers to imagine "living the way they do … signing / five-figure checks on shopping sprees." This subtly advances the argument by introducing not just the money but what it leads to—shopping sprees where tens of thousands of dollars are spent.

In the next stanza, we see the protagonist first contemplating then actively joining the others in buying condoms "just in case," and then "giving hand jobs," for which "the sugar's / pouring in." In the next stanza, we watch "you" progress to bachelor parties, "three most weekends, making it / hand over fist." What exactly happens at those parties is left unsaid, but the end result is clear.

In the penultimate stanza, the protagonist is making porn, after being urged to it by another dancer: "Imagine / your picture on boxes—Not just a job, / a career!" This sentence throws in another possible reason for "why it almost never ends with stripping"—fame, at least of the "your picture on the box of a porn video" sort.

In that last stanza, there's a shift. Up to this point, the other "girls" have been fellow travelers. In the final stanza, however, the protagonist "just sign[s] / to compete with the rest of the gravy- / starved girls." The motive suddenly seems more desperate. The other "girls" are the competition, antagonists. Until now, money was the driving force. The benefits outweighed the costs. In "these days," however, the protagonist apparently *has to* do whatever is asked of her because of the competition. Why the sudden change? The poem doesn't say. Whatever the reason, quitting no longer seems to be even a viable option, and that's the final piece of evidence for this argument.

This poem has grim opinions about the world of adult entertainment and the state of gender relations and sexuality in America. However, is it possible that the poem is arguing that at least part of the reason "why it almost never ends with stripping" has to do with human nature? Perhaps it's because it's so easy to stick with what's familiar even if we know it's not good for us. Perhaps it's because the power of money entices us to compromise our long-term goals, our values, even our own safety and health. Perhaps it's because we always want just a little more than we have. After all, in the world of the poem, there's no coercion, only enticement.

The poem might make other arguments. Finding and analyzing one argument doesn't mean there aren't others. And perhaps the short analysis here is missing something, some element of the poem, some nuance of language, that another reader—perhaps you—will see or hear and incorporate into a deeper understanding of what the poem says to us about ourselves, the world, and each other.

Forming Interpretations

Discussing a poem's meaning isn't a matter of solving a problem or a riddle. It's entering into a conversation. We're not trying to find the one right answer. Instead, we are trying to form an accurate understanding of something external, something coming to us from the outside, sometimes from very far away. We have to be careful and diligent and open-minded so as not to get it wrong, but we shouldn't mistake that for definitively getting it right.

In working your way through this book, you've built a foundation for not getting it wrong. That is, you've developed the skills of attentive reading to see and hear what the poem is saying. It's impossible to understand what someone means if you don't listen carefully to what they're actually saying, and that goes for poems, too.

Beyond that, however, there's a lot of gray area. Literary texts are complex and open to multiple interpretations and analysis. What we bring to a text as a reader necessarily influences how we read it and what it means for us. New readers are always bringing new insights, too, noticing new things, making new connections. Great literature is never fixed. It lives in dialogue with its audiences.

Nonetheless, literary analysis is not a game of make-believe. The poem's text has objective reality, and interpretations have to be grounded in the reality of that text. Some interpretations are obviously wrong because they are not grounded in the text, and putting them forward indicates a failure on the reader's part. Some interpretations are clearly right because they are so clearly grounded in the text. Missing them also indicates a failing on the reader's part. In between what's clearly right and wrong, however, there is a vast continuum. In that continuum are many possible opinions, explanations, and interpretations.

Generally, you judge the validity of an answer that falls into that gray area by the quality of the evidence. Does the interpretation account for everything that is relevant in the text? Does it limit itself to what is actually in the text? The more the interpretation does both of these things, the more valid it becomes. You have to take the text on its own terms and as a totality. You must support your interpretation, relying primarily on the text as your evidence.

As a good habit of thought, you should also try to avoid reducing poems to any one message or moral. Try to describe poems in terms of what they *do*—raise questions, make challenges, or put forward arguments about given subjects—rather than in terms of what they *are*. Instead of saying, for example, that the Beers poem "is an anti-stripping poem," say that the poem "raises serious questions about and challenges to the morality of stripping."

This approach helps keep your mind open about other things the poem might do and makes dialogue easier. It helps you resist the urge to think you have a poem figured out, and reminds you this is a conversation, not an interrogation.

Deepening Your Appreciation

Throughout the book, we've consistently differentiated between understanding and appreciating poetry. This section will talk a little more formally about the appreciation of poetry and present some strategies for deepening your appreciation and talking about the poems you enjoy.

As always, pay attention to your reactions to poems. You don't have to judge or explain or defend your reactions. Just notice them. Maybe say out loud or make a quick note in the margin: "I like this poem," or "I am indifferent to this poem" or "I hate this poem but am strangely drawn to it." Pay attention to reactions to passages or lines that stand out as you read. The point is to bring awareness to the mind as it reacts to what you read and not let those reactions pass by unnoticed.

Discovering Your Reasons

Once you are aware of how you're reacting, ask yourself why and assume there are reasons. Sometimes something calls to us or repels us unexplainably, but with poems, always start by assuming there are reasons that you can understand and articulate if you pay close enough attention. Usually, there's something specific happening in the poem, or in a part of the poem, that connects with and pleases or displeases you for some reason.

Think about your reasons in terms of the elements of the poem. Are you enjoying the story's happy resolution? Do you like the development of a character? Is the figurative language striking? Or, inversely, is the difficult-to-understand archaic diction off-putting? Is the unclear action making you lose interest?

This is a good place to check in with your emotional response to the poem and how that might be influencing your reaction. Do you like it because it makes you happy or fills you with hope? Do you enjoy the sentimental longing it fills you with? Do you dislike it because it makes you angry? Does the poem's depressed, hopeless tone put you off entirely?

Once again, pay attention to the difference between what a poem actually says and what a poem reminds you of. Do you dislike the poem because it reminds you of the grouchy grandparents you never got along with? Do you love this poem because it's set somewhere you lived and are fond of? These associations are a normal, human part of responding to art of any sort. However, if we work towards meeting the poems where they are and setting aside those associations, at least temporarily, we can grow as readers.

Another caution is to ask yourself if you're liking or disliking something because you think you ought to — maybe because other people do, or the teacher does, or for some other reason. It's certainly interesting to listen to other people's opinions, but trying to force yourself to like something never works for very long. If you don't like something, don't like it! That's okay. And if you do, then do. Just look for what in the poem is causing this reaction.

Comparing with Other Poems

A poem can be a complex thing, with lots of moving parts that might lead you to like or dislike it. Sometimes even when you *think* you know why you're reacting to a poem, there might be factors you're not aware of. It's good to cross-check your responses by making comparisons with other poems.

Perhaps you think you dislike a poem because the language is crass and vulgar. Remember that the next time you come across a poem with similar language. Do you have the same reaction? Maybe what you disliked in the first poem was not the vulgarity so much as what was being expressed in that rough language — the misogyny, for example. Sometimes it's hard to identify a cause without comparisons to help you isolate what's really going on.

One of the great things about learning to recognize and explain your own reactions is that you'll start to see patterns in them. When you keep an awareness that you "liked X about this particular poem" and "disliked

Y about that particular poem," you start to realize that these are the things you like and dislike about poems in general. As you progress, you're soon able to develop a list of these preferences, either unconsciously or consciously.

The broader and more complete you make that list, the easier it will be for you to find poetry you like and to deepen your appreciation for and understanding of the elements of poetry you most enjoy. It also gives you a vocabulary for finding and connecting with others. Understanding your own preferences is the first step in being able to talk about them.

Comparisons also give you a sense of new territory you might want to explore. If you notice, for example, that older poetry with archaic diction is *not* something you usually enjoy, that's good to know, and you can direct your reading or explorations toward more contemporary work. On the other hand, if there comes a point in your life when you want to take on a new challenge, you have an idea of where to head—merry old England. Taking the time and effort to master that older vocabulary could unlock a new world of beauty and enjoyment for you, or if you are assigned to study work that you know you haven't liked much in the past, you are at least forewarned. You have a sense of the task ahead and some knowledge of what you can do to make it as painless as possible. Forewarned is forearmed.

Articulating Your Appreciation

The most important reason to articulate what you do and do not enjoy is simply to work through and clarify it for yourself. Clearly explaining something is one of the best ways to develop and cement your knowledge of it.

First, think of your explanation as an argument. Explain your preferences and then show us exactly how the poem fulfills (or fails to meet) them. Focus on discussing the poem, not yourself, and think of the poem as your research material. All the evidence you need is in the poem. So, instead of saying, "I like this poem because it has great flow," try something along these lines:

> I like poems with strong, noticeable, interesting rhythm, even
> if they don't fit into established metrical patterns. I noticed that
> this poem alternates between lines with four to five stressed
> syllables and lines with two to three, regardless of how many
> total syllables there are in each line. The fact that the final
> stressed syllables in each line rhymes ABABCDCD and that
> the initial stressed syllables alliterate in the same base pattern
> really emphasizes the strong, regular rhythm.

Second, be specific in describing the poem. Refer to actual words, passages, or qualities that anyone else could find in the text. Avoid discussing subjective responses to the poem, such as "I like this poem because it is sad." Instead, point out elements of the poem that demonstrate a tone of sadness. Resist the urge to discuss subjective impacts as if they were universal, too, as in "the word choice in this poem would make anyone depressed." Instead, explain what you see in the poem and why you think it might create certain general effects. For example, you might describe the subjective qualities of the poem like this:

> Every image in the poem emphasizes darkness, coldness, and
> dampness; nowhere are light or warmth ever referred to. Most
> people find being cold, dark, and wet unpleasant and upsetting,
> so the poem seems to be projecting a rather depressing and
> dismal mood. It certainly gives me a creepy, sad feeling.

Third, explain your understanding of the poem alongside your appreciation of it, especially if the poem seems difficult to understand or if you feel like you have new insight. Sometimes people like or dislike a poem because they didn't understand it or they formed an impression of it based on a mistaken understanding. If you and your audience have different understandings of the poem, explaining your understanding at least clarifies where you stand. That way you can proceed to a discussion of your differences on firm ground.

Communicating what you enjoy in poetry can be a wonderful tool for developing your self-awareness, finding new poetry to love, and connecting to other people. Don't passively accept that you mysteriously like or don't like some things—investigate your reactions. Learn more about poetry and about yourself. Use what you learn to lead you to new poems and experiences. Feel confident standing up for what you like and explaining yourself and what you enjoy to others!

Final Thoughts

When people talk about what a poem "means," they're generally talking about how it reaches outside of itself and interacts with the world we live in and our shared experience of being human. One way to explore that aspect of the poem without tying it to a chair and beating a confession out of it is through questions: Does the poem raise questions? Does it offer a challenge? Does it make any arguments?

Being attentive to and articulating what you do and do not enjoy in a poem, and in poetry in general, is useful as a reflective act, and to communicate those things to others. Noticing your reactions, asking yourself why you have them, and looking for patterns in those reactions are key steps in developing your self-understanding. When explaining your likes and dislikes, though, be specific. Treat the discussion like an essay. The evidence for your argument must always come from the text of the poem itself.

To finish off the chapter, here is a list of reminders, tips, and tricks to help you as you inquire after the meaning of a poem and articulate your appreciation of it:

- Try not to jump straight into asking or assuming you know what a poem means.

- The foundation of interpreting a poem is always a thorough and attentive conversation with the poem. Make sure you're responding to the poem, not to what you think it says or what it reminds you of. Pay attention to all the elements and all the ways a poem is. Notice how the song or picture elements affect you, for example.

- Remember that it's okay to not understand. What you can explain, explain. What you cannot explain, you can still bear witness to.

- Keep an open, flexible mind. Make proposals about what a poem does, rather than attempting to define what it is.

- Pay attention to your reactions. Make short notes to track them. Don't be passive. Ask yourself why you like or dislike what you read. Always assume there are reasons for your reactions and that reacting to poetry is as explicable an internal process as any other.

We've now come to the end of this book—and the beginning, hopefully, of your deepening relationship with poetry. If you've been paying attention and asking questions, you have everything you need to make poetry your own and enjoy it the rest of your life. It can be among the best of companions, through good times and bad.

You should now know how to read a poem with confidence, free from the anxiety that you have to understand or like all poetry or any particular poem. You know how to carefully read a poem and deepen your understanding of it. You also know that poems aren't riddles or puzzles, that they don't have to be solved. You know that some poems or parts of poems might not be understandable in conventional ways, or at all, and you're comfortable with that. Poetry is yours now, in whatever way and however often you want it.

Having Poetry in Your Life

Having poetry in your life doesn't mean you have to become an English major or read poetry every day. It just means that you're not afraid of it, that you're open to it when you find it, and that you seek it out when you want it. You should always try to have a little poetry in your life. If you have even one or two favorite poems, or passages from poems, print them out or copy them out in your own fair hand. They might be song lyrics or passages from scripture. Put them on the refrigerator or above your desk. Put one on your kids' bedroom door or on the wall beside the TV. Keep them close by.

If you feel some desire to have more poetry in your life, it is not hard to find. The internet is full of poetry. The Poetry Foundation website is a great place to start. This extremely large, comprehensive, diverse, and well-maintained site links to many other of poetry's biggest homes online. *YouTube* is full of poetry readings, too, from sedate and scholarly recitations to intense slam performances and experimental mashups. Giant online booksellers like Powell's Books make it possible to find and buy almost any book of poetry ever published. And the internet is also home to lots of new poetry publishing, in the form of online journals or magazines. Poetry journals can be very old, established, and broad, like the journal *Poetry*. They can also be tiny, raw, amateur, and tightly focused on a subject, a community, a received form, or almost anything else.

If you're lucky to live somewhere with a decent bookstore, browsing the poetry section in person can be a wonderful way to drift into new work or find more by poets you've already learned you like or are curious about. It's also a great way to meet other people in your community who are interested in poetry. Likewise, a library is a good place to find poetry, and sympathetic librarians can help you get anything they don't have on hand from other branches or library systems. Librarians and booksellers are also likely to be good sources of information for poetry readings and other events.

Poetry readings, despite several centuries of gloomy expectations, have not disappeared. Poetry as an oral, performed art form is still part—albeit a small part—of popular culture. If you're interested in seeing and hearing poetry performed, it's out there. Poetry performances need a certain critical mass of people to be generated and sustained, so they're a little easier to find in larger towns or cities, or around colleges or universities: great places to look for poetry being performed and discussed. Most poetry events on a campus are open to the public. Other likely venues include cafes and libraries. Keep an eye on bulletin boards in these places, and websites, of course.

Another way to get more poetry in your life, or in new parts of your life, is to try your hand at writing it. Poetry classes, workshops, writing groups, and online forums abound, and they are likely to be found in, or at least through, the same sorts of places as readings. Colleges have for-credit classes and host noncredit workshops of all sorts. Bigger towns or cities often have dedicated venues for writing workshops.

This book has not pretended to be anything more than an *introduction* to poetry, which is a fantastically old and rich artistic tradition. We've only really talked about a single **genre** of poetry, the **lyric poetry**, and we've only discussed short lyrics written in modern English, which means in the past five hundred years. This is a good place to start, but there is much more to learn. If you want to explore poetry more in an analytical and intellectual way, you're just at the start of an amazing journey. Any one of the elements we introduced in this book can be an entire graduate education in itself. If you're in college, of course, you can look for more classes—ask your professor—but that bookstore or library is also full of books that can teach you a lot.

I hope you will find that whatever you invest in poetry and however much you open yourself to it, it will repay you a hundred times over. And if there's no place for poetry in your life right now, maybe there will be later. It will be there when you're ready.

Exercises

This section gives you the chance to practice your understanding and appreciation of poems through guided readings of three poems and through focused creative writing exercises. Your professor may or may not assign them, but they are also designed to be completed independently.

For Readers

Here are three poems that present clear and interesting situations to practice your understanding and appreciation of poetry. Unless your professor gives you other instructions, try doing this for each poem:

1. Complete the basic reading.

2. Jot down your own initial impressions: What did you understand to be happening on the literal level in this poem? Did you like it? Can you point to specific passages that you liked more or less? Make written notes or mark up the texts.

3. Answer the questions for deeper meaning from the start of this chapter: Does it raise questions? Does it offer challenges? Does it make any arguments?

4. Taking all that together, does the poem raise any larger significances to you? Is it about something? Is it meaningful? Does it have something to say about the world? Does it have something to teach the audience?

5. Pick one poem and write a brief argument that identifies what you think its central theme is. Explain how you came to this conclusion.

Poem 1

This is a quiet poem, but don't be fooled into thinking that means it has nothing to say. Consider this an opportunity to practice being quiet yourself—and to listen carefully. This poem is reaching out to your world with questions, challenges, and arguments a-plenty.

Winter Term

Men reach a certain age and rest:
forty-five for a decade,
seventy-two until death.

Only in academia
5   does this happen to women as well.
Something about the books,
and all that youth to push against.

They reach a certain frowsy middle-agedness
early, and then grow slowly into themselves
10   until, at sixty, they are gorgeous,

their beauty like the poems they read,
difficult to interpret
and enduring.

Karelia Stetz-Waters, 2019

Poem 2

The next poem stands entirely on its own, singing out some interesting questions, challenges, and arguments in a complex and strict form. It also makes an interesting counterpoint to the first exercise poem. Reading the poems together might help you deepen your understanding and appreciation of both of them.

Between Jobs
– OR –
25 Years in HR Management and All I Got Was This Lousy Poem

It's nine a.m. on Monday and I'm still 60 and it's still
December in Western Oregon where we've caught
up from the drought plus a foot or so. Don't talk
to me about Jesus and Christmas and the season
5   of hope. I'll cut you. I've little else to do these days,
and I could easily rationalize an ax murder. It's black

in there — my mind spins records day and night, black
platters, old-school low-down moanin' blues, dead still
between the cuts. Back in the world of work my days
10 were spent managing up and assessing down, caught
on the bottom line. I resigned without notice — a season
and time to every purpose under heaven — a time to talk,

a time to commit career suicide with nothing left to talk
about except the cost of COBRA, that necessary black
15 hole. Truth is, I couldn't do it another day. And my season
for career building is long gone so I find myself still
dressed in sweatpants this morning, cranky and caught
in the Food Network, my waistband expanding, my days

spent watching Ina Garten's fabulous Hamptons life, days

20 of watching her cook for trim gay men. I don't want to talk
to a career counselor. I want to get millennial, get caught
in a desire for crafting, perhaps knitting from skeins of black
yarn stashed in every room, so hip, or maybe felting still-
lifes of wool fruit into little hats—Saturday Market season

25 is almost here and I could use the cash. Loser season
lasts as long as I troll the Internet for jobs and the days
of résumés accrue rejection, compound loss. Yet I still
might dye my silver hair, trim my job history and try to talk
like today is the day my success begins but it gets black
30 early and I have Fritos to eat, and I'd rather not be caught

in chat rooms full of happy-talk job networkers caught
in their Zig Ziglar world. I knew it was end-of-season
when I quit, yet I don't want to give up my title, my black
belt in bootstrapping, my American male tale, my days
35 of stellar evaluations and respectful deference. I talk
about acceptance like I'll get there any day now, but still

there will be no graceful way through, caught in this still,
plush-black analog between songs, the season for talk
lost in bent-blue music. It's how I keep time these days.

David J. S. Pickering, 2019

Poem 3

Let's end with a poem about ending. Keats is not nearly as accessible as the two poets you just read, but he is just as rewarding, and you have the tools you need to enter into a long and rewarding conversation with this poem.

[When I have fears that I may cease to be]

When I have fears that I may cease to be
    Before my pen has gleaned my teeming brain,
Before high-pilèd books, in charactery,
    Hold like rich garners the full ripened grain;
5 When I behold, upon the night's starred face,
    Huge cloudy symbols of a high romance,
And think that I may never live to trace
    Their shadows with the magic hand of chance;
And when I feel, fair creature of an hour,
10   That I shall never look upon thee more,
Never have relish in the faery power
    Of unreflecting love—then on the shore
Of the wide world I stand alone, and think
Till love and fame to nothingness do sink.

John Keats, 1848

For Writers

As in the last chapter, this set of exercises proposes subjects for or approaches for writing actual, whole poems. These exercises are meant to help you create poems which focus on the outside world, rather than the interior world of the speaker.

1. Make a list of things you passionately believe to be true, activities that everyone should try at least once in their life, or places you think everyone should visit. Make the list as long as you can. Look through

the list and ask yourself if you could write a poem about any of them. Then, ask yourself if you should. Is there some reason why this *poem* must be written? Would it be more effective to make the argument in the form of an essay or something else? For arguments that would be best as poems, write a paragraph explanation of the argument and its reasoning. Then pick one of those and write your argument as a poem.

2. Write an occasional poem. This is a poem that commemorates and comments on a historical event. It could be an event you lived through or have only read about. Don't say anything not historically accurate. Write at least twenty-four and no more than forty lines.

3. Write an elegy, which is a lament for the dead. Make the tone and diction formal and elevated. Be completely honest. Don't write more than eight lines. Optionally, write an extended elegy of at least fifty lines, in which you relate key scenes or events from the deceased's life.

4. Write a devotional poem. Try to express how you feel about God. For an extra challenge, don't address the divine directly. You could try writing your devotion as a love poem.

5. Write a poem against love, but don't be bitter. Then try being as bitter as you want, and be more specific, too. Write an angry divorce or break-up poem. Need inspiration? Listen to Bob Dylan's "Idiot Wind." Also, never break up with a poet.

6. Write a poem that to your mind means nothing at all—makes no argument, raises no questions, challenges nothing. Need inspiration? Listen to Bob Dylan's "Million Dollar Bash." Give your poem to people and ask them to explain what it means to you. Record the answers and collect them.

Appendix A

Common Poetic Forms

This appendix includes descriptions of some of the received, historic forms that you are most likely to encounter in undergraduate college textbooks and contemporary American poetry. Because forms are often defined at least in part by patterns in rhyme, stanza, and meter, we use the terms and concepts explained in those chapters of the text without additional explanation.

Anglo-Saxon Meter

Anglo-Saxon meter, which is sometimes called "Old English meter," is inherited not from a distant foreign relation but from a dead ancestor—Anglo-Saxon, also known as Old English, the language spoken by the Germanic invaders of the British Isles who settled there in the Dark Ages. Only a few examples of what was probably a vast body of oral poetry survive, having been written down by literate monks using the Latin alphabet.

It influences us today in two ways. First, some of those remaining poems, such as *Beowulf*, are still read today, and modern poets frequently experiment with the form. Second, that oral tradition passed into the English popular oral tradition and provides the metrical underpinnings of genres as diverse as the nursery rhyme, the ballad, cowboy poetry, and hip-hop.

Anglo-Saxon meter isn't actually metrical. It relies on three major devices for form—alliteration, a fixed number of stressed syllables per line, and a strong caesura. It does not use rhyme and does not count syllables—only stresses. Because of this, it's sometimes called "alliterative verse" or "accentual verse" or some variation of that.

Contemporary Anglo-Saxon meter is generally defined by four stressed syllables per line, a caesura dividing those stressed syllables into two groups of two, and alliteration on three of the four stressed syllables. Like blank verse, it doesn't rely on stanzas for form.

In truth, Anglo-Saxon meter isn't written much any longer in its pure form, and while it has its passionate fans, it can sound too alien to many modern readers. However, there are some good examples, such as Wilbur's "Junk," which is in Chapter 10 of this book, or Pound's "The Seafarer." The following is the first section of this much longer poem:

from "The Seafarer"

May I for my own self song's truth reckon,
Journey's jargon, how I in harsh days
Hardship endured oft.
Bitter breast-cares have I abided,
Known on my keel many a care's hold,
And dire sea-surge, and there I oft spent
Narrow nightwatch nigh the ship's head
While she tossed close to cliffs. Coldly afflicted,
My feet were by frost benumbed.
Chill its chains are; chafing sighs
Hew my heart round and hunger begot
Mere-weary mood. Lest man know not
That he on dry land loveliest liveth,
List how I, care-wretched, on ice-cold sea,
Weathered the winter, wretched outcast
Deprived of my kinsmen;
Hung with hard ice-flakes, where hail-scur flew,
There I heard naught save the harsh sea

And ice-cold wave, at whiles the swan cries,

Did for my games the gannet's clamour,

Sea-fowls, loudness was for me laughter,

The mews' singing all my mead-drink.

Storms, on the stone-cliffs beaten, fell on the stern

In icy feathers; full oft the eagle screamed

With spray on his pinion.

Ezra Pound, 1911

There are others that can be quickly found online, including "The Land" by Rudyard Kipling. Many nursery rhymes, such as "Pat a Cake, Pat a Cake" also conform to Anglo-Saxon meter or are clearly closely derived from it.

Nineteenth-century English poet Gerard Manly Hopkins used a form he called "sprung rhythm" that is essentially an updated Anglo-Saxon meter, relying heavily on alliteration and accentual lines. Some stellar examples are "Spring and Fall," "No Worst, There Is None. Pitched Past Pitch of Grief," in Chapter 4, and "God's Grandeur," which is reprinted here.

God's Grandeur

The world is charged with the grandeur of God.

    It will flame out, like shining from shook foil;

    It gathers to a greatness, like the ooze of oil

Crushed. Why do men then now not reck his rod?

Generations have trod, have trod, have trod;

    And all is seared with trade; bleared, smeared with toil;

    And wears man's smudge and shares man's smell: the soil

Is bare now, nor can foot feel, being shod.

And for all this, nature is never spent;
 There lives the dearest freshness deep down things;
And though the last lights off the black West went
 Oh, morning, at the brown brink eastward, springs—
Because the Holy Ghost over the bent
 World broods with warm breast and with ah! bright wings.

Gerard Manley Hopkins, 1918

Ballad Meter

This multiheaded beast, which also goes by the names "common meter" and "hymn meter," is native to modern English. It probably evolved out of Anglo-Saxon meter in the Middle Ages as Middle English spread and displaced Old English throughout Britain. It emerged into poetry from the oral folk tradition of England and underlies not only a lot of verse but the language rhythms of lots of songs, including hymns in the post-Reformation English church and folk ballads.

The exact definition of ballad meter is not agreed upon by experts. Some think of it as an accentual form, counting only stresses per line, like Anglo-Saxon meter, while most define it according to more modern accentual-syllabic lines. Regardless, something related to this family of forms underlies a lot of popular entertainment today. Church hymn tradition and the folk ballad tradition are the immediate ancestors of the rhythmic and narrative structure of contemporary country, rock, pop, and hip-hop music.

We can point at least to some core common features. Ballad meter is defined by stanza rules, but it can extend indefinitely through any number of stanzas. The ballad stanza is a quatrain, generally rhyming ABCB, though the version used in hymns usually rhymes ABAB. The lines alternate between four stresses and three, so a line with four stresses is followed by one with only three, and then back again. If the meter is accentual syllabic, it is iambic, and again alternating between four and three—but this time three or four feet. The lines thus start with iambic tetrameter and move to iambic trimeter, iambic tetrameter, and iambic trimeter. Ballads tend to have strong stories.

Over time, the ballad stanza has been a very fertile field for experimentation and modification, perhaps because poets can count on a certain basic familiarity with it on the part of much of the audience.

Many anonymous folk ballads are preserved in writing, but most were probably meant to be sung with accompaniment. Some common examples include "The Cruel Mother," "Barbara Allen," and "Sir Patrick Spens." Many nursery rhymes are in ballad meter, such as Mother Goose's "Sing a Song of Sixpence:"

Sing a Song of Sixpence

Sing a song of sixpence,
A pocket full of rye;
Four-and-twenty blackbirds
Baked in a pie.
When the pie was opened
The birds began to sing;
Wasn't that a dainty dish
To set before a king?

Mother Goose (traditional), 1784

Almost all of Emily Dickinson's poems are written in or near hymn meter, and many conform to it quite closely, though perhaps using inventive slant rhymes instead of perfect rhymes.

Some other clear and accessible examples include "The Song of Wandering Aengus" by William Butler Yeats, "The Ballad of Rudolph Reed" by Gwendolyn Brooks, and "Carentan O Carentan" by Louis Simpson. A famous romantic poem in ballad metere is "La Belle Dame sans Merci: A Ballad," by John Keats, which is found on the next page.

La Belle Dame sans Merci: A Ballad

O what can ail thee, knight-at-arms,
    Alone and palely loitering?
The sedge has withered from the lake,
    And no birds sing.

O what can ail thee, knight-at-arms,
    So haggard and so woe-begone?
The squirrel's granary is full,
    And the harvest's done.

I see a lily on thy brow,
    With anguish moist and fever-dew,
And on thy cheeks a fading rose
    Fast withereth too.

I met a lady in the meads,
    Full beautiful—a faery's child,
Her hair was long, her foot was light,
    And her eyes were wild.

I made a garland for her head,
    And bracelets too, and fragrant zone;
She looked at me as she did love,
    And made sweet moan

I set her on my pacing steed,
    And nothing else saw all day long,
For sidelong would she bend, and sing
    A faery's song.

She found me roots of relish sweet,

And honey wild, and manna-dew,
And sure in language strange she said—
   "I love thee true."

She took me to her Elfin grot,
   And there she wept and sighed full sore,
And there I shut her wild wild eyes
   With kisses four.

And there she lullèd me asleep,
   And there I dreamed—Ah! woe betide!—
The latest dream I ever dreamt
   On the cold hill side.

I saw pale kings and princes too,
   Pale warriors, death-pale were they all;
They cried—'La Belle Dame sans Merci
   Thee hath in thrall!'

I saw their starved lips in the gloam,
   With horrid warning gapèd wide,
And I awoke and found me here,
   On the cold hill's side.

And this is why I sojourn here,
   Alone and palely loitering,
Though the sedge is withered from the lake,
   And no birds sing.

John Keats, 1819

Blank Verse

Blank verse is the form used by a great deal of long narrative and dramatic poetry in English. It was invented, as near as we can tell, by translators of classical long narrative poems in the early 1500s. All the great renaissance drama, including Shakespeare's plays, is written in blank verse, and so are epics such as Milton's *Paradise Lost*. It has never gone out of style for both translations and composing in these genres up through today.

Blank verse is unrhymed iambic pentameter lines, not broken into stanzas. It may make use of other patterns of sound repetition for musical effect, but heavy or consistent alliteration is not generally part of bank verse. Artful substitution and variation of trochees and minor ionics are common in blank verse. In the hands of a master like Milton, the subtle music of blank verse can be surprisingly and intensely enjoyable for the attentive listener.

Iambic pentameter is generally thought of as the meter most closely replicating spoken English. Spoken English tends not to tolerate more than three syllables in a row without varying stress, and a "one-two" pattern of "unstress-stress" is common and typical. Ten syllables, many suggest, is something like the average utterance between pauses for breath. Because most of us do not speak in rhyme, blank verse is the form that is most conversational, most natural, while retaining enough structure to create opportunities for artifice.

All of Shakespeare's plays and Milton's *Paradise Lost* are premiere examples of renaissance blank verse and are available online. You can find bite-size samples of both at the Poetry Foundation website. Here is the opening of the Milton poem, with the original seventeenth-century spelling and punctuation preserved:

[OF Mans First Disobedience] from *Paradise Lost*: Book 1

OF Mans First Disobedience, and the Fruit
Of that Forbidden Tree, whose mortal tast
Brought Death into the World, and all our woe,
With loss of Eden, till one greater Man
Restore us, and regain the blissful Seat,
Sing Heav'nly Muse, that on the secret top
Of Oreb, or of Sinai, didst inspire
That Shepherd, who first taught the chosen Seed,
In the Beginning how the Heav'ns and Earth
Rose out of Chaos: or if Sion Hill
Delight thee more, and Siloa's brook that flow'd
Fast by the Oracle of God; I thence
Invoke thy aid to my adventrous Song,
That with no middle flight intends to soar
Above th' Aonian Mount, while it pursues
Things unattempted yet in Prose or Rhime.
And chiefly Thou, O Spirit, that dost prefer
Before all Temples th' upright heart and pure,
Instruct me, for Thou know'st; Thou from the first
Wast present, and with mighty wings outspread
Dove-like satst brooding on the vast Abyss
And mad'st it pregnant: What in me is dark
Illumin, what is low raise and support;
That to the highth of this great Argument
I may assert Eternal Providence,
And justifie the wayes of God to men.

John Milton, 1674

There are many examples of blank verse available, including from contemporary poems. Here are some that should be easy to find: "Special

Treatments Ward," by Dana Gioia, "Epic Simile" by A.E. Stallings, "The Death of the Hired Hand," by Robert Frost, "The Idea of Order at Key West," by Wallace Stevens, and "The Middle Passage" by Robert Hayden. Here is the start of another long blank verse classic:

from "Lines Composed a Few Miles above Tintern Abbey, On Revisiting the Banks of the Wye during a Tour. July 13, 1798"

Five years have past; five summers, with the length
Of five long winters! and again I hear
These waters, rolling from their mountain-springs
With a soft inland murmur. — Once again
Do I behold these steep and lofty cliffs,
That on a wild secluded scene impress
Thoughts of more deep seclusion; and connect
The landscape with the quiet of the sky.
The day is come when I again repose
Here, under this dark sycamore, and view
These plots of cottage-ground, these orchard-tufts,
Which at this season, with their unripe fruits,
Are clad in one green hue, and lose themselves
'Mid groves and copses. Once again I see
These hedge-rows, hardly hedge-rows, little lines
Of sportive wood run wild: these pastoral farms,
Green to the very door; and wreaths of smoke
Sent up, in silence, from among the trees!

William Wordsworth, 1798

Ghazal

The ghazal is an even older form than blank verse, but its arrival in English is very recent. Poems referred to as ghazals are originally found in Arabic and written examples survive reaching as far back as the 600s. The form spread throughout the Islamic world through the Middle Ages, and in the areas now known as Turkey, Iran, and Pakistan, the tradition is especially rich. Regional variations between the versions of the ghazal are significant enough that some scholars consider them different forms sharing a name. In the Persian tradition especially, ghazals are closely associated with the mystical Sufi branch of Islam. Ghazals are often set to music.

The current popularity of the ghazal in English is almost completely thanks to the effort of one man, the Indian-American poet Agha Shahid Ali, who published widely in the 1990s and edited a collection of ghazals titled *Ravishing DisUnities: Real Ghazals in English* in 2000. Lewis Turco's *The Book of Forms*, third edition, which was considered authoritative and complete when it was published in 1999, barely mentions ghazals, but today they are very common and growing in popularity all the time.

A "real ghazal in English," as Ali defined it, is written in couplets. It must be at least ten lines long and is generally not longer than thirty lines. Each couplet ends with the same word, known as the "radif." The words before the radif rhyme, and are known as the "qafia." The lines should all be of the same syllable length, but stressed syllables are not counted or their pattern considered. Finally, the poet's name or a pen name should appear in the final line.

The content of each couplet should not be related in any obvious way to the content of the other couplets. Each is almost an independent poem, linked by the syllable count, the qafia, and the radif. Despite the theoretical disunity, though, the content of many ghazals seems to have at least some common subjects, themes, moods, symbols, or concerns.

Many English-language poets publish ghazals that are basically collections of free-verse couplets linked only by the radif. Some even do away with the actual repletion of the radif and turn it into a rhyming pattern instead.

Example ghazals you can easily find online include: "Miscegenation," by Natasha Tretheway, "Hip Hop Ghazal" by Patricia Smith, "Ghazal of the Better-Unbegun" by Heather McHugh, and "Tonight" by Agha Shahid Ali. We used *Derecho* Ghazal," by Louisa Igloria, as our key example poem for Chapter 2, when we discussed forms. "Ghazal," by Christopher Wicks, provides another contemporary take on this ancient form:

Ghazal

I know that you rejoice to see my stinging pain.
I've never doubted, when I feel this singing pain.

It permeates my nerves and fills my temples
When steeple-bells, too loud, call forth a ringing pain.

It's harsh as your dear voice is light and sweet.
The exquisite thought of you is forever slinging pain.

Like stones to foreheads, adhering to every cell
In my compromised brain, is this my clinging pain.

Like flame or hair-shirt, though, it leads to you
And dangerously does not balk at flinging pain.

From seed in furrows, where I, Christopher, sow,
The sweet fruit soothes not, but is only bringing pain!

Christopher M. Wicks, 2019

Haiku

The haiku is a Japanese form that arose in the early 1600s. In Japanese, the haiku is often part of a collaborative improvised longer poem, the *renga*, or part of a hybrid form that combines short prose pieces and haiku describing a journey, the *haibun*. A trio of Japanese poets writing from the early 1600s to the early 1800s—Basho, Buson, and Issa—cemented the form's enduring status in Japan.

The haiku was unknown in English-language poetry until the start of the twentieth century, when it exploded into the poetry world as part of Modernism's general fascination with east Asian aesthetics. The haiku was deeply influential beyond its adaptation as a form. Its extreme concision and sparseness, with its emphasis on the power of a single image or pair of images, became hallmarks of early twentieth-century poetry in general.

The utter simplicity and accessibility of the form also makes it popular in primary education in the English-speaking world, especially America, and many schoolchildren know how to write a haiku even if they know literally nothing else about poetry.

The structure of the haiku in English is not an uncontested concept. Debate rages among scholars about even so simple a thing—how should the tradition and strictures of the Japanese form be translated into English? This perennial disagreement about details aside, the English-language haiku is generally defined as a single unrhymed tercet. The lines are of a fixed number of syllables—five, seven, and five. Often a content requirement is part of the form—a single image or pair of images of the natural world. Many contemporary English-language haiku loosen the strict syllabic requirement into something like "three lines, all short, maybe the middle a little longer."

Here are some example haikus in English that you can easily find online: "A Dent in a Bucket" by Gary Snyder, "Small Poems for Big" by Chinaka Hodge, "Blackbird Etude" by A. E. Stallings, "Snow in my

Shoe" by Jack Kerouac, and "Whitecaps on the Bay" by Richard Wright. Here's a contemporary example that uses a common approach to the form, which is to present multiple haiku together. Each is independent, but both inform the other as well.

Two Rivers: Two Questions

We walk, Chief Kilchis,
The River bearing your name.
Does absence kill us?

Dead elk decomposed
Along the bank of Elk Creek.
Where does your soul go?

Nancy Slavin, 2015

Sestina

The sestina is a very old form. Sestinas from the late 1100s survive in writing, which means it probably existed even earlier. It was originally written in Occitan, a romance language like Spanish or French that is still spoken today in small pockets throughout southwestern Europe.

Traveling minstrels called "troubadours" from Occitan-speaking areas were famous throughout Europe in the Middle Ages for their skill as poets, musicians, gossips, and comedians. The sestina is only one of many forms they invented, but it is the one which is remembered and commonly used today. It entered English in the Renaissance, but it was not common until the late 1800s. It has remained popular in English ever since.

The stanza is composed of six sestets followed by a final tercet. The final tercet is referred to as the "envoi." The modern English sestina, like the villanelle, has no fixed line length or rhythmic pattern, but also like the villanelle, the lines tend to be around the same length throughout the poem, not either too long or too short. The main defining feature of the sestina is the repetition of the ending words of the first six lines in a fixed pattern. If we assign the end word of each line a number, the pattern is: 123456/615243/364125/532614/451362/246531. The envoi must include two of the six end words in each line, one in the middle of the line somewhere and one at the end, in this pattern: (2)5-(4)3-(6)1.

Example sestinas that you can easily find online include: "Sestina: Altaforte" by Ezra Pound, "Sestina" by Elizabeth Bishop, "Farm Implements and Rutabagas in a Landscape" by John Ashberry, and "Paysage Moralise" by W. H. Auden. The literary magazine *McSweeney's* publishes only sestinas. "Why It Almost Never Ends with Stripping," by Shaindel Beers, the key example poem for Chapters 13 and 14, is a sestina. So is "Like," by A. E. Stallings in Chapter 7. Pioneering American feminist Charlotte Perkins Gilman also wrote a number of poems in this and other demanding forms:

To the Indifferent Women

You who are happy in a thousand homes,
Or overworked therein, to a dumb peace;
Whose souls are wholly centered in the life
Of that small group you personally love;
Who told you that you need not know or care
About the sin and sorrow of the world?

Do you believe the sorrow of the world
Does not concern you in your little homes?—
That you are licensed to avoid the care
And toil for human progress, human peace,
And the enlargement of our power of love
Until it covers every field of life?

The one first duty of all human life
Is to promote the progress of the world
In righteousness, in wisdom, truth and love;
And you ignore it, hidden in your homes,
Content to keep them in uncertain peace,
Content to leave all else without your care.

Yet you are mothers! And a mother's care
Is the first step toward friendly human life.
Life where all nations in untroubled peace
Unite to raise the standard of the world
And make the happiness we seek in homes
Spread everywhere in strong and fruitful love.

You are content to keep that mighty love
In its first steps forever; the crude care
Of animals for mate and young and homes,
Instead of pouring it abroad in life,
Its mighty current feeding all the world
Till every human child can grow in peace.

You cannot keep your small domestic peace
Your little pool of undeveloped love,
While the neglected, starved, unmothered world
Struggles and fights for lack of mother's care,
And its tempestuous, bitter, broken life
Beats in upon you in your selfish homes.

We all may have our homes in joy and peace
When woman's life, in its rich power of love
Is joined with man's to care for all the world.

Charlotte Perkins Gilman, 1911

Sonnet

The word "sonnet" means "little song" in Italian. This form entered English from Italian sometime in the 1500s and has been in use, if not in always in favor, ever since. Its popularity is probably as great right now as it has ever been.

One of the things that accounts for the sonnet's perennial place among commonly used and beloved forms is its combination of strict formal rigor and almost endless flexibility. As soon as it got to Britain, it started mutating in the new climate of English and has never really stopped. Perhaps because it's so compact and has only a couple of fairly straightforward requirements, it readily accepts modification while still remaining recognizable as a sonnet and as part of the tradition.

There are so many varieties and experimental versions of the sonnet that there are a number of books dedicated solely to the subject. But for *this* book, we'll identify some more-or-less core defining features and the rules that govern the two most common types of sonnet.

Core Features

Predictably, there is not even agreement on this. However, for our purposes, we will say that a sonnet is a lyric poem, often a love poem of some kind, that is fourteen lines long, usually rhyming in some pattern, and usually in something close to iambic pentameter.

The content shifts or turns in some dramatic way, usually *from* some sort of argument, question, problem, or dilemma *to* a counterargument, answer, resolution, or solution. That shift in content is generally marked by some formal change as well—a stanza break or a change in rhyme pattern. The shift is called the "volta."

Anytime you see any poem that's fourteen lines long, you ought to investigate rhyme, meter, and content, looking for these or other patterns and start to wonder if you have some sort of sonnet on your hands.

The Italian, or Petrarchan, Sonnet

This is the oldest form of the sonnet in use. It's called "Petrarchan" because it was made famous by a poet named Francesco Petrarch, who wrote a much-celebrated sequence collected under the title *The Songs* in the mid-1300s. *The Songs* was widely read across Europe during the Renaissance. It was translated into English several times in the early 1500s and was widely enough known by Shakespeare's time to be a common target of both imitation and satire.

The Petrarchan sonnet is organized into an octave and a sestet. The volta occurs at the stanza break. The stanza break is often *not* indicated with white space, so at first glance, it seems to be a single unified stanza. The octave traditionally rhymes ABBAABBA. The sestet rhymes two or three new endings, usually CDECDE or CDCCDC, but variations are common. The meter is iambic pentameter.

Here are a couple of example Italian sonnets you can easily find online: "When I Consider How My Light is Spent" by John Milton, "How Do I Love Thee" by Elizabeth Barrett Browning, and "The World is Too Much With Us" by William Wordsworth. These are all a little older, but you can find contemporary ones as well, such as "Design" by Robert Frost, "Leda and the Swan" by W. B. Yeats, and this one, which you might have heard before, at least in part:

The New Colossus

Not like the brazen giant of Greek fame,
With conquering limbs astride from land to land;
Here at our sea-washed, sunset gates shall stand
A mighty woman with a torch, whose flame
Is the imprisoned lightning, and her name
Mother of Exiles. From her beacon-hand
Glows world-wide welcome; her mild eyes command
The air-bridged harbor that twin cities frame.
"Keep, ancient lands, your storied pomp!" cries she

With silent lips. "Give me your tired, your poor,
Your huddled masses yearning to breathe free,
The wretched refuse of your teeming shore.
Send these, the homeless, tempest-tost to me,
I lift my lamp beside the golden door!"

Emma Lazarus, 1883

The English, or Shakespearian, Sonnet

Because the Italian sonnet traditionally only uses four ending rhymes, it's more difficult to write one in English, which has relatively fewer easy rhymes than Italian. English Renaissance poets loved the compact structure and intensity of the sonnet, but they chafed at the rhyme requirements. Various modifications of the Italian version allowing for more rhymes arose, but the form we know as "English" became dominant and was made famous by the playwright William Shakespeare, whose collection of 154 English sonnets, published in 1609, still defines the form for many. This is why this form is also known as "Shakespearian."

The English sonnet is organized into three quatrains followed by a couplet. The rhyme scheme for the entire poem is ABAB/CDCD/EFEF/GG. The volta occurs between the final quatrain and the couplet. Often the first three stanzas describe a situation or dilemma and the final couplet states a conclusion or theme or lesson that can be drawn from the situation. Often each of the quatrains is organized around an extended figure of speech, and sometimes the various figures intertwine. The meter is iambic pentameter.

Shakespeare's sonnets, of course, make excellent examples to study, even though the Elizabethan language may make them a little harder to get at first. Searching online or in a bookstore will easily lead you to all the sonnets you can read, but here are titles of a few other examples that are easy to find online: "Scorn Not the Sonnet" by William Wordsworth, "First Poem for You" by Kim Addonizio, and "America" by

Claude McKay. The British Romantics wrote a lot of sonnets of all sorts, including this charmingly titled, if less well-known, example:

Sonnet: On Being Cautioned Against Walking on an Headland Overlooking the Sea, Because It Was Frequented by a Lunatic

Is there a solitary wretch who hies
    To the tall cliff, with starting pace or slow,
And, measuring, views with wild and hollow eyes
    Its distance from the waves that chide below;
Who, as the sea-born gale with frequent sighs
    Chills his cold bed upon the mountain turf,
With hoarse, half-uttered lamentation, lies
    Murmuring responses to the dashing surf?
In moody sadness, on the giddy brink,
    I see him more with envy than with fear;
He has no nice felicities that shrink
    From giant horrors; wildly wandering here,
He seems (uncursed with reason) not to know
The depth or the duration of his woe.

Charlotte Turner Smith, 1783

Sonnets that hybridize the two basic varieties, or create some other near but new version of either, are common, as in this famous example, which takes up its form as its subject:

[If by dull rhymes our English must be chain'd]

If by dull rhymes our English must be chain'd,
    And, like Andromeda, the Sonnet sweet
Fetter'd, in spite of pained loveliness;
    Let us find out, if we must be constrain'd,

Sandals more interwoven and complete
To fit the naked foot of poesy;
Let us inspect the lyre, and weigh the stress
Of every chord, and see what may be gain'd
By ear industrious, and attention meet:
Misers of sound and syllable, no less
Than Midas of his coinage, let us be
Jealous of dead leaves in the bay wreath crown;
So, if we may not let the Muse be free,
She will be bound with garlands of her own.

John Keats, 1819

Villanelle

The villanelle is a complex form brought into English poetry from French. Published villanelles in French using the currently accepted definition go back to the early 1600s, but after it became popular in Britain in the late 1800s, it has been far more common in English-language poetry than in its original home.

It is very difficult to create a villanelle that fulfills the rigid and artificial formal requirements and that is also sensible, natural, and pleasant. Perhaps this is the reason for the enduring appeal of the form. Like a double-black-diamond ski run, it attracts those eager to set their skill and wits against a real challenge.

The villanelle is composed of five tercets followed by a single concluding quatrain. There is no metrical requirement, but the lines should be roughly the same length and not draw attention to themselves by outlandish or highly varied meter or length.

It should rhyme ABA/ABA/ABA/ABA/ABA/ABAA, which is difficult enough on its own. However, the villanelle demands more. It demands repetition of entire lines, called "refrains." Lines 1 and 3 are each repeated throughout in a fixed pattern. Line 1 is repeated in lines 6, 12, and 18. Line 2 is repeated in lines 9, 15, and 19. Slight variation in the remain lines is acceptable. We can represent the whole pattern like this—notice how the refrains contribute to and are part of the rhyme scheme, too:

1. Refrain 1 (A1)
2. Line 2 (b)
3. Refrain 2 (A2)
4. Line 4 (a)
5. Line 5 (b)
6. Refrain 1 (A1)
7. Line 7 (a)
8. Line 8 (b)
9. Refrain 2 (A2)
10. Line 10 (a)
11. Line 11 (b)
12. Refrain 1 (A1)
13. Line 13 (a)
14. Line 14 (b)
15. Refrain 2 (A2)
16. Line 16 (a)
17. Line 17 (b)
18. Refrain 1 (A1)
19. Refrain 2 (A2)

Some example villanelles you can easily find online include "Video Blues" by Mary Jo Salter, "One Art" by Elizabeth Bishop, "Parsley" by Rita Dove, "The Waking" by Theodore Roethke, and "The House on the Hill" by Edward Arlington Robinson. This recent example takes up the potential for creepiness embedded in repetition and tight forms:

You Don't Love the Voyeur

But you need him, and you think you don't need him.
Without him, you're just bones and blood in a shower.
He drinks the light you reflect, enlivens your skin.

Watching, he makes your fragments whole again,
Counts your pulses, stretches out your hours.
But you go on thinking you don't need him.

Those mornings you get up early, go for a swim?
He is that feeling, humming behind white flowers,
Drinking the light, enlivening your skin.

He forgives—no, savors—your every slip and sin,
But you don't notice, buried under covers
Fast asleep, thinking you don't need him.

He gives you his fullest thoughts, his richest attention,
He crackles beside you all night, a soothing fire
That drinks the light you reflect, enlivens your skin.

He doesn't want to have and hold you, to own
The way your husband does. But he is there,
And you need him, and you think you don't need him.
He is the light you reflect. He lives in your skin.

Jeffrey Bean, 2014

Not Even the Tip of an Iceberg

We have looked at just eight forms in this appendix. Finch & Varnes's *An Exaltation of Forms* lists thirty-five or so, and Lewis Turco's *The Book of Forms* lists about one hundred fifty forms, depending on how you count them. In other words, this is just the dusting of snow on top of the tip of the iceberg.

Even so, beginning students who are familiar with and able to recognize these eight forms and their major variants can congratulate themselves on a job well done—and be ready to move into deeper waters if they want.

Writing about Poetry

The Sun Rising

Busy old fool, unruly sun,
        Why dost thou thus,
Through windows, and through curtains call on us?
Must to thy motions lovers' seasons run?
        Saucy pedantic wretch, go chide
        Late school boys and sour prentices,
    Go tell court huntsmen that the king will ride,
    Call country ants to harvest offices,
Love, all alike, no season knows nor clime,
Nor hours, days, months, which are the rags of time.
        Thy beams, so reverend and strong
        Why shouldst thou think?
I could eclipse and cloud them with a wink,
But that I would not lose her sight so long;
        If her eyes have not blinded thine,
        Look, and tomorrow late, tell me,
    Whether both th' Indias of spice and mine
    Be where thou leftst them, or lie here with me.
Ask for those kings whom thou saw'st yesterday,
And thou shalt hear, All here in one bed lay.
    She's all states, and all princes, I,
        Nothing else is.

Princes do but play us; compared to this,
All honor's mimic, all wealth alchemy.
   Thou, sun, art half as happy as we,
    In that the world's contracted thus.
   Thine age asks ease, and since thy duties be
    To warm the world, that's done in warming us.
Shine here to us, and thou art everywhere;
This bed thy center is, these walls, thy sphere.

John Donne, 1633

This poem has a lot going on. The language is archaic and challenging. The story is told in an indirect way. The music is rich and complex. It's making some interesting, arrangement choices. It's emotionally intense. It seems to be making some arguments about the world we live in.

As you engage in a long and possibly intense conversation with this dashing, mysterious, and fascinating stranger, you're going to have all kinds of interesting realizations, insights, and questions. You're going to understand and appreciate this poem in a way all your own—a way that's worth sharing with the world. You might even be able to help the rest of us get to know your new friend better.

How? You will write about the poem.

Writing is a great tool to share what you understand, think, and feel about poetry. As a student, writing is how you communicate to your professors your understanding of the poems you read in their classes. As a poet, writing allows you to communicate with other poets about their work. If you happen to be an English major, writing about poetry might be a big part of your professional life.

When English majors write about poetry for other English majors, they call it "criticism," and literary criticism is an interesting, worthwhile, and complex activity. However, this book isn't trying to teach you to do literary criticism. It instead offers just a couple of specific and careful techniques for writing about poetry that will help you understand and appreciate it—and to communicate your ideas to others.

If you look back at the process for reading a poem we learned back in chapter one, you'll see that writing about poetry is already embedded right in the reading process. Summarizing and paraphrasing are two important steps in that process, and that's what we're going to learn now. First, though, you need to learn a few rules and expectations for writing about poetry.

Conventions for Writing about Poetry

The following guidelines are designed to help you communicate clearly with others, especially professor types, by giving you a shared set of expectations. However, they also help you keep your thinking clear as you work through the process, so they're worth learning and following any time you're writing about a poem. Here we go:

1. Do not refer to the voice speaking within the poem as the author. While it's true that a poem may be autobiographical or use personal details from the poet's life, resist the urge to equate the poem's voice with the poet. Instead, remember to refer to the voice of the poem as the speaker. When the voice in a poem is a fictional character or one from history, we sometimes call it a persona. Refer to the speaker by the gender pronoun of author if there is no contrary indication within the poem itself.

2. The titles of poems are indicated by enclosing them in quotation marks, and the titles of books of poetry are indicated by italics. For example, you would write that "Introduction to Poetry" by Billy Collins was published originally in *The Apple That Astonished Paris*. When writing about a poem, be sure to provide these important details up front, including the author's first and last name. After that, refer to the author by last name only, unless more is necessary for clarity.

3. When you quote more than one but fewer than three lines, quote within your own paragraph, but be sure to show where the line

breaks occur by using a forward slash (/) with space on either side. For example, you would write that in Collins's poem, the speaker invites readers to "drop a mouse into a poem / and watch him probe his way out." To show stanza breaks, use a double forward slash (//). For example, you would write that the speaker in Collins's poem instructs readers to "hold it up to the light / like a color slide // or press an ear against its hive."

4. **For four lines or more, quote the poem in verse as a block quotation**. Do not add quotation marks to the block quotation. Introduce the block quotation with a sentence that lets readers know what to expect. For example, you would write that in Collins's poem, students have other plans for the poem:

> But all they want to do
> is tie the poem to a chair with rope
> and torture a confession out of it.
>
> They begin beating it with a hose
> to find out what it really means.

When quoting either short or long passages, retain the original capitalization at the beginning of lines, as shown above. When referring to specific words, phrases, or fact or ideas, always reference line numbers. For example, Collins's choice of "confession" (line 14) prepares the reader for the final metaphor comparing reading to torture.

5. **When scanning a line or writing about the rhythm of a line, use the appropriate symbols to show how the meter works.** There are two traditional **diacritical symbols**—marks written in the white space above a letter—to indicate if a syllable is stressed or unstressed. The **breve** (˘) indicates unstressed syllables, and the **acute accent** (´) indicates stressed syllables. When creating a word-processed document, however, the process of inserting these characters is quite time-consuming, so you can use either bold, underline, or both to indicate the stressed syllables and leave the unstressed syllables unmarked, just as we've done in this

book. A single upright line (|), also known as a **pipe**, is used to divide the feet, and a double pipe (||) indicates a caesura.

6. When writing about literature, write in the present tense because works of literature continue to live on in the reader's imagination.

7. Write in the third person—he, she, it, and they—unless an assignment calls for a personal response or discussion of some sort. When you explain your ideas, the reader understands that these are your ideas, so you never need to say "I think that. . ."

8. Always use the terminology of the discipline for greater precision, clarity, and concision. Don't say "paragraph," for example, when you mean "stanza." Don't use a vague term like "flow" to describe the sound of a line. Instead, explain what makes it "flow" by identifying the sound elements at work such as rhythm or assonance. You've worked hard to learn these terms, so use them—even in your notes to yourself.

Paraphrase and Summary

All successful writing rests on a strong analysis. These two techniques, paraphrasing and summarizing, are designed to help you achieve and share your analysis with others.

Paraphrase

Paraphrasing retells a poem in your own words and in your own most natural prose style, but it does so without omitting, altering, explaining, or interpreting anything, including the point of view of the original. It may be helpful to think of a paraphrase as a "translation" of the poem from its own verse style into your own straightforward prose style. A paraphrase doesn't involve any research or external sources other than looking up definitions, allusions, and references.

Paraphrase is most useful when the poem in question is somewhat inaccessible on the literal level, especially if it uses archaic or elevated or experimental diction and syntax. A poem written in a straight-forward conversational modern idiom is difficult to paraphrase, but more importantly, there is little value in doing so.

A paraphrase can be longer than the original poem, but it doesn't have to be. If the original contains a lot of compact figurative language or dense vocabulary or syntax, many extra words may be required to make it clear. On the other hand, a poem which uses lots of repetition in its original may come out shorter in paraphrase. The key either way is that you should not alter or remove any content, nor add on any of your own explanation or interpretation.

Sometimes dealing with language in the original that is figurative or unclear is difficult in paraphrase. There is no quick and easy resolution to this difficulty. More than one poet has argued that one of the essential features of a poem is that it *can't* be paraphrased. Be that as it may, the attempt is still a useful tool, and "do your best" is your only guideline. As a rule, err on the side of writing a paraphrase which is unclear rather than one in which you risk altering the meaning of the original.

Creating a Paraphrase

Don't try to start your paraphrase until you've gone through the first steps of the basic reading from chapter one. Noting and answering questions is crucial. You can't retell what you don't understand. You can't understand a poem until you understand all the words, phrases, and sentences that make it up.

A good first step in a paraphrase is to simply copy the poem into conventional prose lines and paragraphs, using stanza breaks as a guideline for where the paragraph breaks should be. Depending on how closely the poet followed conventions of punctuation, you may need to make additions just to get to regular sentences. As long as you read carefully, the logic of the words usually tells you where the punctuation should go even when it's missing.

After that, concentrate on vocabulary. Replace words that you didn't know or wouldn't use in your everyday speech with words or phrases you do know and would use every day. Don't use a thesaurus! Read the word's definitions in a dictionary. Think about what usage makes sense. Figure out what the word means in that place, then think of a word you already know and use that would express the same meaning. If you need to use multiple words to explain the idea, that's fine. This is essentially the process presented in detail in Chapter 6, using the speech from *Romeo and Juliet* as an example.

Observe how the poet uses the allusion or reference and what it means in the context. Add in explanations or alternative references if they're needed to make the meaning clear.

Now go back and reread it. It should be starting not just to make more sense, but to sound more like you. Rewrite any sentences that seem awkward or have gotten muddled through the substitutions. Break up long complex or compound sentences. Keep repeating—revise, read, contemplate, question. Do this until you have accurately reproduced the content of the original but in your own voice and your own words. That's a paraphrase.

Paraphrasing "The Sun Rising"

Here is a paraphrase of our opening poem from this chapter:

> Busybody sun, why are you poking through our windows
> and curtains? Do lovers have to answer to your schedule?
> Teacher's pet, brownnoser, go yell at late schoolboys and
> grumpy apprentices, go tell the king's horse handlers to get
> up because the king wants to ride, tell farmers it is time to get
> to work on the harvest. Love can't tell the difference between
> times or seasons. It doesn't notice hours, days, or months,
> which are the outward signs of time.
>
> Why do you think your beams are so majestic and strong?
> I could block them out with a wink, but I don't want to lose
> sight of her for even that long! If *her* eyes have not blinded *you*,
> go look, and tomorrow tell me, whether both the East Indies

and the West Indies are still where you left them, or lie here with me. Ask for the kings you saw yesterday and you will hear, everyone was here in our bed!

All the nations of the world are right here, and I am ruler of them all. Nothing and no one else exists. All the rulers of the world are just playing at being us. Compared to this, all honor is false, all wealth an illusion. You, sun, get to share in our happiness since the world has shrunk down to fit in this bed. You're old, and you should take it easy. Your duty is to warm the world, but once you warm us, you're done! Shine here and you are everywhere! This bed is the center of your existence, and the walls of this room, its outer limits.

Once you have a paraphrase you like, you're in good shape to move on to a summary.

Summary

In any academic field, a summary is a short explanation of a longer work that highlights the most important things about the original. A summary of an essay, for example, tells the audience what the essay's main idea and most important supporting points are. Summarizing a poem isn't always so clear cut because it may not be obvious what the most important things to know about the poem are.

A summary of a prose work is almost always significantly shorter and simpler than the original. A summary of a poem, however, is not necessarily because poems are so nonliteral, compressed, and complicated formally. Poems leave lots of things out that we often put back into the summary, and poems have many important characteristics, like form, sound elements, and visual elements, which have to be put into words. For the purposes of this book, a summary should include the following elements:

1. A two- to three-sentence introduction to the poem's history and

context, which may include the title, when and where it was originally published, the author's name, and maybe one or two facts about the author's life or the context in which the poem was written or published, if they seem relevant.

2. A description of the poem's form, especially identifying any received or closed form the poem is in. If you can't find a specific form, just describe the structure of the poem, whatever gives it form. Remember, not all poems are formal, but all poems have form.

3. An explanation of the situation, including:

    a. a description of the persona "telling" the poem (the speaker)

    b. the relationship of the speaker to the action (the point of view)

    c. the overall mood and feeling of the poem, as well as the apparent attitude or feelings of the author toward the poem, if that's at odds with the feelings of the speaker (the tone)

    d. where and when it takes place (the setting)

    e. who is mentioned in the poem (the characters)

    f. what's happening in the poem (the action)

4. A description of any other elements that seem to be pervasive or important. For example, if the poem makes extensive use of symbols, mention but don't otherwise analyze or explain that. This is somewhat subjective. Just use your own experience of listening to the poem as a starting point. What leapt out at you in reading the poem? What, as you reread it, seemed to be most important for understanding and enjoying the poem? Go with that.

Creating a Summary

No special knowledge or secret skill is required. Just read slowly and carefully, thinking about what you read and looking up words and references that are unclear. Everything you need to summarize the poem is in the poem or in a reference work like a dictionary or *Wikipedia*. You just need to slow down, be quiet, and listen attentively for the answers.

Some of these elements to be covered in a summary may be missing from a poem, or there may be little or no information about them. For example, many times there is no particular setting for a poem — it could be taking place anytime or anywhere, and no clues are given. That's fine. Just say so in your summary. For example, "The poem gives us no clues to its setting." There's a crucial difference between seeing that you looked for an element and correctly surmised it was absent from the poem and not knowing if you even know what the element is.

Sometimes finding some of these elements is going to be easy, and in other cases, even when they are present, discovering them may require several long conversations with the poem. Students often give up too easily on discovering the situation in a poem, for example. There are often subtle clues.

It's important to include all of those elements in your summary, but it's just as important not to let your summary expand beyond those borders. Your summary should *not* include:

1. Your own reaction, opinion, or evaluation. Summaries and responses often go together — many assignments ask you to summarize *and respond* to a text — but keep those two actions separate. Don't let them mingle!

2. Any interpretation, explication, or analysis. Do not try to explain what the poem means. That's a separate activity, too.

3. Any research or external sources, except to a limited extent for providing context, as above. It especially should not refer to or be based on other people's analysis, reviews, commentary and so on.

Summarizing "The Sun Rising"

Let's take a look at a summary of our opening poem:

"The Sun Rising," by John Donne, was written sometime in the late sixteenth or early seventeenth century, according to the Poetry Foundation "Poem Guide" by Stephen Burt. The same source tells us that it was not published until after his death.

The poem is divided into three ten-line stanzas. Each stanza rhymes ABBACDCDEE. The rhythm of the lines is basically iambic, and most of the lines are pentameter, but there is a pattern of variation. The number of feet per line varies, but the pattern stays the same across the three stanzas: 4,2,5,5,4,4,5,5,5,5. This seems to be a nonce form.

The poem addresses the sun directly, as if it were a character (1), making this an apostrophe. In addition, since the poem takes place at dawn in the bed of two lovers waking up together (2), it is an aubade.

The situation of the poem is simple. There is a participant speaker; the first-person pronouns, plural and singular, are used throughout (e.g., 1, 13–14, 21), and the speaker clearly situates himself in the action. We know that he is in love (4, 9). The way the speaker addresses the sun, an infinitely powerful cosmic force, in dismissive, humorous language shows us how full of self-confidence he is (e.g., 1, 5, 13). The tone is joyful, exuberant, brash, excited—full of the energy of erotic love.

The poem is set in the speaker's bedroom at dawn (3, 20, 30). We don't know where or when, otherwise, though the references in the poem construct an image of a pre-modern, medieval world: princes (21), kings and huntsmen (7), apprentices (6), alchemy (24), and so forth. However, it also refers to both the "west" and "east Indies" (27), meaning it is sometime after Columbus and the beginning of the colonial era, so probably the late Renaissance—the same time as the author lived.

The only other real character is his lover, who is a woman (14). There's no real action. The sun rises, the speaker addresses him. The speaker expounds about how strong and perfect his love is.

The diction and syntax of this five hundred-year-old poem are unfamiliar, complex, and somewhat inaccessible to the modern reader. This poem is built around a series of long, sophisticated extended metaphors. It makes extensive use of hyperbole and exaggeration. The figurative language is complicated, but vivid and original.

Examples of Paraphrase and Summary

Summaries and paraphrases are not intrinsically complicated, but they do require practice. You will also find that the characteristics of a good paraphrase or summary of one poem might be different from an equally good paraphrase or summary of a different poem. Studying multiple examples will thus help you see how this works as you begin to build your skills. We'll look at three examples of summary and paraphrase in this section.

Poem 1

[I think i could turn and live with animals] from "Song of Myself," section 32

I think I could turn and live with animals, they are so placid
    and self-contain'd;
I stand and look at them long and long.

They do not sweat and whine about their condition;
They do not lie awake in the dark and weep for their sins;

They do not make me sick discussing their duty to God;

Not one is dissatisfied — not one is demented with the mania
   of owning things;

Not one kneels to another, nor to his kind that lived thousands
   of years ago;

Not one is respectable or industrious over the whole earth.

Walt Whitman, 1855

Paraphrase

"I Think I Could Turn and Live with Animals," by Walt Whitman

I might go and live with the animals, they're so calm and quiet. I like to be in their company. They don't complain about their circumstances. They don't feel guilty about who they are or torment themselves about their actions; they don't disgust me talking about all the things they have to do for God. None of them are dissatisfied with what they have, and none of them are obsessed with owning things. They have no hierarchy. They don't care about tradition or leaders of the past, and none of them care about what other animals think or try to make or build things all over the world.

Summary

"I Think I Could Turn and Live with Animals," by Walt Whitman, is presented here as if it were a stand-alone poem; in fact, this is merely the first eight lines of section 32 of the 1892 version of "Song of Myself," a much longer poem (*Whitman: Collected Poetry and Prose*, p. 218).

According to *Wikipedia*, Whitman is "a part of the transition between transcendentalism and realism, incorporating both views in his works." That page also describes him as one of the most important figures in American literary history, a pioneer of free verse and a champion for a uniquely American literature.

This short poem is in free verse; there is no rhyme or meter; the lines are long. However, it does use repetition of line-beginning words or phrases to create a structure. The starting words and phrases are: I, I, They do not, They do not, They do not, Not one, Not one. The lines are end stopped, though all eight lines contain only two long sentences.

The situation in the poem is simple. The participant speaker is describing his feelings about animals and comparing humanity to animals, favorably for the animals. There are no characters or action other than the speaker and his thoughts. We have no information about the setting of the action, though he says "I stand and look at them," so perhaps he is actually on a farm or in a barnyard, as he's having these thoughts.

The poem is abstract and philosophical. The tone is mostly reserved and intellectual. It reads almost more like an essay than a poem. It lists a variety of behaviors human beings engage in that animals do not, and the speaker clearly doesn't respect people for these behaviors. This fact introduces a little bit of feeling into the poem; there are undertones of anger and frustration expressed in phrases like "make me sick" and "demented with the mania of owning things."

There is no figurative language, symbolism, or imagery to speak of. The repetition and parallel structure between lines are the most obvious "poetic" elements and give the poem a chantlike feel.

Poem 2

Rondeau

Jenny kissed me when we met,
  Jumping from the chair she sat in;
Time, you thief, who love to get
  Sweets into your list, put that in:
Say I'm weary, say I'm sad,
  Say that health and wealth have missed me,
Say I'm growing old, but add,
  Jenny kissed me.

Leigh Hunt, 1838

Paraphrase

"Rondeau," by Leigh Hunt

Jenny jumped out of her chair to kiss me when we met. Time, you love to steal things, so take this too: in many ways, life has passed me by, and I'm getting older, without health or wealth. But at least Jenny kissed me.

Summary

"Rondeau," by Leigh Hunt, was first published in 1838 in a British magazine, and is now, according to the Poetry Foundation website, an often-anthologized poem. The same web page tells us that Hunt was a member of the Romantic poetry movement, though he was never as successful or well-known.

The title of the poem is obscure, and somehow misleading; for although the term "rondeau" describes a specific poetic form, this poem is not a rondeau, which according to the Poetry Foundation, should have ten or fifteen lines in two or three stanzas of five lines and rhyme abbaabC abbaC, (the ten-line version), or aabbaaabC aabbaC, the fifteen-line version (in each case the capital C stands for a repeated line, or refrain). The poem is an apostrophe, because it is addressed to a personified "Time."

What we do have here is eight lines, in a single stanza (an octave); the rhyme scheme is ababcdcd (where the boldface stands for a repeated final word). The base meter of the poem is trochaic tetrameter, though the odd-numbered lines all drop the final syllable. The last line is only two trochees, which adds emphasis to the last line's thought.

There is little information about setting; a room with a chair. There are two real characters, the participant speaker, about whom we know nothing objective, and "Jenny," a woman he's pleased to be kissed by. What we can infer about the speaker is that he's somewhat unsuccessful, unhappy, and conscious of getting older.

The speaker is reflecting back on a happy moment when a woman leapt out of her chair on meeting him to give him a kiss. He describes the event in the opening two lines, without much detail; in the next line, he addresses "Time" and tells him not to leave this out when making the list of his life, which otherwise includes weariness, sadness, ill health, poverty, and old age. He ends by repeating and reaffirming—"Jenny kissed me."

The most noticeable feature of this poem is how the tone created by the rhythm and rhyme (jaunty, light, happy) are in contrast to much of the subject matter (weariness, sadness, sickness, poverty, the "thievery" of time), which are all dark and grim.

Poem 3

[Sonnet 25]

Let those who are in favour with their stars,
Of public honour and proud titles boast,
Whilst I whom fortune of such triumph bars
Unlooked for joy in that I honour most;

Great princes' favourites their fair leaves spread,
But as the marigold at the sun's eye,
And in themselves their pride lies buried,
For at a frown they in their glory die.

The painful warrior famoused for fight,
After a thousand victories once foiled,
Is from the book of honour razed quite,
And all the rest forgot for which he toiled:

Then happy I that love and am beloved
Where I may not remove nor be removed.

William Shakespeare, 1609

Paraphrase

"Sonnet 25," by William Shakespeare

Let the lucky people brag about their public recognition and titles while I, who am not as lucky as them, find joy in what I really care about—you. The princes' favorites, who enjoy their high positions, are like marigolds that blossom when the sun shines on them; however, their pride is fragile. A single frown from their patron will destroy them. The once famous warrior who endured pain and won a thousand battles is overcome. His pride and honor are destroyed, and all his hard work is forgotten. When I think about all this, I am so happy that I love and am loved back in a place I cannot leave nor be removed from.

Summary

"Sonnet 25," by William Shakespeare, was written sometime in the Elizabethan era in England. Shakespeare is one of the most famous writers in the world.

This poem is obviously a Shakespearean sonnet. Just in case we were afraid the author is tricking us by being Shakespeare and giving us a poem titled "Sonnet #x," we can see that the poem conforms to all the rules for the Shakespearean Sonnet given in the Glossary of Forms: it is fourteen lines long, has four stanzas (three quatrains and one couplet), is written in iambic pentameter, and rhymes in the following pattern: ABAB/CDCD/EFEF/GG.

The poem is told from a first-person perspective; there is a participant speaker. What we can tell about the speaker is not much. He is not very fortunate, at least as far as public honors go (2–3). He finds joy in his loving relationship with whomever he is addressing in the poem. The tone seems guardedly joyful; the speaker is happy in his love, but seems a little defensive about his lack of other, more worldly glories.

Besides those two main characters—the speaker and his beloved—there are no other specific characters. The poem references categories of people: famous warriors, princes, and so on.

The poem has no specific setting. We can infer it's set in some time and place in which the patronage of princes is important, and in which one can gain glory and fame by being a warrior. Of course, both "prince" and "warrior" could be figurative.

There is no action in the poem. The speaker is just ruminating on fortune and happiness.

The archaic diction and convoluted syntax of this poem make it difficult to read and understand at first. It took real work to get to a literal understanding of this poem.

Checklists for Paraphrase and Summary

One problem for many students when it comes to paraphrasing and summarizing poems is that one thought and observation often leads to another — and another — all of them interesting in their own rights. Before long, the poor student writer has wandered far from the material that he or she needed to cover.

In a certain way, this isn't a problem — no thinking about a poem is bad. However, understanding and appreciating poetry well rests on a methodical approach to the reading process that carefully attends to and accounts for everything that is actually present in the poem — and everything that isn't.

The following checklists will help you to attend carefully and completely to all the basics before you launch into flights of fancy further afield.

Paraphrase Checklist

When you write a paraphrase of a poem, be sure to take the following actions:

- ❑ Write in prose, not verse.
- ❑ Start with the title and author of the poem.
- ❑ Use the same point of view as the poem (for example, first-person pronouns, participant speaker, and so on).
- ❑ Provide all the same content—action, characters, etc.
- ❑ Give the same level of detail and information.
- ❑ Write in conventional, fluid, conversational syntax and diction.
- ❑ Use direct, easy-to-read diction and syntax.
- ❑ Make extensive use of a good dictionary to explore the meaning-in-context of the original.

When writing a paraphrase, do *not* take the following actions:

- ❑ Do *not* leave out or alter any of the literal information or content.
- ❑ Do *not* substitute guesses, interpretations, or wishful thinking for ambiguous or mysterious passages in the original.
- ❑ Do *not* add any extra content that doesn't appear in the original.
- ❑ Do *not* use a thesaurus to find and replace words from the original.

Summary Checklist

When you write a summary of a poem, be sure to include the following items:

- ❑ A two- or three-sentence introduction to the poem, the poet, and their history and context.

- ❑ A mention of the source(s) for this information.

- ❑ A description of the poem's form, especially identifying any received or closed form the poem is in or seems to be close to.

- ❑ An explanation of the situation:

    - ❑ a description of the speaker person who is "telling" the poem

    - ❑ the relationship of the speaker to the action (point of view)

    - ❑ attitudes and feelings of the author towards the poem (tone)

    - ❑ where and when is it set (setting)

    - ❑ who is mentioned in the poem (characters)

    - ❑ what's happening in the poem (action)

    - ❑ a brief mention of any other elements that seem to be pervasive or important

When you write a summary, do *not* include the following items:

- ❑ Your own reaction, opinion, or evaluation.

- ❑ Any interpretation—do not try to explain what the poem means.

- ❑ Other people's analysis, reviews, commentary, and so on.

Beyond Paraphrase and Summary

Writing paraphrases and summaries are just the beginning of all the fun, interesting, and challenging writing about poetry to be done. However, they are a good and useful start and will give you a solid foundation to build on. If you want to try your hand at some other ways to write about poetry, here are some common assignments you could explore.

Analysis: This is a super summary. It picks up where the summary leaves off and extends it into all of the elements, giving a careful description of each. Then it deepens the description of each element by explaining how it works with the other elements in creating the total effect of the poem. Sometimes an analysis is not comprehensive, but focuses only on a single element in the poem.

Explication: This is like an analysis, in that it attempts to carefully and thoroughly explain the separate parts and total effect of the poem. However, instead of being organized element by element, it proceeds from start to end through the poem, line by line. Consequently, examining and explaining sequencing of ideas, events, and language becomes more important, as is attention to line and stanza structure, breaks, and enjambment.

Interpretation: This is an argument about the meaning or meanings of a poem—the questions it asks, the challenges it raises, and most of all the arguments it makes. Most arguments focus on identifying and explaining a theme of a poem, but broadly an interpretation is any argument about what a poem means—how it relates to or instructs us about the world and our lives.

Review: Just like a movie review or a restaurant review, a review is an argument about the relative merits of a poem. Not the same as simply explaining whether or not you liked it and why, which is a reaction. A review attempts to establish and appeal to nominally objective aesthetic standards and then evaluate the poem accordingly. Sometimes reviews don't appeal only to aesthetic standards, but to others, for example, ethical standards: is the poem morally despicable?

Students often think of writing about poetry as an end in itself. They have an assignment to complete, and they regard any value in writing about poetry as derived from some external reward, like a grade.

However, we would like you to consider—just consider!—an alternate possibility, that writing about poetry is a means to other ends, ends that might be intrinsically rewarding. Those ends include better understanding and appreciation of the poetry you read and being able to share what you understand and appreciate with others. These things are not only worth doing in and of themselves, they really are pleasures, once you learn to think of them that way.

Poet Biographies

ANONYMOUS is the unknown author of the text of the *Gerechtigkeitsspirale*, or Spiral of Justice.

José Angel Araguz is the author of many chapbooks and poetry collections including 2019 Oregon Book Awards finalist *Until We Are Level Again*.

Elizabeth Austen's debut poetry collection *Every Dress a Decision* was a 2012 Washington State Book Awards finalist. She was the Washington State Poet Laureate from 2014–16.

Justus Ballard teaches writing at Chemeketa Community College in Oregon. He has an MFA in creative writing, and has written *The Cubist Infant* and *Roboctopus: A Rock Opera for Kids*.

Jeffrey Bean is professor of English/creative writing at Central Michigan University and author of the poetry collections *Diminished Fifth* and *Woman Putting on Pearls*.

Amy Beeder is a world traveler and former University of New Mexico professor. She has published the poetry collections *Now Make an Altar* and *Burn the Field*.

Shaindel Beers teaches English at Blue Mountain Community College in Pendleton, Oregon. Her most recent collection of poetry is *Secure Your Own Mask*.

Hilaire Belloc (1870–1953) was born in France but lived most of his life in England. A politician and prolific writer in many genres, he is best remembered today for his light verse.

David Biespiel has won numerous awards for his poetry and is the Poet in Residence at Oregon State University. His latest collection is *Republic Café*.

Jerry Brunoe is a poet in case you didn't know it. His poetry has appeared in literary magazines, and he is the Supreme Chancellor of the *Toe Good Arts*.

Catherine Bull has a full-length collection, *Muskoxen Slow It Down*, and a chapbook, *Rambo/Rimbaud*. Her poetry has appeared in *Bellingham Review, FIELD*, and others.

Samuel Taylor Coleridge (1772–1834) was a founder of Romanticism and a member of the Lake Poets. He frequently collaborated with William Wordsworth.

Billy Collins, dubbed "America's favorite poet" by the *Wall Street Journal*, was the 2001–03 US Poet Laureate and has published twelve collections of poetry.

Brittney Corrigan is the author of the poetry collections *Navigation* and *40 Weeks*. She is both an alumna and employee of Reed College.

LeAnna Crawford is an American poet and a writing instructor at Chemeketa Community College in Salem, Oregon. She has an MFA from Antioch University Los Angeles.

E. E. Cummings (1894–1962) was a modernist American poet famous for his minimalist style and innovative experiments with form and language.

Oliver de la Paz is a Filipino American poet whose prize-winning poetry has appeared in five collections, most recently *The Boy in the Labyrinth*.

Danielle Cadena Deulen is an associate professor at Willamette University. Her latest publication is the poetry collection *Our Emotions Get Carried Away Beyond Us*.

John Donne (1572–1631) was an English lawyer, politician, poet, and Anglican priest renowned for his extended figures of speech and the emotional intensity of his love and religious poems.

T. S. Eliot (1888–1965) won the 1948 Nobel Prize in Literature and was one of the most distinguished writers of the twentieth century, best known for his poem *The Waste Land*.

Robert Frost (1874–1965) was one of the most beloved American poets of all time, melding difficult, complex topics and clear language. He was a four-time Pulitzer Prize winner.

Charlotte Perkins Gilman (1860–1965) was an American writer, activist, and feminist social theorist best known for her short story "The Yellow Wallpaper."

Heidi Schulman Greenwald is a Portland poet. When she's not writing, she is taming her backyard, practicing yoga, and spending time with her family.

Mother Goose is an imaginary person to whom numerous rhymes and fairytales of unknown origin are attributed, dating back to seventeenth-century France.

Thomas Hardy (1840–1928) was a Victorian realist whose novels and poetry explored the difficulties of reconciling individual desire with social constraints and fate.

George Herbert (1593–1633), John Donne's godson, was a politician, orator, and Anglican priest now remembered mostly for his religious poetry, full of complex figurative language and formal innovation.

Andrea Hollander is the author of five full-length poetry collections, including *Blue Mistaken for Sky*, a finalist for the 2018 Best Book Award in Poetry.

Gerard Manley Hopkins (1844–1889) was a Jesuit priest whose innovative poems such as "The Windhover" were mostly published posthumously.

Leigh Hunt (1784–1859) was an English journalist, critic, playwright, and poet, best remembered as a supporter and friend to the major writers of British Romanticism.

Bette Lynch Husted is an award-winning essayist, novelist, and poet living in Pendleton, Oregon. Her full-length poetry collection is titled *At This Distance: Poems*.

Luisa A. Igloria is a Filipina American poet and the author of more than fourteen poetry collections. She is a professor at Old Dominion University.

Lawson Fusao Inada was the 2006 Oregon Poet Laureate. Many of his poems address his experience in Japanese internment camps as a child.

John Keats (1795–1821), who published only fifty poems during his short life, is now widely considered one of the major writers of British Romanticism and one of the most influential and well-loved English poets.

Jennifer Kemnitz is an American poet whose work has been featured in the feminist journal *CALYX*, as well as *Pilgrimage Magazine*. She has served as managing editor of *VoiceCatcher*.

Robert Lashley describes his experiences growing up in the African American community in Tacoma, Washington, in his poetry collections *Up South* and *The Homeboy Songs*.

Emma Lazarus (1849–1887) was a Jewish-American poet and activist. Lines from her sonnet "The New Colossus" are engraved on the pedestal of the Statue of Liberty.

Annie Lighthart believes poetry can change the world. She hopes you'll find a poem to love in this book, even if it's not one she wrote.

Amy Lowell (1874–1925) was a poet, critic, and editor. She was a fierce advocate of Imagism, free verse, and the avant-garde. Her collection *What's O'Clock* won the 1926 Pulitzer Prize.

Tod Marshall was the 2016 Washington State Poet Laureate. He lives in Spokane, Washington, and is a professor at Gonzaga University.

Carolyn Martin's love for words inspires an eclectic style seen in her most recent work *A Penchant for Masquerades*.

Michael McGriff focuses on the state of American ruin in his contemporary poetry. He has published four poetry collections and is a creative writing professor.

Jessica Mehta is an award-winning poet whose work addresses the inequalities experienced by indigenous people. She experiments with VR-technology for an immersive experience for her readers.

David Melville is a Portland poet. His poems have appeared in *Pilgrimage, The Timberline Review*, and other publications. For many years, he earned his living as an attorney.

Corey Mesler is widely published in various journals. He has written ten novels, four short-story anthologies, numerous prose chapbooks, and four poetry collections.

Edna St. Vincent Millay (1892–1950) was an American poet and playwright. She was a progressive feminist and one of the most successful writers of her generation. She won the Pulitzer Prize in 1923.

John Milton (1608–1673) was an English poet and playwright whose work included *Paradise Lost,* considered one of the greatest epic poems of all time.

A. Molotkov's books are *The Catalog of Broken Things, Application of Shadows* and *Synonyms for Silence.* He co-edits The Inflectionist Review. Visit him at AMolotkov.com.

Lisa Marie Oliver lives in Portland, Oregon. She has studied at the University of Oregon and The Attic Institute.

Wilfred Owen (1893–1918) was an infantry officer during World War I, and was killed in action. He is now considered the greatest of the British World War I poets.

Darlene Pagán authored the poetry collection *Setting the Fires.* Her poems and essays have appeared in various journals.

David J. S. Pickering's poetry has been published in the *Gold Man Review, Raven Chronicles, Verseweavers, Portland Review, Gertrude Journal,* and in the collection *Salt.*

Edgar Allan Poe (1809–1849) was an influential poet, short-story writer, and critic. His work has had a lasting influence on crime, gothic, and horror literature.

Jessie Pope (1868–1941) was an English humorist poet remembered for her jingoistic poems during World War I.

Ezra Pound (1885–1972), a founder of Modernism, was famous for his pioneering poetry and his criticism and promotion of, and collaboration with, other writers.

Tiah Lindner Raphael is a Portland writer. Her work has been published in *Spoon River Poetry* Review and *CutBank*, among others.

Susan Rich is a Fulbright Fellowship recipient for South Africa. She has authored five collections of poetry and teaches creative writing and film studies at Highline College.

Virginia Robinson received her MA in creative writing from the University of California, Davis. She continues to teach and write in North Carolina.

Alida Rol is a retired OB-GYN and holds an MFA in writing from Pacific University. Her poems have won several awards.

Walt Schaefer is a poet and writer who lives in Queens, New York.

Caitlin Scott's poems have appeared in magazines such as *FIELD, Threepenny Review, Cloudbank,* and *Measure*. She is interested in the connection between writing and dreams.

William Shakespeare (1564–1616) is considered the greatest writer in the English language. The prolific playwright also penned 154 sonnets, including the illustrious "Sonnet 18."

Scot Siegel is the author of three poetry collections and three poetry chapbooks. He most recently published *The Constellation of Extinct Stars and Other Poems*.

Brian Simoneau's poems have appeared in numerous journals and the anthology *Two Weeks*. His poetry collection *River Bound* won the 2013 De Novo Prize.

Stephen Siperstein is an environmental educator with an interest in the emotional dimensions of climate change, as seen in both his poetry and scholarly work.

Nancy Slavin is a poet, violence-prevention educator, and English teacher who lived on the Oregon coast for twenty-one years, inspiring her poetry collection *Oregon Pacific*.

Charlotte Smith (1749–1806) was a translator, essayist, novelist, and Romantic poet. She helped repopularize the English sonnet and was an early influential Gothic writer.

kosal so escaped to America from Pol Pot's regime. His work is published in the Oregon State Penitentiary poetry anthology *Men Still in Exile*.

A. E. Stallings is a MacArthur Fellow, poet, and translator who has published four collections of poetry, *Archaic Smile*, *Hapax*, *Olives*, and, most recently, *Like*.

George Starbuck (1931–1996) was an American professor and witty poet of the New Formalism movement. He was also an important antiwar and civil liberty activist.

Clemens Starck, a lifelong union carpenter and construction foreman, received the William Stafford Memorial Poetry Award and the Oregon Book Award for his first collection *Journeyman's Wages*.

Karelia Stetz-Waters is a contemporary lesbian romance writer and an English and composition instructor at Linn-Benton Community College.

Cindy Stewart-Rinier's manuscript, *A Desire for Color, for Wings* was a finalist for the 2016 Philip Levine Prize for Poetry contest.

Jonathan Swift (1667–1745) was an Irish writer famous for his satirical wit in essays like "A Modest Proposal" and his acclaimed novel *Gulliver's Travels*.

Allison Tobey teaches writing at Chemeketa Community College in Salem, Oregon. Her work has been published in many national reviews.

Chrys Tobey is a Portland poet whose collection of feminist poems, A *Woman is a Woman is a Woman is a Woman*, was published in 2017.

Jan VanStavern is an Oregonian whose poetry chapbook *The Long Birth* captures her experience with adopting a child from China and being adopted herself.

W. Vandoren Wheeler's collection of poems, *The Accidentalist*, won the Dorothy Brunsman Poetry Prize in 2012. He currently teaches writing and literature at Portland Community College.

Walt Whitman (1819–1892) was one of America's most quintessential poets and thinkers. He revised and expanded his single collection of poems, *Leaves of Grass*, throughout his lifetime.

Christopher M. Wicks is a six-time self-published Oregon poet known more recently for his collection *365 Sonnets*, which he wrote over twenty-two years.

Richard Wilbur (1921–2017) was a revered US Poet Laureate and two-time Pulitzer Prize winner remembered for his collection *Things of This World*.

John Sibley Williams has authored four poetry collections. His most recent, As One Fire Consumes Another, won the Orison Poetry Prize in 2019.

Dawn Diez Willis has an MFA from the University of Oregon. Her poetry collection *Still Life with Judas & Lightning* was a 2015 Oregon Book Awards finalist.

William Wordsworth (1770–1850) founded English Romanticism with *Lyrical Ballads*, a collection of poems co-written with Samuel Taylor Coleridge.

Sir Thomas Wyatt (1503–1542) was a poet and translator who brought the sonnet to England. He was a politician and ambassador in the court of Henry VIII of England.

William Butler Yeats (1865–1939) was an Irish poet hailed as one of the most influential writers of the twentieth century for his fusion of innovative, symbolic writing and mythological subjects.

İsmail Zühdü (ca. 1745–1806) was the Ottoman Court Calligrapher throughout the late 1700s. His work can be seen on mausoleums, in rare editions of the Q'ran, and other shorter works.

Poem Index

Authors   *Titles*   First Lines

S

Y

Yak, The: 5
Yeats, W. B.: 187
You Don't Love the Voyeur: 361
You start out doing it for the bucks: 295
You who are happy in a thousand homes: 353
Young Couple Marries in July: 236
Your family stitched the sagai together just like that: 310
Your son shermed to death in makeshift car: 78
Yr Appt: <u>*10:30 Thursday*</u> *: 278*

Z

Zühdü , Ismâîl: 282

Key Terms: Glossary & Index

A

Accentual Rhythm: The sound pattern created by the stressed and unstressed syllables in the poem.
244

Accentual-Syllabic Rhythm / Meter: a system, dominant in English-language poetry from the renaissance to the *20*th century, that organizes and names lines according to number of total syllables, number of stressed syllables, and the pattern of stressed and unstressed syllables.
247

Action: The sequence of logically-related events that unfolds in the lives of the story's characters. Synonymous with "plot."
95

Addressee: a character to whom the speaker of a poem is speaking directly, when the speaker is addressing a specific character within the poem. Not all poems have an addressee.
56

Alliteration: The repetition of sounds at the beginning of words, generally the initial consonant sound.
216

Allusion: A reference to something outside the poem that may take on significance, and possibly symbolic value, within the poem.
164

Anapest: a three-syllable, or treble, **foot** made up of a sequence of two unstressed syllables followed by one **stressed syllable**.
251

Analyze: broadly, to discover the structure that lies behind a function or beneath the surface of a system by identifying its **elements**, studying each closely, and explaining how they work together. The noun is **analysis**.
10

Appreciation: Your emotional and aesthetic response to a poem.
10

Arrangement: The placement of a poem's words on the page relative to each other and to the surrounding white space.
268

Assonance: A pattern of repetition of a vowel sound occurring at any point in the words, independent of surrounding consonant sounds.
222

B

Basic Reading: a systematic approach to reading a poem explained in chapter 1, page 14-16, of this book.
14

Beloved, the: traditional term for the addressee in a love poem.
57

C

Caesura: A break or pause in the sound or rhythm of a line of poetry that comes from the content or the grammatical structure, usually marked with punctuation.
24

Character: Any person-like being in a poem.
91

Conceit: A complex web of overlapping and extended figures of speech.
153

Concrete Poetry / Poem: A poem in which the visual elements create a pictorial representation of the poem's content.
281

Connotation: The meaning of a word suggested through association.
113

Consonance: A pattern of repeating consonant sounds in the middle of words. The pattern may include, but cannot be made up solely of, consonant sounds in the middle of words echoing consonants at the start or end of words as well.
222

Content (i.e. as a concept, vs. "Form"): The information, ideas, emotions, and so on that an author wants the audience to understand.
20

Content Word: A word that has meaning in and of itself, including nouns, main verbs, most modifiers, and some pronouns (especially personal pronouns) — contrast with **function word**.
198

Couplet: A two-line stanza.
25

D

Dactyl: a three-**syllable**, or **treble**, **foot** made up of a sequence of one **stressed syllable** followed by two unstressed **syllables**.
252

Denotation: The meaning of a word based on what it refers to literally.
113

Diction: The word choice or vocabulary of a poem or passage of a poem.
112

Dominant Foot: The foot most commonly occurring in a given line or passage of a poem; a term used in **scansion**.
257

Double Iamb: another name for the **Minor Ionic.**
253

Duple Foot: a **foot** with two **syllables**. The duple feet are the **iamb, trochee, spondee,** and **pyrrhic.**
250

E

Element: a piece or process that make up a larger, more complex system. A term used in **analysis.**
11

End Rhyme: A pattern of rhymes occurring at the ends of lines; can be exact or slant and can be mingled with **internal rhyme.**
201

End-stopped (line): A line that ends at the end of a grammatical unit — that is, a clause or phrase.
22-23

Enjambed (line): A line that breaks in the middle of a grammatical unit — that is, a clause or phrase — interrupting it. The noun is **enjambment.**
23

Exact Rhyme: A rhyme that is created when we hear the same vowel sound followed by the same consonant sound repeating in a proximity and to a degree such that a pattern is established.
204

Extended Figure of Speech: a linked group of figures of speech that share **tenors** and **vehicles,** some of which may be implied. One thing may be explained by comparing it to many other things, or many things may be explained by comparing them all to a single thing, or the same thing can be explained by one thing and explain something else simultaneously.
148

F

Figure of Speech / Figurative Language: The definition, explanation, or presentation of one thing (the **tenor**) by comparison to or in terms of another thing (the **vehicle**). A **figure of speech** is one particular instance of figurative language. See also **Extended Figure of Speech, Implied Figure of Speech**.

144

Foot: An unit for describing **accentual-syllabic meter** that measures a discrete pattern of stressed and unstressed syllables that is repeated throughout the line.

249

Form: How a poem is presented as distinguished from the content it presents. Specifically, "form" also refers to a small set of conventional formal poetic elements. It can also be used to talk about formal patterns within a poem or to refer to a historical, established pattern for the use of those formal tools (see **Received Form**).

3-4

Formal Poem: a poem that uses formal elements to crate patterns.

26

Free Verse: Poetry that doesn't follow any apparent structural patterns, especially regular rhythm or rhyme patterns or a **Received Form**. Also called "**open form**."

33

Function Word: A word that has no inherent meaning but serves to connect or otherwise "assist" **content words**. This includes conjunctions, articles, helping verbs, prepositions, demonstratives, most modifiers, and most pronouns.

198

G

Genre: A broad category of poem that's defined by similarities in some key aspects — perhaps **form**, perhaps length, perhaps style, perhaps **content**, perhaps some combination of those, or something else. Genre is a broader category than **form** into which to sort poems.
331

H

Heptameter: A line composed of seven **feet**; a term used in **scansion** and the discussion of **accentual-syllabic meter**.
255

Hexameter: A line composed of six **feet**; a term used in **scansion** and the discussion of **accentual-syllabic meter**.
255

I

Iamb: a two-**syllable**, or **duple, foot** made up of a sequence of one unstressed **syllable** followed by one **stressed syllable**.
250

Imagery: The description of concrete objects with language that appeals to the five senses. Imagery refers to anything in a poem that gives the reader concrete description of the world. An **image** is one particular instance of imagery.
140

Implied Figure of Speech: All **figures of speech** have two parts: the **tenor** and the **vehicle**. When one of these parts is not written on the page, it may be "implied," meaning it's logically demanded by the context.
146

Internal Rhyme: A pattern of **rhymes** occurring within a single line or between the interiors multiple lines; can be **exact** or **slant** and can be mingled with **end rhyme**.
201

Interpretation: A specific kind of discussion of a poem focused on identifying and explaining a poem's argument(s) (often but not consistently called **theme(s)** in this context).
319

Irony: A **tone** created when what people say and what they actually mean are purposefully different, different from what was intended, or different than what was reasonably expected.
77

L

Line: The basic unit of structure in a poem. This is one of the fundamental things that separates verse poetry from **prose**. Lines may be defined with sound, such as number of syllables or ending **rhyme**, or visually, such as with white space or other layout choices, or both.
22

Lover, the: Traditional term for the **speaker** in a love poem.
57

Lyric Poem (a **Genre**): A short poem, usually less than one hundred lines, that is focused on the thoughts, feelings, and experience of a single speaker. There may be action, and other characters may appear, but a lyric is internally focused and concerned with thinking and feeling more than reporting events.
331

M

Meter: A more precise term than **rhythm** that describes the actual pattern or structure of **stressed syllables** in a line of verse. The adjective is **metrical**.
246

Minor Ionic: A pair of **feet** functioning together as a unit, composed of a **pyrrhic** followed by a **spondee**. Sometimes called a "**double iamb**."
253

Monometer: A **line** composed of one **foot**; a term used in **scansion** and the discussion of **accentual-syllabic meter**.
255

Multiple Rhyme: A pattern of **rhyme** created by sets of more than one rhyming syllable in a sequence. Sometimes known as feminine rhyme.
202

N

Neologism: A word created by the poet just for that poem. See also **Portmanteau Word**.
117

Non-participant Speaker: A **speaker** who is not also a **character** in the poem; a **speaker** not directly involved in the **action** of the poem.
49

O

Octameter: A **line** composed of eight **feet**; a term used in **scansion** and the discussion of **accentual-syllabic meter**.
255

Octave/Octet: An eight-line **stanza**.
25

Onomatopoeia: The use or creation of words to mimic natural sounds directly.
232

Open Form: Poetry that doesn't strictly follow an apparent defining structural pattern, especially poetry that doesn't follow any regular rhythm or rhyme patterns or a traditional form. Also known as "**free verse**."
33

P

Paraphrase / Paraphrasing: Restating a poem in one's own prose language without omitting, altering, explaining, or interpreting anything. A sort of translation.

16, 383 (instructions on how to make a formal paraphrase.)

Participant Speaker: A **speaker** who is also a **character** in the poem; a **speaker** directly involved in the **action** of the poem. See also **Unreliable Speaker**.

49

Pentameter: A **line** composed of five **feet**; a term used in **scansion** and the discussion of **accentual-syllabic meter**.

255

Personification: A particular kind of **implied figure of speech** in which a non-human creature is assigned human qualities, or an object is assigned human or animal qualities.

146

Point of View: The particular perspective from which the story of a poem is told. Point of view describes the relationship of the speaker to the action.

49

Portmanteau Word: A specific kind of **neologism** created by joining together two existing words, such as "spork" (spoon + fork).

117

Prose: Writing made from conventional sentences and paragraphs. Novels, essays, and journalism are all examples of writing in prose.

3

Pyrrhic: a **foot** made up of two unstressed **syllables**.

253

Q

Quatrain / Quartet: A four-line **stanza**.

25

Quintain /Quintet: A five-line **stanza**.
25

R

Received Form: A pre-existing set of rules that define some aspects of a poem, like a poem recipe. Received forms often have traditional names, such as "sonnet" or "haiku." Also called "fixed," "traditional," or "closed" form — or just "a form." That's not confusing at all.
26

Refrain: A word, phrase, or **line** repeated multiple times within a poem, often at the end of a **stanza**.
195

Rhyme: Broadly, rhyme refers to the repetition of ending sounds in multiple words, occurring in such a way as to suggest a pattern. See also **End Rhyme, Exact Rhyme, Internal Rhyme, Multiple Rhyme, Single Rhyme,** and **Slant Rhyme.**
201

Rhyme Scheme: A traditional method and system of notation for identifying, representing, and discussing the rhyming pattern in a poem.
205

Rhythm: Any recognizable pattern of repetition and variation of anything within a poem. Usually used to describe patterns of sound, and, specifically, patterns of **stressed** and **unstressed syllables**.
244

S

Scansion: The process of examining a line of poetry or entire poem in order to discover and analyze its meter. The verb is to **scan**.
256

Schwa: the unstressed "uh" vowel sound represented by \ ə \ in pronunciation guides. Many unstressed **syllables** are pronounced with a schwa sound, regardless of spelling.
193-194

Setting: The particular places and times in which a poem takes place.
    88

Single Rhyme: A pattern of **rhyme** created by one rhyming **syllable** in a sequence. Sometimes known as masculine rhyme.
    202

Situation: A simple overview of the story **elements** in a poem — **setting, characters, action, speaker,** and **point of view.**
    87

Slant Rhyme: A rhyme that is created when the ending consonant sounds of a set of words are the same, or nearly the same, but the preceding vowel sounds are not.
    204

Speaker: Every story has a teller, and in discussing poetry, we usually refer to the storyteller as the speaker. The speaker is the voice that tells or "speaks" the poem, a fictional poem-speaking persona created by the author. Not to be confused with the author.
    47

Spondee: a **foot** made up of two stressed **syllables.**
    253

Stanza: A recognizably distinct set of lines, often but not always separated by white space, either between lines or through some form of indentation.
    24

Stressed Syllable: A syllable that is more fully vocalized, louder, or longer. The vowel sound is usually more distinctly and clearly pronounced. The added emphasis is referred to as "stress." Also called "accented syllable."
    196

Syllable: The basic unit of speech and word formation, comprising a single vowel sound, with or without surrounding consonants.
    195

Symbol: Something that represents or stands for something else. In literature, a symbol is often a concrete thing that refers to something abstract, or a familiar thing that refers to something unknown.
172

Syntax: The arrangement of words into larger units of meaning such as phrases, clauses, and sentences. It also refers to the rules that govern making those arrangements sensible.
125

T

Tenor (Figure of Speech): In a figure of speech, the thing being explained or defined (as opposed to the **vehicle**).
145

Tercet: A three-line **stanza**.
25

Tetrameter: A **line** composed of four **feet**; a term used in **scansion** and the discussion of **accentual-syllabic meter**.
255

Theme: a slippery word that can refer to the overall subject or topic of a poem, any discrete topic or subject it takes up, any abstract concept it refers to, or, most specifically, an argument a poem makes, analogous to a thesis in an essay. See **interpretation**.
319

Tone: Narrowly, the attitude that the author takes or feelings the author has towards the content of the story. Broadly, the general emotional aspect, mood, or feeling of the poem. Not to be confused with the way the poem makes you feel.
68

Treble Foot: a **foot** with three **syllables**. The treble feet are the **dactyl** and the **anapest**.
251

Trimeter: A **line** composed of three **feet**; a term used in **scansion** and the discussion of **accentual-syllabic meter**.

255

Triplet: A **rhyming tercet** (AAA).

25

Trochee: a two-**syllable**, or **duple**, **foot** made up of a sequence of one **stressed syllable** followed by one unstressed **syllables**.

250

Typography: The typefaces or fonts used and choices within the typeface such as size, capitalization, bolding, color, and so on.

277

U

Understanding: the comprehension of a poem's diction, syntax, context; its literal situation and its figurative content; awareness of its elements and their function; insight into challenges, questions, and arguments it might raise.

10

Unreliable Speaker: a special kind of **participant speaker** who cannot be fully trusted to tell the truth about the **situation** in the poem, whether due to incapacity, malice, or their own misunderstanding.

51

V

Vehicle (Figure of Speech): In a **figure of speech**, the **vehicle** is what the **tenor** is being compared to or defined as.

145

Contents in Detail

Chapter 4: **The Feeling of a Poem** 67

Chapter 5: **The Situation of a Poem** 87

Acknowledgments

"Quinceañera" by José Angel Araguz appears in *Small Fires* © 2017 by FutureCycle Press. Reprinted by permission of José Angel Araguz. First published in *Luna Luna* 2014.

"Humans" by Elizabeth Austen is copyrighted work and may not be reproduced without permission from Blue Begonia Press. Reprinted by permission of Elizabeth Austen and Blue Begonia Press. First published in *Crab Creek Review* and in *Every Dress a Decision* from Blue Begonia Press.

"The Man and How We Plan to Stick It to Him" by Justus Ballard is copyrighted work and may not be reproduced without permission from the author. Reprinted by permission of Justus Ballard.

"You Don't Love the Voyeur" by Jeffrey Bean is copyrighted work and may not be reproduced without permission from the author. Reprinted by permission of Jeffrey Bean. First published in *The Willow Magazine*.

"Captain Haddock vs. the PTA" by Amy Beeder appears in *Now Make an Altar* © 2012 by Amy Beeder. Reprinted with the permission of The Permissions Company, Inc., on behalf of Carnegie Mellon University Press, www.cmu.edu/universitypress.

"Why It Almost Never Ends With Stripping" by Shaindel Beers appears in *A Brief History of Time* © 2009 by Shaindel Beers. Reproduced with permission of the Licensor through PLSclear.

"Hunters" by Andrea Hollander is copyrighted work and may not be reproduced without permission from the author. Reprinted by permission of Andrea Hollander. First published in *DoubleTake*.

"Watershed" by Bette Lynch Husted is copyrighted work and may not be reproduced without permission from the author. Reprinted by permission of Bette Lynch Husted. First published in *Windfall*.

"Derecho Ghazal" by Luisa A. Igloria appears in *Ode to the Heart Smaller than a Pencil Eraser* © 2014 University Press of Colorado. Reprinted by permission of University Press of Colorado and Luisa A. Igloria.

"The Grand Silos of Sacramento" by Lawson Fusao Inada is reprinted by permission from *Drawing the Line* (Coffee House Press, 1997). Copyright © 1997 by Lawson Fusao Inada.

"Cryophilia" and "Kali Yuga" by Jennifer Kemnitz are copyrighted work and may not be reproduced without permission from the author. Reprinted by permission of Jennifer Kemnitz. "Cryophilia" was first published in *Cirque*. "Kali Yuga" was first published in *The Kerf*.

"Anti-Elegy" and "Funeral Blues for Whitney" by Robert Lashley are copyrighted work and may not be reproduced without permission from the author. Reprinted by permission of Small Doggies Press.

"Sown" by Annie Lighthart is copyrighted work and may not be reproduced without permission from Airlie Press. Reprinted by permission of Airlie Press. First published in *Iron String*.

"smiley face" and "Bugle" by Tod Marshall are copyrighted work and may not be reproduced without permission from the author. Reprinted by permission of Tod Marshall and Canarium Books. First published in *Bugle* from Canarium Books.

"Shall I Compare Thee to a Summer's Day?" and "What the Old Mole Said" by Carolyn Martin are copyrighted work and may not be

"Inheritance" by Darlene Pagán is copyrighted work and may not be reproduced without permission from the author. Reprinted by permission of Darlene Pagán.

"Prince Credo" by Oliver de la Paz is copyrighted work and may not be reproduced without permission from the author. Reprinted by permission of Oliver de la Paz. First published in *Seattle Review of Books*.

"Between Jobs -OR- 25 Years in HR Management and All I Got Was This Lousy Poem" by David J.S. Pickering is copyrighted work and may not be reproduced without permission from the author. Reprinted by permission of David J.S. Pickering.

"Burying Our Daughter's Teeth" by Tiah Lindner Raphael first appeared in *Ink Node* 2013. Reprinted by permission of Tiah Lindner Raphael.

"Invitation to Mr. W" by Susan Rich is copyrighted work and may not be reproduced without permission from Whitd Pine Press. Reprinted by permission of Susan Rich and White Pine Press. First published in *Cures Include Travel* from White Pine Press.

"Cleaning Magazines" by Virginia Robinson is copyrighted work and may not be reproduced without permission from Swan Scythe Press. Reprinted by permission of Swan Scythe Press. First published in *Carrier* from Swan Scythe Press.

"Yoked" (excerpt) by Alida Rol is copyrighted work and may not be reproduced without permission from the author. Reprinted by permission of Alida Rol.

"Yr Appt: 10:30 Thursday" by Walt Schaefer is copyrighted work and may not be reproduced without permission from the author. Reprinted by permission of Walt Schaefer.

"Weekend Swim with Wedding Band" by Caitlin Scott is copyrighted work and may not be reproduced without permission from the